Lecture Notes in Computer Science

Lecture Notes in Artificial Intelligence   15501

Founding Editor

Jörg Siekmann

Series Editors

Randy Goebel, *University of Alberta, Edmonton, Canada*
Wolfgang Wahlster, *DFKI, Berlin, Germany*
Zhi-Hua Zhou, *Nanjing University, Nanjing, China*

The series Lecture Notes in Artificial Intelligence (LNAI) was established in 1988 as a topical subseries of LNCS devoted to artificial intelligence.

The series publishes state-of-the-art research results at a high level. As with the LNCS mother series, the mission of the series is to serve the international R & D community by providing an invaluable service, mainly focused on the publication of conference and workshop proceedings and postproceedings.

Han Yu · Xiaoxiao Li · Zenglin Xu ·
Randy Goebel · Irwin King
Editors

Federated Learning in the Age of Foundation Models - FL 2024 International Workshops

FL@FM-WWW 2024, Singapore, May 14, 2024;
FL@FM-ICME 2024, Niagara Falls, ON, Canada, July 15, 2024;
FL@FM-IJCAI 2024, Jeju Island, South Korea, August 5, 2024; and
FL@FM-NeurIPS 2024, Vancouver, BC, Canada, December 15, 2024
Revised Selected Papers

Springer

Editors
Han Yu 🆔
Nanyang Technological University
Singapore, Singapore

Xiaoxiao Li 🆔
University of British Columbia
Vancouver, BC, Canada

Zenglin Xu
Fudan University
Shanghai, China

Randy Goebel 🆔
University of Alberta
Edmonton, AB, Canada

Irwin King 🆔
The Chinese University of Hong Kong
Shatin, Hong Kong

ISSN 0302-9743   ISSN 1611-3349 (electronic)
Lecture Notes in Artificial Intelligence
ISBN 978-3-031-82239-1   ISBN 978-3-031-82240-7 (eBook)
https://doi.org/10.1007/978-3-031-82240-7

LNCS Sublibrary: SL7 – Artificial Intelligence

This Springer imprint is published by the registered company Springer Nature Switzerland AG
The registered company address is: Gewerbestrasse 11, 6330 Cham, Switzerland

If disposing of this product, please recycle the paper.

Preface

Federated learning (FL) has emerged as a groundbreaking approach in artificial intelligence, enabling collaborative model training across distributed and privacy-sensitive data environments. The rapid evolution of foundation models—large-scale pre-trained models capable of tackling diverse tasks—has further amplified the potential of FL, unlocking new possibilities for efficient, scalable, and versatile applications. This book, *Federated Learning in the Age of Foundation Models*, presents a collection of research that explores this confluence, addressing both theoretical and practical challenges.

The chapters in this volume focus on several key areas of research:

- **Efficient Model Adaptation and Personalization**: Techniques for tailoring foundation models to diverse multilingual and personalized federated learning settings, including strategies for handling heterogeneous and resource-constrained environments.
- **Data Heterogeneity and Incomplete Data**: Novel approaches to managing the challenges posed by heterogeneous data distributions, including clustering, synthetic data generation, and benchmarking methodologies for data heterogeneity evaluation.
- **Integration of Specialized Neural Architectures**: Exploration of cutting-edge neural network designs, such as convolutional and spiking neural networks, to enhance learning in heterogeneous and resource-constrained federated systems.
- **Frameworks and Tools for Federated Learning**: Insights into the use of advanced frameworks such as Flower and NVIDIA FLARE to streamline FL workflows, making them accessible and scalable.
- **Applications in Domain-Specific Contexts**: Real-world use cases, including a benchmark for legal natural language processing and leveraging unstructured text data for instruction tuning of large language models.
- **Unsupervised and Lightweight Learning**: Innovations in unsupervised and lightweight federated learning, enabling effective model training with limited resources and minimal supervision.
- **Causal Discovery and Black-Box Optimization**: Advanced methodologies for causal discovery in federated environments with limited local samples and the exploration of black-box foundation models for personalized learning.

This collective exploration of the intersection of federated learning and foundation models aims to offer readers both a deeper understanding of the field and practical guidance for addressing its challenges. It is our hope that this book will serve as an indispensable resource for researchers, practitioners, and students who are passionate about advancing the frontiers of distributed and privacy-preserving machine learning.

The chapters have been selected from papers presented in the FL@FM-WWW'24, FL@FM-ICME'24, FL@FM-IJCAI'24, and FL@FM-NeurIPS'24 workshops. Each of them has been thoroughly reviewed by at least two reviewers. We are deeply grateful to the authors for their invaluable contributions, the reviewers for their critical insights, and the broader research community for its continued commitment to innovation in federated learning.

December 2024

Han Yu
Xiaoxiao Li
Zenglin Xu
Randy Goebel
Irwin King

Organization

FL@FM-TheWebConf'24

General Co-chairs

Irwin King   Chinese University of Hong Kong, China
Guodong Long   University of Technology Sydney, Australia

Program Co-chairs

Zenglin Xu   Harbin Institute of Technology, China
Han Yu   Nanyang Technological University, Singapore

Publication Co-chairs

Lixin Fan   WeBank, China

Publicity Co-chairs

Xu Guo   Nanyang Technological University, Singapore

Local Arrangement Co-chairs

Xiaoli Tang   Nanyang Technological University, Singapore

FL@FM-ICME'24

General Co-chairs

Randy Goebel   University of Alberta, Canada
Xiaoxiao Li   University of British Columbia, Canada

Program Co-chairs

Han Yu	Nanyang Technological University, Singapore
Jane Z. Wang	University of British Columbia, Canada
Ross Mitchell	University of Alberta, Canada

FL@FM-IJCAI'24

Steering Committee

Steering Co-chairs

Qiang Yang	Hong Kong University of Science and Technology/WeBank, China
Yaochu Jin	Westlake University, China

Organizing Committee

General Co-chairs

Randy Goebel	University of Alberta, Canada
Lixin Fan	WeBank, China

Program Co-chairs

Xiaoxiao Li	University of British Columbia, Canada
Han Yu	Nanyang Technological University, Singapore

Publication Co-chairs

Ying Wei	Nanyang Technological University, Singapore
Zengxiang Li	ENN Group, China

Publicity Co-chairs

Alysa Ziying Tan	Nanyang Technological University, Singapore
Jiankai Sun	Pinterest, USA

FL@FM-NeurIPS'24

Co-chairs

Sai Praneeth Karimireddy	University of Southern California, USA
Xiaoxiao Li	University of British Columbia, Canada
Songtao Lu	IBM Thomas J. Watson Research Center, USA
Stacy Patterson	Rensselaer Polytechnic Institute, USA
Pascal Poupart	University of Waterloo, Canada
Han Yu	Nanyang Technological University, Singapore

Contents

FedHLT: Efficient Federated Low-Rank Adaption with Hierarchical Language Tree for Multilingual Modeling

Zhihan Guo[1], Yifei Zhang[1], Zhuo Zhang[2(✉)], Zenglin Xu[2], and Irwin King[1]

[1] The Chinese University of Hong Kong, Sha Tin, Hong Kong SAR, China
{zhguo22,yfzhang,king}@cse.cuhk.edu.hk
[2] Harbin Institute of Technology, Shenzhen, China
iezhuo17@gmail.com, xuzenglin@hit.edu.cn

Abstract. Federated Multilingual Modeling (FMM) has become an essential approach in natural language processing (NLP) due to increasing linguistic diversity and the heightened emphasis on data privacy. However, FMM faces two primary challenges: 1) the high communication costs inherent in network operations, and 2) the complexities arising from parameter interference, as languages exhibit both unique characteristics and shared features. To tackle these issues, we introduce a communication-efficient framework for Multilingual Modeling (MM) that combines low-rank adaptation with a hierarchical language tree structure. Our method maintains the base model's weights while focusing on updating only the Low-rank adaptation (LoRA) parameters, significantly reducing communication costs. Additionally, we mitigate parameter inference by organizing languages based on their familial ties rather than merging all LoRA parameters together. Our experimental findings reveal that this novel model surpasses established baseline models in performance and markedly decreases communication overhead.

CCS CONCEPTS

• **Computing methodologies → Natural language processing.**

Keywords: Federated Multilingual Modeling · Low-rank Adaption · Hierarchical Federated Learning

1 Introduction

The growing emphasis on multilingual modeling within natural language processing (NLP) is driven by the increasing diversity of languages present online [21]. However, the acquisition of multilingual data often faces significant challenges, including high costs associated with its dispersed nature and data privacy concerns [11,33]. To overcome these obstacles, we leverage the potential of Federated Learning (FL) to develop a multilingual model utilizing various institutional and data sources [4,10,39]. Central to FL is the concept of exchanging model

© The Author(s), under exclusive license to Springer Nature Switzerland AG 2025
H. Yu et al. (Eds.): FL 2024 Workshops, LNAI 15501, pp. 1–18, 2025.
https://doi.org/10.1007/978-3-031-82240-7_1

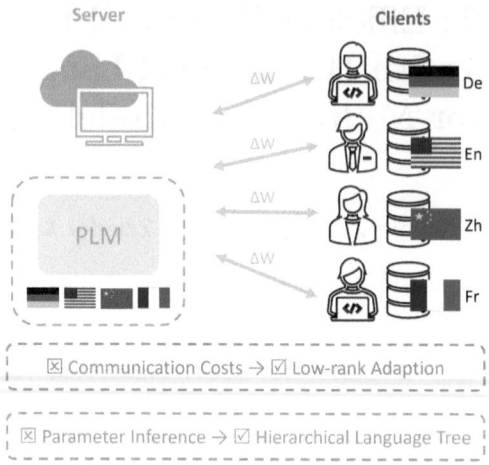

Fig. 1. Traditional Federated Learning (FL) encounters two primary challenges in the context of Federated Multilingual Modeling (FMM). 1. Huge communication cost: the necessity for large models to learn multilingual knowledge leads to significant communication costs due to the transfer of extensive model parameters across clients. 2. Parameter inference: various languages exhibit unique characteristics while also sharing commonalities. Our FedHLT model addresses these 2 challenges through the introduction of Low-Rank Adaptation (LoRA) and multilingual hierarchical language tree learning strategy, respectively.

parameters instead of direct data sharing, which ensures the preservation of data privacy [36,40].

The application of large pre-trained language models (PLMs) in fine-tuning Federated Multilingual Models (FMM) within a federated environment encounters notable difficulties, especially when dealing with limited data [41]. A primary challenge lies in transmitting the PLMs' extensive parameters across the network, leading to communication bottlenecks [18]. Additionally, FMM is inherently prone to non-IID (Non-Independently and Identically Distributed) issues due to the diverse linguistic and cultural characteristics [38]. For languages closely related linguistically, parameters can be mutually beneficial despite minor conflicts. In contrast, for languages that are more distantly related, while there are more parameter inference, there is also a mutual benefit. For example, languages like English and German, which have a close relationship in the language family tree (see Fig. 2), show significant similarities. However, English and Chinese, belonging to different language families, exhibit considerable distributional differences. Though Chinese and English are distant in the language tree, they also share mutual benefits. For instance, the use of inversions is common in English and Chinese, but rare in German. In this scenario, parameters between Chinese and English can assist each other, whereas English and German parameters might experience minor conflicts. These disparities can hinder the model's specific language adaptation, leading to significant Parameter Inference (PI) problems [5,23], adversely affecting transfer performance [35], as depicted in Fig. 1.

In response to these challenges, we introduce a novel, communication-efficient federated learning framework for multilingual modeling, utilizing hierarchical language tree learning strategy (HLT). Drawing inspiration from parameter-efficient fine-tuning (PEFT) strategies [14, 16, 29, 31], our approach involves fine-tuning a select subset of parameters via Low-Rank Adaptation (LoRA) techniques, while keeping the original pre-trained language model (PLM) parameters intact. This marks a groundbreaking implementation of LoRA in the context of federated learning (FL). By limiting the number of trainable parameters in the LoRA adapter, our method substantially reduces communication overhead, as illustrated in Fig. 2. To alleviate the issue of interference among diverse languages, we suggest organizing languages into clusters based on their linguistic family affiliations, a concept visually represented in Fig. 2. The empirical results demonstrate that our method not only achieves enhanced performance but also boasts greater efficiency compared to a range of baseline models.

In this research, we make significant strides in the field of federated multilingual modeling, marked by the following contributions:

i. **FedHLT Framework.** We introduce the groundbreaking FedHLT framework, a novel and communication-efficient approach to federated learning for multilingual modeling. OA pivotal aspect of our contribution is the pioneering application of Low-Rank Adaptation (LoRA) within the realm of Federated Learning (FL), which has successfully achieved a remarkable reduction in communication overhead by a factor of 100.

ii. **Hierarchical Language Tree Learning Strategy.** We employed a language hierarchical language tree strategy to alleviate parameter interference in the context of federated multilingual modeling.

iii. **Experimental Results.** We have rigorously tested the FedHLT framework across a suite of downstream tasks, *i.e.*, language modeling, machine translation, and text classification. The results from these experiments conclusively demonstrate the superior performance of our FedHLT framework.

2 Related Work

2.1 Federated Learning in NLP

Federated learning (FL) [19, 25], a distributed machine learning framework, consists of a central server and several client nodes. In this model, clients' raw data is kept local to address privacy concerns. The training process involves exchanging parameters among clients instead of data [22]. However, the non-IID (not Independently and Identically Distributed) nature of data across these clients hampers FL's performance, often leading to less accuracy than centralized training models [17]. Recent advancements have seen federated multilingual models being increasingly deployed in a variety of tasks, such as medical transcript analysis [24], enhancing multilingual natural language understanding through knowledge composition [33], applying pre-trained models in multilingual federated settings [34], multilingual emoji prediction [12], and machine translation

[23]. Nonetheless, these models often suffer from inefficiency due to the extensive data exchanged between the server and clients during training. Current solutions, like adapter tuning, unfortunately introduce additional latency during inference. In our work, we integrate LoRA [15], an approach for parameter-efficient fine-tuning, to substantially decrease the number of trainable parameters by a factor of 100 and reduce GPU memory requirements by a factor of 3, thereby enhancing both efficiency and performance in federated multilingual modeling.

2.2   Parameter-Efficient Fine-Tuning

Parameter-Efficient Fine-Tuning (PEFT) is a technique designed to modify a minimal subset of parameters in pre-trained language models (PLMs) for specific tasks, as opposed to retraining the entire model [3,14,15,20,41]. PEFT methods are generally divided into three categories [8]. The first category, addition-based methods, incorporates additional trainable parameters not originally present in the model. However, these can introduce challenges such as inference latency in adapters [14,16] and limited input sequence handling in prefix-tuning [20]. The second category, specification-based methods, includes BitFit [3] and diff pruning [13], which selectively make certain original model parameters trainable while freezing the rest. The third category, reparameterization-based methods like LoRA [15], transforms existing parameters into a more efficient form through reparameterization techniques. Despite their advantages, PEFT models can reduce the performance of language models, as shown by Zhang et al. [41] and our experiments. This decrease in performance is mainly attributed to parameter inference among different languages, a significant challenge that needs to be addressed in multilingual contexts.

3   Methodology

We introduce FedHLT, a communication-efficient federated learning framework specifically tailored for Multilingual Modeling. FedHLT distinguishes itself through two fundamental innovations: (1) federated low-rank fine-tuning, which offers an effective approach to learning in federated multilingual settings, and (2) hierarchical tree learning strategy, which addresses the challenges of parameter inference that often arise in multilingual learning. In the following sections, we delve deeper into the intricacies and implementation of FedHLT. Section 3.1 introduces the overarching setting of Federated Multilingual Modeling. Subsequently, in Sect. 3.2, we provide a detailed exposition on the federated low-rank fine-tuning aspect, explaining its significance and mechanics. Finally, Sect. 3.3 thoroughly discusses our HLT learning strategy, showcasing its role in mitigating parameter inference in multilingual scenarios.

3.1   Federated Multilingual Modeling

We begin by introducing the formulation of Federated Multilingual Modeling (FMM) [34]. Given N language datasets $\{D_i\}_{i=1}^{N}$, the goal of FMM is to collaboratively train a multilingual FL model that achieves high performance in the downstream tasks. Specifically, in the setting of FMM, we assume there are N client $\{C_i\}_{i=1}^N$. Each client C_i owns only one language D_i and the different client has different languages. Let Θ_i be the trainable parameters of the local model in C_i. At each training round l, the server initially performs a weighted aggregation of the LoRA parameters for client C_i (in the language family tree, its node is T_i) and its parent nodes $P = \{T_i^1, \ldots, T_i^n\}$ (where T_i^1 is the parent node of T_i at different levels), then sends the result to the corresponding language's client. The client C_i trains the local FL model with parameter $\Theta^{(l)}$ on its own dataset D_i and then sends parameters to the server S. The server S then aggregates these parameters to update parent nodes $P = T_i^1, \ldots, T_i^n$ of C_i $\Theta^{(l+1)}$ and sends $\Theta^{(l+1)}$ to client C_i for the subsequent training round. FedAvg is employed for aggregation by default [25] and is computed as follows:

$$\Theta^{(l+1)} = \sum_{i=1}^N \frac{1}{N} \Theta_i^{(l)}. \tag{1}$$

3.2   Federated Efficient Fine-Tuning with Low-Rank Adaption

In FMM, training the entire FL model incurs substantial communication costs as it involves computing/exchanging a large number of parameters through the networks. The success of fine-tuning on PLMs motivates us to explore adjustment of the small portion of parameters in the FMM.

FMM with Low-Rank Adaption. It has been shown that PLMs exhibit a low "intrinsic dimension" when adapting to specific tasks [1] and can still learn efficiently despite a random projection to a smaller subspace. Inspired by this, in FMM, we hypothesize the local updates to the weights Θ for each client also have such low "intrinsic rank" during training. Therefore we employ the Low-Rank Adapter (LoRA) for efficient FMM fine-tuning – instead of training and exchanging Θ for each client, we only adjust the parameters of adapter $\Delta\Theta$ in propagation. Specifically, the forward process for the linear layer in the FMM model is computed as follows:

$$h = \Theta x + \Delta\Theta x = \mathbf{B}\mathbf{A}x, \tag{2}$$

where x represents the output of the previous layer, h is the hidden state. Note that $\Theta \in \mathbb{R}^{d \times k}$ is parameters of the PLM used in the local model, which is frozen. $\Delta\Theta$ is the parameters of the adapter, which is updated during training rounds. $\Delta\Theta$ can be factorize into two matrix $\mathbf{B} \in \mathbb{R}^{d \times r}$ and $\mathbf{A} \in \mathbb{R}^{r \times k}$ As the intrinsic rank $r \ll min(d, k)$ is small, $\Delta\Theta = \mathbf{B}\mathbf{A}$ has fewer parameters to communicate.

Federated Parameter-Efficient Fine-Tuning. Our approach involves freezing a pre-trained model and solely training adapters, which is more parameter-efficient. For each client C_i, we add a LoRA module with trainable parameter $\Delta\Theta_i$ in parallel to the PLMs parameter Θ_i. In each training round l, we freeze the parameters of the PLM, $\Theta_i^{(l)}$ and only update LoRA parameters $\Delta\Theta_i^{(l)}$. At the end of each training round, clients transfer their updated LoRA parameters to the server. When the server receives the parameters of all clients, it aggregates LoRA parameters as

$$\Delta\Theta^{(l+1)} = \sum_{i=1}^{N} \frac{1}{N}\Delta\Theta_i^{(l)}. \tag{3}$$

3.3 Updating LoRA Parameters with Hierarchical Language Tree Learning Strategy

The PI issue is common in FMM. The presence of languages from different sources in diverse distributions introduces a non-i.i.d. (non-independent and identically distributed) nature, which leads to conflicts when aggregating parameters trained on different datasets, denoted as D_i. The update of the parameter Θ_i from one client may have an adversarial effect on the others, yielding sub-optimal performance.

Hierarchical Language Tree Learning Strategy (HLT). To address the PI issue prevalent in FMM, we introduce the HLT approach. Prior cluster-based methods have demonstrated effectiveness in reducing PI [23,28,32]. Our LFC method not only considers the benefits of clustering languages within the language family tree, where closely related languages aid each other, but it also acknowledges the potential conflicts and occasional assistance between more distantly related languages. This approach resonates with findings in FL research, where clustering a subset of clients with similar distribution strategies can mitigate PI. LFC shares similarities with existing clustering strategies. In language modeling, languages are grouped based on linguistic similarities, forming language families. Our method follows the categorizations in the language family tree as outlined in [26]. We aggregate the LoRA parameters according to this family tree, as depicted in Fig. 2. For instance, languages in the Germanic family, including English and German, are clustered together, as are languages in the Italic family (Spanish, French, and Portuguese), the Balto-Slavic family (Russian, Polish, Czech, and Lithuanian), the Sino-Tibetan family (including Chinese), the Uralic family (including Finnish), the Afro-Asiatic family (including Arabic), and the Japonic family (including Japanese). This clustering allows us to capitalize on the synergies within language families while minimizing conflicts, thereby enhancing the overall efficiency and effectiveness of our FMM approach.

Let $\{\mathcal{G}_m\}_{m=1}^{M}, (M \leq N)$ denotes the parent nodes of a client node at each hierarchical level in the language tree. Each $\mathcal{G}_m$ contains a set of index i indicating the i-th clients with datasets D_i belong to the m-th language tree path. The aggregation in Eq. 3 then change to

$$\Delta\Theta^{m,(l+1)} = \sum_{i\in\mathcal{G}_m} \frac{1}{|\mathcal{G}_m|}\Delta\Theta_i^{(l)}. \tag{4}$$

Regarding our implementation, we have M LoRA adapters associated with different language tree path $\mathcal{G}_m$. For downstream tasks in specific languages, we

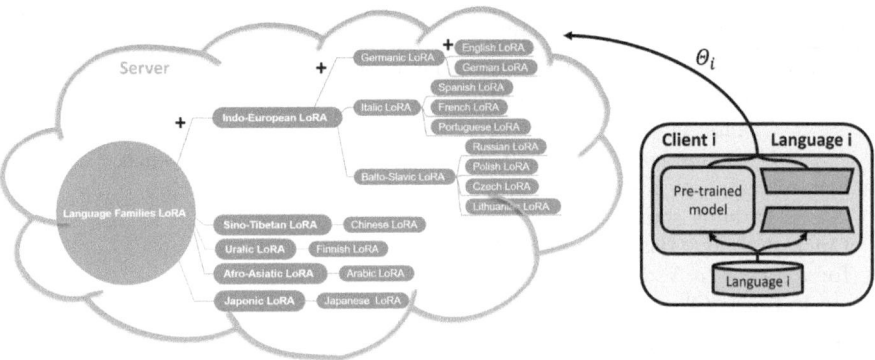

Fig. 2. The overall framework of FedHLT. FedHLT is a communication-efficient framework designed for Federated Multilingual Learning, comprising two key designs: federated low-rank fine-tuning and HLT approach. Specifically, languages are divided into a family tree based on their language families. At the outset, both the server and client sides possess an identical pre-trained language model, and maintain a set of LoRA parameters for each language tree node. During the federated learning process, for each language, the server initially performs a weighted aggregation of the LoRA parameters for that language's node in the language tree and its parent nodes, then sends the result to the corresponding language's client. Each client then updates the LoRA parameters and sends the updated parameters back to the server. The server, upon receiving these LoRA parameters, performs a weighted aggregation and uses it to update the nodes of that particular language in the language tree and all its parent nodes. The parameter-efficient fine-tuning design with the divide-and-conquer strategy in FedHLT effectively resolves the parameter inference arising from multilingual learning and reduces the communication costs in federated learning.

utilize the corresponding $\Delta\Theta^{m,(l\mid 1)}$ for inference. The comprehensive algorithm detailing this process is presented in Algorithm 1.

4   Experiment

We conduct a thorough evaluation of our model across three widely recognized tasks in NLP, *i.e.*, Language Modeling (LM), Machine Translation (MT), and Text Classification (TC). For these evaluations, we utilize four distinct datasets: Europarl, MTNT, UN Corpus, and News Classification. Detailed statistics and the specific evaluation metrics for each dataset are provided in Table 1.

To offer a comprehensive understanding of our evaluation process, we have organized the following sections accordingly. In Sect. 4.1, we present detailed descriptions of each task, elaborating on the specific challenges and objectives associated with LM, MT, and TC. Section 4.2 is dedicated to discussing the evaluation metrics employed in our study, providing insights into how the performance of the model is quantitatively assessed across different tasks. Section 4.3 delves into the datasets, highlighting their relevance, composition, and the ratio-

---

Algorithm 1: Hierarchical Language Tree Aggregation

Input: The hierarchical language tree nodes set G;
   Initial LoRA parameters Θ^0;
   Clients set $\{C_i\}_{i=1}^N$;
   In the language tree, the parent nodes of a client node at each
hierarchical level in each path g;
   Training round L.
Output: LoRA Parameters $\{\Theta_i^L\}_{i=1}^N$.

1   **for** i *from* 1 *to* N **do**
2   Initialize Θ_i^0 with Θ^0;

3   **for** l *from* 1 *to* L **do**
4   **for** i *from* 1 *to* N **do**
    // local update of client i
5   update Θ_i^{l-1} with local data;

   // language tree nodes aggregation of LoRA parameters
6   **foreach** g *in* G **do**
7     $\Theta_g^l = \sum_{id \in g} \frac{1}{|g|} \Theta_{id}^{l-1}$;
8   **foreach** id *in* g **do**
9      $\Theta_{id}^l = \Theta_g^l$;

---

nale behind their selection for this research. Section 4.4 provides comprehensive details about the training process in our study, including the framework, GPU type, learning rates, training durations, and the use of pre-trained models. Section 4.5 analyzes the performance of three settings (*Centralized Model*, *FedAvg*, and *Standalone*) and the standard *Adapter* approach. Lastly, in Sect. 4.6, we analyze the main results presented in Tables 3, 4, 5, and 6 for LM, MT, and TC experiments, highlighting our consistently superior performance compared to other federated learning methods, and discussing key observations.

4.1 Tasks

Language Modeling (LM). The LM task involves predicting the subsequent word in a given sequence, and its evaluation metric, perplexity (PPL), serves as a measure of model performance. It tests the model's ability to understand contextual dependencies, capture semantic relationships, and generate coherent and meaningful sequences of words. For example, given the sentence "The acting in this movie is", the model would predict the next word, such as "excellent". When the language model effectively captures and understands complex language patterns and dependencies, leading to more accurate predictions of the next word, the PPL will be low. In our study, we employ the UN Corpus and Europarl datasets to conduct LM experiments.

Machine Translation (MT). The MT task involves automatically translating text from a source language to a target language, with BLEU serving as an evaluation metric. For example, given a source text in English, such as "Hello", the desired output in French would be "Bonjour". A higher BLEU score in MT indicates better translation quality. In our research, we have utilized the UN Corpus and MTNT datasets.

Text Classification (TC). The TC task involves assigning predefined labels to text data, and accuracy is a metric used to evaluate the performance of the classification model by measuring the percentage of correctly predicted class labels compared to the total number of predictions. For example, if the input text is "This movie is fantastic!", the output label should be "movie". In our study, we adopt News Classification datasets.

We adopt these three tasks to verify the proposed method can provide a comprehensive performance improvement in FMM setting.

4.2   Evaluation Metric

In evaluating our model across three fundamental NLP tasks-LM, MT, and TC-we employed different datasets and metrics. For the language modeling task, we use perplexity (PPL) as the evaluation metric [34]. For neural machine translation task, we use BLEU as evaluation metrics, using ScareBLEU package [27]. For the text classification task, we use accuracy as an evaluation metric.

Table 1. Datasets and metric information for the three experiment tasks.

Task	Dataset	# Train	# Dev	# Test	Metric
LM	Europarl	160,000	40,000	40,000	PPL
	UN	300,000	30,000	30,000	PPL
MT	MTNT	11,210	1,798	2,019	sacreBleu
	UN	30,000	15,000	15,000	sacreBleu
TC	NC	40,000	5,000	5,000	Accuracy

Table 2. Memory usage for FL experiments on four tasks. Bold numbers indicate the best memory usage. The proposed FedHLT demonstrates superior memory efficiency compared to the FedAvg baseline, thanks to parameter-efficient fine-tuning. Compared to PEFT methods, *e.g.*, Adapter and LoRA, FedHLT achieves comparable memory efficiency.

Methods	LM		MT		TC
	UN	Europarl	MTNT	UN	NC
FedAvg	25.7G	25.7G	54.9G	31.0G	27.2G
+ Adapter	**21.0G**	**21.0G**	**54.2G**	28.8G	21.6G
+ LoRA	21.3G	21.3G	54.8G	28.8G	20.8G
FedHLT	21.3G	21.3G	54.8G	**28.8G**	**20.8G**

4.3   Datasets

In our study, we utilized four diverse datasets to evaluate our model. The News Classification dataset from the XGLUE benchmark encompasses articles in five languages (English, Spanish, French, German, and Russian) for Text Classification tasks. The Machine Translation of Noisy Text (MTNT) dataset, including noisy Reddit comments, focuses on language pairs <English, French> and <English, Japanese> to test Machine Translation resilience. The UN Corpus, with United Nations documents in six languages, is used for both Language Modeling and Machine Translation tasks. For Language Modeling, we also employ the Europarl corpus, containing European Union meeting transcripts in 11 languages, with a focus on eight specific languages. Each dataset offers a rich, multilingual environment crucial for assessing our model's performance in understanding and categorizing complex linguistic data.

4.4   Implementation Details

In our federated learning setup, we employed the FedLab framework [37][1], adhering to the training methodology outlined in [34]. Experiments were conducted on a 4 GPU cluster with A100 GPUs, each having 80 GB memory. The maximum sequence length was set to 512, and the AdamW optimizer was used. Training involved each client completing an epoch of local learning before synchronization with the server. We tested four learning rates (1e−4, 5e−4, 1e−3, 5e−3), with 5e-4 proving most effective. Training durations varied per task: 20 epochs for LM, 25 for MT, and 30 for TC. The FedAvg algorithm was employed for FL training, with the adapter bottleneck at 128 and the LoRA module set to a rank of 64, alpha of 32, and dropout of 0.1.

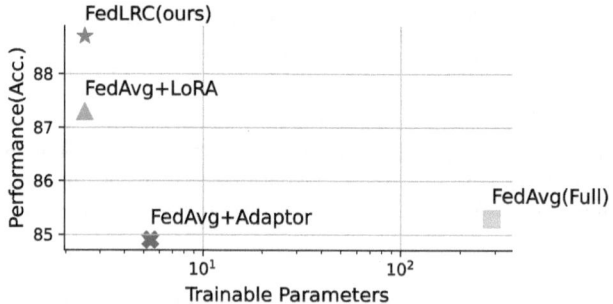

Fig. 3. Comparison of trainable parameters and performance between FedHLT and baselines on the Text Classification task. FedHLT achieves less than 1% parameter count compared to FedAvg and demonstrates significant performance improvements compared to other PEFT solutions, *e.g.*, LoRA and Adapter.

---

[1] https://github.com/SMILELab-FL/FedLab/.

Pre-trained Models. We use different pre-trained models for different tasks, *i.e.*, mBERT [7,30] (distilbert-base-multilingual-cased[2]) for language modeling, M2M100 [9] (facebook/m2m100_418M[3]) for machine translation, and XLM-RoBERTa [6] (FacebookAI/xlm-roberta-base[4]) for text classification.

4.5   Baselines

In our experiment, we utilized three distinct settings: *Centralized Model*, *FedAvg*, and *Standalone*, each offering unique insights into the performance of our model. The *Centralized Model*, following the approach of Weller et al. [34], involves consolidating all data in a single location for training. *FedAvg* adopts the Federated Averaging method as described by McMahan et al. [25], distributing data across various clients within the federated learning framework. Both these settings train a conventional multilingual model utilizing all parameters. The *Standalone* setting diverges by focusing on training data in just one language and assessing its performance across multiple languages. This scenario, as explored by Weller et al. [34], simulates a model trained solely with data from a single client. To highlight the effectiveness of our LRH and LoRA methods, we also include scenarios where the parameters of PLMs are frozen in both the *Centralized* and *FedAvg* settings. Additionally, we compare the performance of the *LoRA* method [15] and the standard *Adapter* approach [14] without LRH to further demonstrate the superiority of our proposed techniques.

4.6   Main Results

In this section, we delve into the results and observations outlined in Tables 3, 4, 5, and 6, which correspond to our experiments in language modeling, neural machine translation, and text classification. A thorough analysis of these tables reveals that our approach consistently outperforms other FL methods across the majority of tasks. Following are several key observations.

FMM Model Outperform Standalone. In our study, the standalone model acts as the lower performance benchmark. Our results indicate that models trained with FedAvg generally outperform the standalone setup. This finding emphasizes the value of FMM in real-world language training, as it efficiently leverages diverse data sets across languages without the constraints of data barriers, highlighting its practical superiority in federated learning environments.

Parameters Efficient FT *vs.* Full-Parameters FT. Our results, as shown in Tables 3, 4, 5, and 6, demonstrate that our model utilizing LoRA for PEFT not only aligns with but, in certain tasks like text classification (Table 6), surpasses the performance of conventional full fine-tuning models. This enhanced performance is likely due to LoRA's focused approach in mitigating overfitting,

---

[2] https://huggingface.co/distilbert-base-multilingual-cased.
[3] https://huggingface.co/facebook/m2m100_418M.
[4] https://huggingface.co/FacebookAI/xlm-roberta-base.

Table 3. Results for LM experiments on the UN Corpus. A comparison was made between our proposed method and the baseline methods. PPL was chosen as the performance metric, with bold numbers indicating the best results. ↑ means higher is better, ↓ means lower is better. Our method consistently achieved lower PPL scores than FedAvg + Adapter and FedAvg + LoRA across all languages, indicating its superior performance. Furthermore, our model demonstrated the lowest memory usage for TP, highlighting its efficiency.

Method	# TP ↓	En ↓	Es ↓	Zh ↓	Ru ↓	Ar ↓	Fr ↓	Avg ↓
Standalone	-	$33.0_{\pm0.8}$	$16.1_{\pm1.2}$	$43.0_{\pm1.5}$	$10.3_{\pm0.8}$	$10.8_{\pm0.2}$	$14.0_{\pm0.3}$	$25.4_{\pm0.9}$
Centralized	-	$7.4_{\pm0.2}$	$4.8_{\pm0.4}$	$6.9_{\pm0.2}$	$3.9_{\pm0.1}$	$5.2_{\pm0.3}$	$4.6_{\pm0.3}$	$5.6_{\pm0.3}$
+ Adapter	-	$10.4_{\pm0.6}$	$6.2_{\pm0.5}$	$9.0_{\pm0.2}$	$4.7_{\pm0.5}$	$7.2_{\pm0.4}$	$5.9_{\pm0.2}$	$7.0_{\pm0.3}$
+ LoRA	-	$11.3_{\pm0.5}$	$6.7_{\pm.7}$	$9.7_{\pm1.0}$	$5.0_{\pm0.5}$	$7.6_{\pm0.3}$	$6.4_{\pm0.1}$	$7.5_{\pm0.6}$
FedAvg	135.4M	$\mathbf{8.7}_{\pm0.2}$	$\mathbf{4.2}_{\pm0.5}$	$\mathbf{5.4}_{\pm0.1}$	$4.1_{\pm0.2}$	$\mathbf{4.2}_{\pm0.7}$	$5.1_{\pm0.5}$	$\mathbf{5.1}_{\pm0.6}$
+ Adapter	2.5M	$22.8_{\pm0.5}$	$14.9_{\pm0.5}$	$17.0_{\pm0.4}$	$9.9_{\pm0.5}$	$17.2_{\pm0.1}$	$14.3_{\pm0.7}$	$15.5_{\pm0.6}$
+ LoRA	1.2M	$10.8_{\pm0.9}$	$6.6_{\pm0.3}$	$9.3_{\pm0.5}$	$5.0_{\pm0.6}$	$8.1_{\pm0.5}$	$6.3_{\pm0.6}$	$7.5_{\pm0.8}$
FedHLT	**1.2M**	$9.4_{\pm0.5}$	$5.6_{\pm0.7}$	$8.0_{\pm0.4}$	$\mathbf{4.0}_{\pm0.6}$	$6.0_{\pm0.1}$	$\mathbf{5.1}_{\pm0.2}$	$6.3_{\pm0.3}$

Table 4. Results for LM experiments on the Europarl. Illustration is the same as Table 3. Our method consistently achieved lower PPL scores than FedAvg + Adapter and FedAvg + LoRA across all languages, indicating its superior performance. Furthermore, our model demonstrated the lowest memory usage for TP, highlighting its efficiency.

Method	# TP ↓	En ↓	Cs ↓	Lt ↓	Es ↓	Pl ↓	Fi ↓	Pt ↓	De ↓	Avg ↓
Standalone	-	$9.4_{\pm0.9}$	$2.8_{\pm0.4}$	$2.6_{\pm1.2}$	$4.3_{\pm0.6}$	$2.8_{\pm0.5}$	$3.0_{\pm0.2}$	$3.7_{\pm0.6}$	$3.5_{\pm0.8}$	$4.0_{\pm0.2}$
Centralized	-	$9.8_{\pm0.5}$	$3.8_{\pm0.6}$	$4.8_{\pm0.1}$	$6.0_{\pm0.2}$	$3.9_{\pm0.8}$	$5.8_{\pm0.4}$	$9.2_{\pm0.6}$	$8.4_{\pm0.5}$	$5.9_{\pm0.5}$
+ Adapter	-	$10.6_{\pm0.6}$	$7.1_{\pm0.5}$	$8.2_{\pm0.5}$	$7.3_{\pm0.2}$	$5.8_{\pm0.8}$	$7.6_{\pm0.8}$	$7.6_{\pm0.5}$	$7.9_{\pm0.5}$	$7.7_{\pm0.2}$
+ LoRA	-	$10.7_{\pm0.8}$	$6.9_{\pm0.9}$	$8.0_{\pm0.2}$	$7.3_{\pm0.2}$	$5.7_{\pm0.6}$	$7.4_{\pm0.4}$	$7.5_{\pm0.5}$	$8.0_{\pm0.8}$	$7.6_{\pm0.6}$
FedAvg	135.4M	$10.4_{\pm0.6}$	$6.4_{\pm0.5}$	$9.2_{\pm0.2}$	$\mathbf{5.9}_{\pm0.1}$	$5.9_{\pm0.3}$	$7.8_{\pm0.6}$	$7.5_{\pm0.5}$	$7.9_{\pm0.8}$	$7.7_{\pm0.6}$
+ Adapter	2.5M	$12.0_{\pm0.8}$	$10.6_{\pm0.2}$	$14.2_{\pm0.6}$	$8.3_{\pm0.4}$	$7.5_{\pm0.8}$	$10.7_{\pm0.2}$	$9.4_{\pm0.4}$	$9.2_{\pm0.6}$	$10.1_{\pm0.5}$
+ LoRA	1.2M	$11.4_{\pm0.8}$	$8.8_{\pm0.6}$	$11.3_{\pm0.4}$	$7.8_{\pm0.5}$	$6.6_{\pm0.2}$	$9.3_{\pm0.5}$	$8.5_{\pm0.8}$	$8.8_{\pm0.6}$	$8.9_{\pm0.4}$
FedHLT	**1.2M**	$\mathbf{10.4}_{\pm0.5}$	$\mathbf{6.1}_{\pm0.6}$	$\mathbf{6.3}_{\pm0.6}$	$7.1_{\pm0.2}$	$\mathbf{5.4}_{\pm0.3}$	$\mathbf{6.4}_{\pm0.5}$	$\mathbf{7.2}_{\pm0.2}$	$\mathbf{7.7}_{\pm0.4}$	$\mathbf{7.1}_{\pm0.5}$

which in turn maintains the pre-trained model's generalization capabilities and leads to an overall improvement in effectiveness.

Comparison with Adapter-Based PEFT Method. We observed a notable trend in our experiments: not all PEFT methods are equal in their effectiveness within FMM contexts. Specifically, Adapter-based methods often do not reach the performance levels of full fine-tuning (FT). For instance, in text classification (Table 6), while FedAvg with FT achieves an average accuracy of 85.3% across

Table 5. Results for FL experiments on the machine translation task. We evaluated our model's performance on the UN Corpus and MTNT datasets. A comparison was made between our proposed method and the baseline methods. The BLEU score was chosen as the performance metric, with bold numbers indicating the best results. ↑ means higher is better, ↓ means lower is better. Our method consistently achieved higher BLEU scores than all baseline models, indicating that the clustering strategy employed significantly improves performance. Furthermore, our method demonstrated the highest efficiency in terms of memory utilization for TP, highlighting the effectiveness of our model.

Method	# TP ↓	MTNT ↑			UN ↑			
		En-Fr	En-Ja	Avg	En-Fr	Ar-Es	Ru-Zh	Avg
Centralized	-	$32.2_{\pm0.5}$	$32.3_{\pm0.2}$	$32.1_{\pm0.7}$	$39.3_{\pm0.6}$	$37.5_{\pm0.9}$	$24.0_{\pm0.2}$	$33.8_{\pm0.6}$
+ Adapter	-	$31.9_{\pm0.5}$	$30.4_{\pm0.3}$	$31.7_{\pm0.1}$	$36.9_{\pm0.9}$	$34.0_{\pm0.6}$	$20.3_{\pm0.2}$	$30.4_{\pm0.3}$
+ LoRA	-	$32.3_{\pm0.6}$	$32.5_{\pm0.2}$	$32.2_{\pm0.6}$	$37.6_{\pm0.3}$	$34.9_{\pm0.3}$	$20.2_{\pm0.2}$	$31.3_{\pm0.6}$
Standalone	-	$27.1_{\pm0.5}$	$28.1_{\pm0.7}$	$27.6_{\pm0.6}$	$34.6_{\pm0.5}$	$33.8_{\pm0.5}$	$18.5_{\pm0.6}$	$29.0_{\pm0.4}$
FedAvg	483.9M	$32.9_{\pm0.2}$	$33.3_{\pm0.8}$	$32.9_{\pm0.6}$	$38.2_{\pm0.4}$	$35.9_{\pm0.3}$	$\underline{21.1}_{\pm0.1}$	$31.1_{\pm0.7}$
+ Adapter	12.7M	$32.6_{\pm0.4}$	$33.0_{\pm0.2}$	$32.6_{\pm0.6}$	$35.8_{\pm0.9}$	$31.9_{\pm0.6}$	$19.2_{\pm0.8}$	$29.2_{\pm0.4}$
+ LoRA	9.4M	$33.3_{\pm0.6}$	$32.5_{\pm0.5}$	$33.2_{\pm0.8}$	$36.3_{\pm0.6}$	$32.7_{\pm0.5}$	$19.8_{\pm0.7}$	$29.5_{\pm0.7}$
FedHLT	**9.4M**	$\mathbf{34.0}_{\pm0.2}$	$\mathbf{33.6}_{\pm0.1}$	$\mathbf{33.8}_{\pm0.4}$	$\mathbf{38.0}_{\pm0.1}$	$\mathbf{37.5}_{\pm0.6}$	$20.7_{\pm0.2}$	$\mathbf{32.1}_{\pm0.6}$

five languages, the combination of FedAvg and Adapter yields sligHLTy lower effectiveness at 84.9%. In contrast, FedAvg paired with LoRA achieves a higher accuracy of 87.3%, outperforming FT. This clearly demonstrates LoRA's distinct advantages in FMM, emphasizing its efficiency and uniqueness. Additionally, our LoRA-based method significantly enhances efficiency over traditional adapter-based PEFT methods. For text classification, FedAvg with FT requires a hefty 278.1 million trainable parameters (TP), and using an Adapter demands 5.4 million TP. In stark contrast, LoRA manages the same task with just 2.5 million TP, as detailed in Table 6. This dramatic reduction in TP not only speaks to LoRA's heightened efficiency but also underscores its effectiveness compared to other PEFT methods.

Model Efficiency and Communication Costs. The proposed FedHLT demonstrates high efficiency across several key dimensions, as shown in Fig. 3. (1) Trainable Parameters: regarding trainable parameters, integrating LoRA results in a significant reduction compared to conventional full fine-tuning, decreasing to less than 1%. This also cuts the parameter count needed for Adapter-based methods by half, as shown in Tables 3, 4, 5, and 6. Such a drastic reduction is vital for minimizing communication costs in federated learning environments. (2) GPU Memory: in terms of GPU memory usage, as detailed in Table 2, FedHLT surpasses the FedAvg baseline in terms of memory efficiency. For instance, in a text classification task, FedHLT uses only 20.8G of GPU memory, while the baseline consumes 27.2G. This efficiency is attributed to our model's optimized

Table 6. Results for FL experiments on the text classification task. We test the model on NC datasets and compare our proposed method with the baseline methods. ↑ means higher is better, ↓ means lower is better. We use accuracy as the adopted metric, with bold numbers indicating the best results. Our method consistently outperforms full fine-tuning, Adapter, and LoRA in terms of accuracy across multiple languages, providing strong evidence for the effectiveness of our framework. Furthermore, our approach demonstrates superior efficiency by utilizing the lowest memory usage for TP, further highlighting the efficiency of our method.

Method	# TP ↓	En ↑	Es ↑	Fr ↑	De ↑	Ru ↑	Avg ↑
Centralized	-	$93.5_{\pm0.7}$	$86.3_{\pm0.5}$	$82.9_{\pm0.3}$	$89.6_{\pm0.1}$	$88.5_{\pm0.4}$	$88.1_{\pm0.2}$
+ Adapter	-	$92.7_{\pm0.4}$	$86.7_{\pm0.6}$	$81.7_{\pm0.1}$	$88.5_{\pm1.0}$	$87.4_{\pm0.5}$	$87.4_{\pm0.3}$
+ LoRA	-	$91.8_{\pm0.4}$	$83.7_{\pm0.3}$	$80.4_{\pm0.5}$	$86.4_{\pm0.4}$	$85.3_{\pm0.1}$	$85.5_{\pm0.1}$
Standalone	-	$22.8_{\pm1.2}$	$40.8_{\pm0.7}$	$40.8_{\pm0.1}$	$40.8_{\pm0.5}$	$77.1_{\pm0.2}$	$44.5_{\pm0.3}$
FedAvg	278.1M	$90.7_{\pm0.4}$	$84.3_{\pm0.2}$	$80.5_{\pm0.3}$	$87.6_{\pm0.1}$	$83.4_{\pm0.5}$	$85.3_{\pm0.2}$
+ Adapter	5.4M	$91.5_{\pm0.5}$	$85.7_{\pm0.7}$	$79.1_{\pm0.2}$	$86.9_{\pm0.7}$	$81.3_{\pm0.8}$	$84.9_{\pm0.7}$
+ LoRA	2.5M	$\mathbf{93.8}_{\pm0.3}$	$85.8_{\pm0.6}$	$80.7_{\pm0.3}$	$89.4_{\pm0.7}$	$86.7_{\pm0.3}$	$87.3_{\pm0.2}$
FedHLT	**2.9M**	$93.5_{\pm0.1}$	$\mathbf{\underline{86.6}}_{\pm0.1}$	$\mathbf{\underline{82.7}}_{\pm0.5}$	$\mathbf{\underline{90.1}}_{\pm0.1}$	$\mathbf{\underline{91.0}}_{\pm0.1}$	$\mathbf{\underline{88.7}}_{\pm0.1}$

fine-tuning approach. When compared with other PEFT methods like Adapter and LoRA, FedHLT remains competitive in memory usage. (3) Training Time: the training time for FedHLT is substantially shorter than traditional models. PEFT training with FedHLT for a single client takes only 1–3 h on an A100 GPU, depending on when the model converges. This is a drastic improvement over the 24–48 h typically needed for full fine-tuning models. This reduction in training time is not just a matter of convenience; it significantly contributes to reducing the communication overhead in federated learning scenarios, making FedHLT a highly efficient choice for such applications.

Hierarchical Language Tree Learning Strategy Improves Performance. Incorporating a LRH strategy in our model results in varied performance improvements across different languages, particularly benefiting those with limited resources. As evidenced in Tables 3 and 5, languages such as Arabic (Ar), Czech (Cs), Lithuanian (Lt), and Finnish (Fi) show a substantial decrease in PPL, Ar (8.1→6.0), Cs (8.8→6.1), Lt (11.3→6.3), and Fi (9.3→6.4). These languages often correspond to medium or low-resource datasets in real-world applications, indicating that LRC is particularly advantageous for languages with fewer resources.

Performance Discrepancy Between Language Modeling and Machine Translation for FedHLT on UN Corpus. The varying performances in our tasks can likely be attributed to the different pre-trained models used. For language modeling, we utilize mBERT, an encoder-only model, whereas for machine translation, we opt for M2M100, an encoder-decoder model. This difference in underlying architectures affects FedHLT's performance in two key ways: (1) different models have varying degrees of adaptability to PEFT; (2) the HLT learning strategy varies across different tasks.

FL Methods Outperforms Centralized Methods. Centralized models are typically regarded as the performance upper bound in various tasks. Nonetheless, findings by Weller et al. [34] indicate that in some instances, a FedAvg-model in a FedNLP framework can exceed the performance of a centralized model. We attribute this occurrence to parameter interference. Within the language family tree, closely related languages often share more similarities in parameters, whereas languages with distant relationships, despite some conflicts, can still mutually assist each other. Aggregating parameters indiscriminately from all languages tends to diminish these characteristics, potentially leading to poorer model performance [2]. In contrast, employing a HLT learning strategy capitalizes on these characteristics, resulting in improved model performance. This phenomenon is also evident in the three tasks of our experiments, showcasing the nuanced interplay of language relationships and parameter management in federated learning.

5   Conclusion

In conclusion, this paper presented an innovative approach in FMM, introducing a highly efficient federated learning framework, FedHLT. Our method leverages the strengths of LoRA and a hierarchical language tree learning strategy, addressing key challenges in the realm of multilingual natural language processing. The significant reduction in trainable parameters, enhanced GPU memory utilization, and reduced training times, as demonstrated in our experiments, underline the efficacy of FedHLT in a federated setting. Experimental results demonstrate the efficiency and effectiveness of our proposed model, resulting in a remarkable reduction of communication overhead by a factor of 100.

Acknowledgments. The work described in this paper was partially supported by InnoHK initiative, The Government of the HKSAR, and Laboratory for AI-Powered Financial Technologies. The research presented in this paper was also partially supported by the Research Grants Council of the Hong Kong Special Administrative Region, China (CUHK 14222922, RGC GRF 2151185).

A   Appendix

A.1   Limitations

In this research, we have primarily evaluated our approach using mBERT, M2M100, and XLM-RoBERTa as PLMs. For future studies, we aim to extend our analysis to encompass Large Language Models (LLMs). Additionally, our current methodology involves equal data usage from each language for fine-tuning, a scenario that might not completely mirror real-world language distributions. To overcome this limitation, future studies will focus on testing our model's effectiveness with datasets that have varying volumes of language data. Moreover, our current approach centers around a HLT learning strategy, where the LoRA parameters for each node are averaged in the aggregation method. A promising direction for future research involves exploring learnable aggregation weights. This adjustment has the potential to optimize the performance of our model further, and we plan to rigorously test this in forthcoming experiments.

References

1. Aghajanyan, A., Gupta, S., Zettlemoyer, L.: Intrinsic dimensionality explains the effectiveness of language model fine-tuning. In: Proceedings of the 59th Annual Meeting of the Association for Computational Linguistics and the 11th International Joint Conference on Natural Language Processing (Volume 1: Long Papers) (2021)
2. Bari, M.S., Haider, B., Mansour, S.: Nearest neighbour fewshot learning for cross-lingual classification. arXiv preprint arXiv:2109.02221 (2021)
3. Zaken, E.B., Goldberg, Y., Ravfogel, S.: BitFit: simple parameter-efficient fine-tuning for transformer-based masked language-models. In Proceedings of the 60th Annual Meeting of the Association for Computational Linguistics (Volume 2: Short Papers) (2022)
4. Chen, G., et al.: Win-win: a privacy-preserving federated framework for dual-target cross-domain recommendation. In: Williams, B., Chen, Y., Neville, J. (eds.) Thirty-Seventh AAAI Conference on Artificial Intelligence, AAAI 2023. AAAI Press (2023)
5. Chronopoulou, A., Stojanovski, D., Fraser, A.: Language-family adapters for low-resource multilingual neural machine translation. In: Proceedings of the The Sixth Workshop on Technologies for Machine Translation of Low-Resource Languages (LoResMT 2023), pp. 59–72 (2023)
6. Conneau, A., et al.: Unsupervised cross-lingual representation learning at scale. CoRR (2019)
7. Devlin, J., Chang, M.-W., Lee, K., Toutanova, K.: BERT: pre-training of deep bidirectional transformers for language understanding. In: Burstein, J., Doran, C., Solorio, T. (eds.) Proceedings of the 2019 Conference of the North American Chapter of the Association for Computational Linguistics: Human Language Technologies, Volume 1 (Long and Short Papers), pp. 4171–4186. Association for Computational Linguistics, Minneapolis (2019). https://doi.org/10.18653/v1/N19-1423
8. Ding, N., et al.: Delta tuning: a comprehensive study of parameter efficient methods for pre-trained language models. arXiv preprint arXiv:2203.06904 (2022)
9. Fan, A., et al.: Beyond English-centric multilingual machine translation. J. Mach. Learn. Res. $22(1)$, 4839–4886 (2021)
10. Fu, X., King, I.: FedHGN: a federated framework for heterogeneous graph neural networks. arXiv preprint arXiv:2305.09729 (2023)
11. Gala, J., Gandhi, D., Mehta, J., Talat, Z.: A federated approach for hate speech detection. In: Proceedings of the 17th Conference of the European Chapter of the Association for Computational Linguistics, pp. 3248–3259. Association for Computational Linguistics, Dubrovnik (2023). https://doi.org/10.18653/v1/2023.eacl-main.237

12. Gamal, K., Gaber, A., Amer, H.: Federated learning based multilingual emoji prediction in clean and attack scenarios. arXiv preprint arXiv:2304.01005 (2023)

13. Guo, D., Rush, A., Kim, Y.: Parameter-efficient transfer learning with diff pruning. In: Proceedings of the 59th Annual Meeting of the Association for Computational Linguistics and the 11th International Joint Conference on Natural Language Processing (Volume 1: Long Papers), pp. 4884–4896. Association for Computational Linguistics (2021). https://doi.org/10.18653/v1/2021.acllong.378

14. Houlsby, N., et al.: Parameter-efficient transfer learning for NLP. In: International Conference on Machine Learning, pp. 2790–2799 (PMLR) (2019)

15. Hu, E.J., et al.: LoRA: low-rank adaptation of large language models. In: International Conference on Learning Representations (2022). https://openreview.net/forum?id=nZeVKeeFYf9

16. Hu, Z., et al.: LLM-adapters: an adapter family for parameter-efficient fine-tuning of large language models. arXiv preprint arXiv:2304.01933 (2023)

17. Kairouz, P., et al.: Advances and open problems in federated learning Found. Trends® Mach. Learn. **14**, 1–2 (2021). 1–210

18. Kim, Y., Kim, J., Mok, W.-L., Park, J.-H., Lee, S.: Client-customized adaptation for parameter-efficient federated learning. In: Findings of the Association for Computational Linguistics: ACL 2023 (2023)

19. Konečný, J., McMahan, H.B., Yu, F.X., Richtárik, P., Suresh, A.T., Bacon, D.: Federated learning: strategies for improving communication efficiency. CoRR abs/1610.05492 (2016). arXiv:1610.05492

20. Li, X.L., Liang, P.: Prefix-tuning: optimizing continuous prompts for generation. In: Proceedings of the 59th Annual Meeting of the Association for Computational Linguistics and the 11th International Joint Conference on Natural Language Processing (Volume 1: Long Papers) (2021)

21. Limisiewicz, T., Balhar, J., Mareček, D.: Tokenization impacts multilingual language modeling: assessing vocabulary allocation and overlap across languages. In: Findings of the Association for Computational Linguistics: ACL 2023, pp. 5661–5681. Association for Computational Linguistics, Toronto (2023). https://doi.org/10.18653/v1/2023.findings-acl.350

22. Lin, B.Y., et al.: FedNLP: benchmarking federated learning methods for natural language processing tasks. In: Findings of the Association for Computational Linguistics: NAACL 2022, pp. 157–175. Association for Computational Linguistics, Seattle (2022). https://doi.org/10.18653/v1/2022.findings-naacl.13

23. Liu, Y., Bi, X., Li, L., Chen, S., Yang, W., Sun, X.: Communication efficient federated learning for multilingual neural machine translation with adapter. In Findings of the Association for Computational Linguistics: AC 2023, pp. 5315–5328. Association for Computational Linguistics, Toronto (2023). https://aclanthology.org/2023.findings-acl.327

24. Manoel, A., et al.: Federated multilingual models for medical transcript analysis. In: Mortazavi, B.J., Sarker, T., Beam, A., Ho, J.C. (eds.) Proceedings of the Conference on Health, Inference, and Learning. Proceedings of Machine Learning Research, vol. 209, pp. 147–162. PMLR (2023). https://proceedings.mlr.press/v209/manoel23a.html

25. McMahan, B., Moore, E., Ramage, D., Hampson, S., y Arcas, B.A.: Communication-efficient learning of deep networks from decentralized data. In: Singh, A., Zhu, J. (eds.) Proceedings of the 20th International Conference on Artificial Intelligence and Statistics. Proceedings of Machine Learning Research, vol. 54, pp. 1273–1282. PMLR (2017). https://proceedings.mlr.press/v54/mcmahan17a.html

26. Paul, L.M., Simons, G.F., Fennig, C.D., et al.: Ethnologue: languages of the world. SIL International, Dallas (2009). www.ethnologue.com/. Accessed 19 June 2011
27. Post, M.: A call for clarity in reporting BLEU scores. In: Proceedings of the Third Conference on Machine Translation: Research Papers (2018)
28. Ruan, Y., Joe-Wong, C.: FedSoft: soft clustered federated learning with proximal local updating. In: Proceedings of the AAAI Conference on Artificial Intelligence, vol. 36, pp. 8124–8131 (2022)
29. Ruder, S., Pfeiffer, J., Vulić, I.: Modular and parameter efficient fine-tuning for NLP models. In: Proceedings of the 2022 Conference on Empirical Methods in Natural Language Processing: Tutorial Abstracts, pp. 23–29 (2022)
30. Sanh, V., Debut, L., Chaumond, J., Wolf, T.: DistilBERT, a distilled version of BERT: smaller, faster, cheaper and lighter. ArXiv abs/1910.01108 (2019)
31. Sung, Y.-L., Cho, J., Bansal, M.: LST: ladder side-tuning for parameter and memory efficient transfer learning. In: Advances in Neural Information Processing Systems, vol. 35, pp. 12991–13005 (2022)
32. Vahidian, S., et al.: Efficient distribution similarity identification in clustered federated learning via principal angles between client data subspaces. In: Proceedings of the AAAI Conference on Artificial Intelligence (2023)
33. Wang, H., Zhao, H., Wang, Y., Yu, T., Gu, J., Gao, J.: FedKC: federated knowledge composition for multilingual natural language understanding. In The ACM Web Conference 2022 (2022)
34. Weller, O., Marone, M., Braverman, V., Lawrie, D., Van Durme, B.: Pretrained models for multilingual federated learning. In: Proceedings of the 2022 Conference of the North American Chapter of the Association for Computational Linguistics: Human Language Technologies, pp. 1413–1421. Association for Computational Linguistics, Seattle (2022). https://doi.org/10.18653/v1/2022.naacl-main.101
35. Xu, R., Luo, F., Chang, B., Huang, S., Huang, F.: S4-tuning: a simple crosslingual sub-network tuning method-tuning: a simple cross-lingual sub-network tuning method. In: Proceedings of the 60th Annual Meeting of the Association for Computational Linguistics (Volume 2: Short Papers), pp. 530–537 (2022)
36. Xu, Z., et al.: Federated learning of gboard language models with differential privacy. In: Proceedings of the 61st Annual Meeting of the Association for Computational Linguistics (Volume 5:Industry Track) (2023)
37. Zeng, D., Liang, S., Hu, X., Wang, H., Xu, Z.: FedLab: a flexible federated learning framework. J. Mach. Learn. Res. (2023)
38. Zhang, T., Liu, C., Lee, W.-H., Su, Y., Sun, H.: Federated learning for semantic parsing: task formulation, evaluation setup, new algorithms. In: Proceedings of the 61st Annual Meeting of the Association for Computational Linguistics (Volume 1: Long Papers), pp. 12149–12163. Association for Computational Linguistics, Toronto (2023). https://doi.org/10.18653/v1/2023.acllong.678
39. Zhang, Y., Zeng, D., Luo, J., Xu, Z., King, I.: A survey of trustworthy federated learning with perspectives on security, robustness and privacy. In: Companion Proceedings of the ACM Web Conference 2023 (Austin,TX, USA) (WWW 2023 Companion), pp. 1167–1176. Association for Computing Machinery, New York (2023). https://doi.org/10.1145/3543873.3587681
40. Zhang, Z., et al.: FEDLEGAL: the first real-world federated learning benchmark for legal NLP. In: Proceedings of the 61st Annual Meeting of the Association for Computational Linguistics (Volume 1: Long Papers) (2023)
41. Zhang, Z., et al.: FedPETuning: when federated learning meets the parameter efficient tuning methods of pre-trained language models. In: Findings of the Association for Computational Linguistics: ACL 2023 (2023)

ZooPFL: Exploring Black-Box Foundation Models for Personalized Federated Learning

Wang Lu[1(✉)], Hao Yu[1], Jindong Wang[2,3], Damien Teney[4], Haohan Wang[5], Yao Zhu[1], Yiqiang Chen[6], Qiang Yang[7], Xing Xie[3], and Xiangyang Ji[1]

[1] Tsinghua University, Beijing, China
newlw230630@gmail.com
[2] William & Mary, Williamsburg, USA
[3] Microsoft Research Asia, Beijing, China
[4] Idiap Research Institute, Martigny, Switzerland
[5] University of Illinois Urbana-Champaign, Champaign, USA
[6] Institute of Computing Technology, CAS, Beijing, China
[7] Hong Kong University of Science and Technology, Sai Kung, Hong Kong

Abstract. When personalized federated learning (FL) meets large foundation models, new challenges arise from various limitations in resources. In addition to typical limitations such as data, computation, and communication costs, access to the models is also often limited. This paper endeavors to solve both the challenges of *limited resources* and *personalization.* i.e., distribution shifts between clients. To do so, we propose a method named **ZooPFL** that uses **Z**eroth-**O**rder **O**ptimization for **P**ersonalized **F**ederated **L**earning. ZooPFL avoids direct interference with the foundation models and instead learns to adapt its inputs through zeroth-order optimization. In addition, we employ simple yet effective linear projections to remap its predictions for personalization. To reduce the computation costs and enhance personalization, we propose input surgery to incorporate an auto-encoder with low-dimensional and client-specific embeddings. We provide theoretical support for ZooPFL to analyze its convergence. Extensive empirical experiments on computer vision and natural language processing tasks using popular foundation models demonstrate its effectiveness for FL on black-box foundation models.

Keywords: Federated Learning · Black-box · Personalization

1 Introduction

Recently, growing emphasis on data privacy and security has led to the emergence of federated learning (FL) [36]. FL enables collaborative learning while

---

W. Lu and H. Yu—Equal contribution.

H. Yu et al. (Eds.): FL 2024 Workshops, LNAI 15501, pp. 19–35, 2025.
https://doi.org/10.1007/978-3-031-82240-7_2

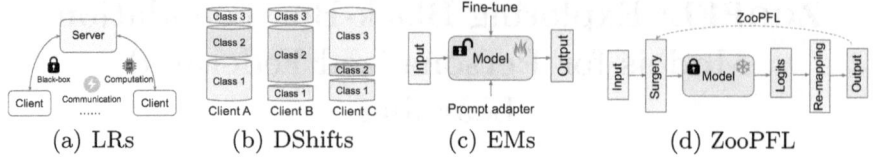

(a) LRs	(b) DShifts	(c) EMs	(d) ZooPFL

Fig. 1. ZOOPFL addresses federated learning with foundation models while coping with limited resources(LRs) in communication, computation, and model accessibility (a) and being robust to distribution shifts (b) (Dshifts). Most existing methods (EMs) rely on white-box model access (c).ZOOPFL is applicable to black-box models by using input surgery and semantic output re-mapping (d).

safeguarding privacy and security across distributed clients [53]. However, FL faces two key issues: *limited resources* and *distribution shifts* (Fig. 1(a, b)).

The rise of large foundation models [4] has amplified these challenges. The computational demands and communication costs associated with such models hinder the deployment of existing FL approaches (Fig. 1a).[1] Most of them require fine-tuning the models on every client.[2] Moreover, foundation models, often proprietary [40], grant only *black-box* access, making FL resource-efficient applications a pressing research area.

Recent efforts in FL [50] have attempted to reduce the number of optimized parameters to minimize computational and communication costs. As illustrated in Fig. 1 (c), existing methods use prompts [25] or adapters [6] to fine-tune foundation models [50]. Other approaches [55] focus on limiting the number of communication rounds. They however depend on white-box access to the foundation models. Moreover, distribution shifts are an additional challenge for FL since the data across clients is not necessarily i.i.d. [23] (Fig. 1b). Direct aggregations e.g., with FedAVG [31] often result in slow convergence and poor performance in each client [14]. Some methods have been designed to address the personalization of large foundation models [38]. However, they cannot deal with black-box models. The method proposed in this paper is designed to cope with label shift, i.e. variations in the distribution of labels among clients (Fig. 1b).

In this paper, we propose ZOOPFL to cope with limited resources and personalization for federated learning and black-box foundation models. To cope with black-box models, ZOOPFL proposes two strategies, *input surgery* and *semantic re-mapping*, and learning through zeroth-order optimization (ZOO). To reduce the computational costs of ZOO and share information among clients, we employ an auto-encoder with low embedding dimensions to represent transformations. For better personalization, the client-specific embeddings and semantic re-mapping are preserved by each client. Figure 1(d) illustrates that our pro-

---

[1] Communication costs can be estimated as $C = p \times K \times T$, where p, T, K respectively denote the number of parameters, rounds, and clients. With GPT-3 for example [5], $p = 175$ billion parameters, making the communication of entire models impractical.

[2] Training GPT-2-small [35] requires at least two A100 GPUs for 16 h, a resource unavailable to many.

Table 1. Comparisons of different methods.

Type	Method	Model scale	Model accessibility	Communication	Computation	Personalization
Base	FedAVG	Limited	White-box	Inefficient	High	Unsupported
	FedBN					Supported
Large model for FL	FedPrompt, FedCLIP	Unlimited	White-box	Efficient	Low	Supported
	PromptFL, pFedPG				High	
Zero-order for FL	FwdLLM, BAFFLE	Unlimited	White-box	Efficient	Low	Supported
	FedZO	Limited				
Model reprogramming	Reprogrammable-FL	Unlimited	White-box	Efficient	High	Supported
Black-box foundation FL	ZooPFL (Ours)	Unlimited	Black-box	Efficient	Low	Supported

posed method learns transformations on the inputs and mappings of the outputs through *zeroth-order optimization* [26]. This bears similarities with model reprogramming [9] and Reprogrammable-FL [2], but the latter is unsuitable for black-box models and personalization. To the best of our knowledge, our method is the first to achieve federated learning with large black-box models, a challenging setting that is becoming increasingly relevant to the real world (Table 1).

In summary, our contributions are four-fold.

1. **Scenario Exploration:** We delve into the challenges posed by fully black-box foundation models in FL. Our contribution lies in understanding and navigating this complex scenario.
2. **ZooPFL Framework:** We introduce ZooPFL, a comprehensive solution tailored for FL in resource-constrained and personalized settings. This framework encompasses input surgery and semantic re-mapping. ZooPFL employs strategic input manipulations, leveraging dedicated embeddings, and employing zeroth-order optimization while it project outputs for specific task and personalization.
3. **Theoretical Support:** We provide theoretical support, enhancing ZooPFL's credibility and offering insights into its workings.
4. **Empirical Validation:** ZooPFL is rigorously evaluated through computer vision and natural language processing experiments, demonstrating the effectiveness and versatility of ZooPFL.

2   Preliminaries

2.1   Black-Box Federated Learning with Large Foundation Models

What is the Setting? Foundation models can be viewed as black-box that can only provide the outputs according to inputs. It is not allowed to access any internal information on the foundation models, which means, *no backpropagation* is allowed. Each client preserves the same foundation model *locally*. We do *not consider* the storage of large models and the additional costs associated with inference. We aim to utilize large black-box foundation models for better personalized FL. [3]

Why is it Practical? To make the best of large foundation models, we can either fine-tune/adapt the models in their own data or perform FL on the cloud. Therefore, the value of our work lies primarily in two aspects. 1. **Fine-tuning or adapting locally is extremely expensive.** Fine-tuning on client side requires high computation and communication costs. Moreover, foundation model providers are not willing to share all information of model resources and it is a possible way that they can provide foundation models in an encrypted form. 2. **FL on the cloud is not the ideal solution.** One cannot trust the cloud providers by uploading all the training data to the cloud. So, the best practice is to perform computation *locally*. Combining the above situations. i.e., updating models locally with low cost, one can conclude that our proposed black-box FL is the only solution. Specifically, note that "black-box" does not only mean we do not have model access; it is a more broad technique for model update when local BP cannot be performed due to large model sizes. In this situation, our proposed method is a preliminary attempt and exploration.

3   Methodology

In this section, we articulate our proposed ZOOPFL. We begin with problem formulation in Sect. 3.1. Then, we show the motivation of designing ZOOPFL in Sect. 3.2. Next, Sect. 3.3 introduces the details of our approach. Finally, we propose some discussions in Sect. 3.4.

3.1   Problem Formulation

We assume there are n different clients $\{C_1, \cdots, C_n\}$ in personalized federated learning scenarios. Each client C_i has its own data $\mathcal{D}_i = \{\mathbf{x}_{i,j}, y_{i,j}\}_{j=1}^{n_i}$ where n_i means the number of data in the ith client. Data in different clients have different distributions, i.e. $P(\mathcal{D}_i) \neq P(\mathcal{D}_j)$. In the personalized FL setting, there exists the same black-box large foundation model in each client, g, which we know nothing inside and can only obtain logit outputs with fixed-size inputs. Our goal is to achieve personalized (i.e., satisfying) performance with black-box foundation models on each client by learning a significant transformation s_i on

---

[3] The real-life dilemma provided here illustrates the importance of direction. On the one hand, powerful LLMs, such as GPT4 [1] and Gemini [11], only provide APIs, that can be viewed black-box [19]. The data owners are unwilling to upload the raw data to APIs. On the other hand, the model suppliers are reluctant to expose all information about their models to others [43]. And clients usually cannot afford the back-propagation costs of LLMs. We believe that encrypting large models into black boxes and running them locally, similar to software [41], may be a solution. Therefore, we propose ZOOPFL, an initial exploration of this subdirection.

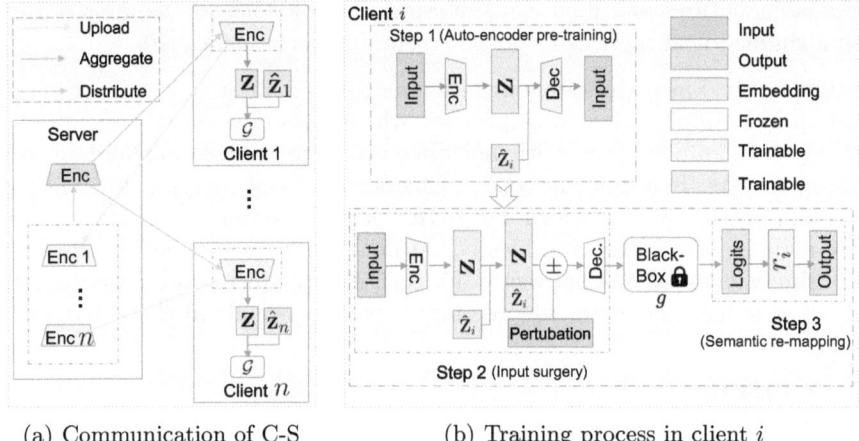

(a) Communication of C-S   (b) Training process in client i

Fig. 2. The framework of ZooPFL. Communications occur during step 2.

inputs and a re-mapping r_i on outputs without accessing g for each client $\mathcal{D}_i$. Specifically, denote ℓ a loss function, the learning objective is:

$$\min_{s_i, r_i} \frac{1}{n} \sum_{i=1}^{n} \frac{1}{n_i} \sum_{j=1}^{n_i} \ell(r_i(g(s_i(\mathbf{x}_{i,j}))), y_{i,j}). \tag{1}$$

3.2 Intuition

Input Designs Affect the Performance of Foundation Models. Different representations with the same inputs can induce foundation models to make completely different predictions, which illustrates that adding interference or reconstructing inputs can be utilized for adaptation. However, most methods that add interference are performed at the sample level [2,28], i.e. special design for each sample, that are unsuitable to exchange information among clients and cannot cope with unseen samples. Therefore, it is necessary to reconstruct samples via an auto-encoder to adapt input with unchanged dimensions for foundation models. The exchange of auto-encoder parameters can facilitate the sharing of input transformation information across different clients.

Semantic Re-mapping Generates More Semantically Meaningful Logits. Although large foundation models have been trained on a huge amount of samples [34], there still exists some classes or situations that foundation models cannot cover [48]. However, these new scenarios or classes can be made of existing fundamental elements or similar to some existing categories, which means foundation models can extract remarkable features.[4] Considering layers between

---

[4] Some popular language models such as BERT [12] and GPT-2 [35] in Huggingface utilize a random projection between extracted features and logits.

remarkable features and final logits as random projecting, re-mapping outputs with a simple linear layer can achieve acceptable performance [20].

Design Logic. Since access to foundation models is restricted, we rely on zeroth-order optimization to train auto-encoders, which leads that directly operating on the outputs of auto-encoders with high dimensions can exhaust unaffordable computational costs. To reduce the costs, we fix decoders and compute differences on embedding with low dimensions. For better personalization, we preserve semantic re-mapping in clients. Specifically, we preserve a client-specific embedding, i.e., a simple one-dimensional vector, for each client, which can be concatenated with embedding to generate adapted inputs with personalized characteristics.

3.3 ZOOPFL

In this paper, we propose ZOOPFL to learn input surgery and semantic re-mapping for black-box large foundation models in federated learning. ZOOPFL aims to adapt inputs to models and project outputs to meaningful semantic space. ZOOPFL mainly consists of three steps, namely, auto-encoder pre-training, input surgery, and semantic re-mapping.[5] Figure 2 shows the pipeline of our approach, where Fig. 2(a) describes the communications between clients and the server and Fig. 2(b) provides details on how to perform training on a local client.

The local training process is described as follows, where steps 2–3 are iterative.

1. Auto-encoder pre-training: this step directly utilizes inputs to pre-train the auto-encoder which then serves as the input surgery function.
2. Input surgery: this step updates encoders of auto-encoder and client-specific embeddings to transform the input consistent with the foundation model.
3. Semantic re-mapping: this step endeavors to re-map logits into meaningful semantic spaces with a simple linear projection.

Auto-Encoder Pre-training. Before input surgery and semantic re-mapping that are assisted by labels, ZOOPFL firstly utilizes inputs of samples to pre-train auto-encoders for better initial understanding of client data and we will fix decoders in the next two steps. For client C_i, we denote $\hat{\mathbf{z}}_i$ as the ith client-specific embedding and $s_i = o_i \circ q_i$ where q_i and o_i represent the encoder and the decoder respectively. This step is unsupervised and each client utilizes MSE loss to train local s_i:

$$\ell_{MSE} = \mathbb{E}_{(\mathbf{x},y)\sim\mathbb{P}(\mathcal{D}_i)} \left\| o_i([q_i(\mathbf{x}), \hat{\mathbf{z}}_i]) - \mathbf{x} \right\|_2^2, \tag{2}$$

where $[\cdot, \cdot]$ denotes the concatenation operation. The updated encoder and decoder of each client are then transmitted to the server. The server aggregates the collected auto-encoders and distributes the aggregated one, s, to each client.

---

[5] Note that the pre-training here is different from the pre-training of large foundation models such as self-supervised pre-training. This step is much more efficient than pre-training a large foundation model since we only train a little auto-encoder.

$$w(s) = \frac{1}{n} \sum_{i=1}^{n} w(s_i), \tag{3}$$

where $w(s)$ represent parameters of s. We assume that all clients contribute equally and participate in training. The above pre-training is iterative and we can obtain well-trained auto-encoders finally.

Input Surgery. After pre-training, input surgery optimizes encoders, q_i, to transform inputs consistent with foundation models. This step only exchanges encoders of clients to share common knowledge while each client preserves a client-specific embedding to represent personalized knowledge. In Fig 2, the foundation model, g, is black-box and the decoder is frozen. In the following, we elaborate on the whole training process in local clients.

In client C_i, an input $\mathbf{x}$ is first fed into the encoder q_i, generating an embedding vector $\mathbf{z} = q_i(\mathbf{x})$. Then we concatenate $\mathbf{z}$ with the client-specific embedding, $\hat{\mathbf{z}}_i$, and obtain the final embedding feature, $\tilde{\mathbf{z}} = [\mathbf{z}, \hat{\mathbf{z}}_i]$, which is then sent to the decoder. Once processed by the decoder, we can obtain $\tilde{\mathbf{x}} = o_i(\tilde{\mathbf{z}})$ with the same dimension as $\mathbf{x}$, and then the adapted input, $\tilde{\mathbf{x}}$, goes through the foundation model and the re-mapping layer, which generates the final prediction, $\tilde{\mathbf{y}}$. We utilize the cross-entropy loss ℓ_{cls} to guide the optimization:

$$\ell_1 = \mathbb{E}_{(\mathbf{x},y) \sim \mathbb{P}(\mathcal{D}_i)} \ell_{cls}(r_i(g(o_i([q_i(\mathbf{x}), \hat{\mathbf{z}}_i]))), y). \tag{4}$$

However, the above objective cannot be directly optimized using the standard stochastic gradient descent since the foundation model g is frozen, preventing us from computing its gradient using back-propagation. We adopt the zeroth-order optimization method, specifically, the coordinate-wise gradient estimate (CGE), to learn q_i and $\hat{\mathbf{z}}_i$ [15,27]. To make the process clear and easy to understand, we freeze r_i and view o_i, g, and r_i as a whole module, $\mathcal{G}$, in this step.

Assume $\mathbf{z} \in \mathbb{R}^{d_1}$ and $\hat{\mathbf{z}}_i \in \mathbb{R}^{d_2}$. According to CGE, by adding a perturbation to $\tilde{\mathbf{z}}$, we obtain the new embedding and the corresponding classification loss,

$$\tilde{\mathbf{z}}_1 = \tilde{\mathbf{z}} + \rho \mathbf{e}_j, \ell_{\mathbf{x},1} = \ell_{cls}(r_i(g(o_i(\tilde{\mathbf{z}}_1, y)))), \tag{5}$$

where $\mathbf{e}_j = (0, 0, \cdots, 1, 0, 0 \cdots, 0) \in \mathbb{R}^{d_1 + d_2}$ denotes the jth elementary basic vector and ρ is a hyperparameter that describes the extent of the perturbation. Similarly, we can obtain $\tilde{\mathbf{z}}_2$ and $\ell_{\mathbf{x},2}$.

$$\tilde{\mathbf{z}}_2 = \tilde{\mathbf{z}} - \rho \mathbf{e}_j, \ell_{\mathbf{x},2} = \ell_{cls}(r_i(g(o_i(\tilde{\mathbf{z}}_2, y)))). \tag{6}$$

Then, we have the gradient of $\mathcal{G}$ w.r.t. $\tilde{\mathbf{z}}$ computed as:

$$\nabla_{\tilde{\mathbf{z}}} \mathcal{G}(\tilde{\mathbf{z}}) = (\nabla_{\tilde{\mathbf{z}}} \mathcal{G}(\tilde{\mathbf{z}})_1, \nabla_{\tilde{\mathbf{z}}} \mathcal{G}(\tilde{\mathbf{z}})_2) \approx \sum_{i=1}^{d_1 + d_2} \frac{\ell_{\mathbf{x},2} - \ell_{\mathbf{x},1}}{2 \times \rho} \mathbf{e}_j. \tag{7}$$

For $\hat{\mathbf{z}}_i$, we directly update it with corresponding parts of $\nabla_{\tilde{\mathbf{z}}} \mathcal{G}(\tilde{\mathbf{z}})$ via a learning rate γ_2, $\hat{\mathbf{z}}_i^{new} = \hat{\mathbf{z}}_i - \gamma_2 \times \nabla_{\tilde{\mathbf{z}}} \mathcal{G}(\tilde{\mathbf{z}})_2$ where $\nabla_{\tilde{\mathbf{z}}} \mathcal{G}(\tilde{\mathbf{z}})_2$ denotes the last d_2

dimensions of $\nabla_{\tilde{\mathbf{z}}}\mathcal{G}(\tilde{\mathbf{z}})_1$. For $\nabla_{\tilde{\mathbf{z}}}\mathcal{G}(\tilde{\mathbf{z}})_1$, we can update q_i with the chain rule for differentiation.

$$\nabla_{q_i}\ell_1 = \frac{d\tilde{\mathbf{z}}}{dq_i}\frac{d\mathcal{G}}{d\tilde{\mathbf{z}}} \approx \frac{d\mathbf{z}}{dq_i}\nabla_{\tilde{\mathbf{z}}}\mathcal{G}(\tilde{\mathbf{z}})_1 \approx \frac{d\nabla_{\tilde{\mathbf{z}}}\mathcal{G}(\tilde{\mathbf{z}})_1\mathbf{z}}{dq_i}. \tag{8}$$

Finally, we can update the encoder, $w(q_i^{new}) = w(q_i) - \gamma_1 \times \nabla_{q_i}\ell_1$. Once all clients have updated encoders, we can aggregate encoders in the server and then distribute the aggregated encoder:

$$w(q) = \frac{1}{n}\sum_{i=1}^{n} w(q_i^{new}). \tag{9}$$

Semantic Re-mapping. In the last step, we train the encoder that enables the input consistent with foundation models. Here, we perform semantic re-mapping similar to [20]. This step only occurs in each client and no communication exists for simplicity and personalization. We view all parts before r_i as a whole module, $\mathcal{F}$, with two functions, including extracting features and mapping extracted features to a random space and we freeze $\mathcal{F}$. These two functions correspond to artificial features and the first layer in [20] respectively and we only update r_i corresponding to the second layer of ELM:

$$\ell_2 = \mathbb{E}_{(\mathbf{x},y)\sim\mathbb{P}(\mathcal{D}_i)}\ell_{cls}(r_i(\mathcal{F}(\mathbf{x})), y). \tag{10}$$

Since this part is behind g, $w(r_i)$ can be updated directly.

3.4   Discussion

We perform step 2 and step 3 iteratively. There also exist other zeroth-order optimization methods, e.g., the randomized gradient estimate (RGE) [26]. However, the concrete implementation of zeroth-order optimization is not our focus and we thereby choose CGE for deterministic and stability [27]. We assume foundation models exist on clients in the form of encrypted assets and we do not upload transformed inputs. Moreover, we do care about communication costs and GPU demands instead of training time in clients. To reduce training time, some techniques, such as RGE, random selections on $\mathbf{e}_j$, reduction on d_1+d_2, etc., can be adopted and we leave this as our future work. Besides, our algorithm converges and the asymptotic convergence rate is $\mathbf{O}(\frac{1}{\sqrt{T}})$.

4   Experiments

4.1   Setup

Datasets and Baselines.
We evaluate ZooPFL on 8 classification benchmarks with two modalities including computer vision (CV) and natural language processing (NLP). The benchmarks are COVID-19 (C-19) [37], APTOS [21], Terra100 (T-100) [3], Terra46 [3], SST-2 [39, 47], COLA [47, 49], Financial-phrasebank (Financial) [30], and Flipkart [45].

Table 2. Information of benchmarks.

Modality	Dataset	Samples	Classes	Clients	Selected Samples
CV	COVID-19	9,198	4	20	9,198
	APTOS	3,662	5	20	1,658
	Terra100	5,883	10	20	5,883
	Terra46	4,741	10	20	4,741
NLP	SST-2	67k	2	20	9,763
	COLA	8.5k	2	20	5,700
	Finanical	4,840	3	10	3,379
	Flipkart	205,053	3	20	3,048

Brief information can be found in Table 2.[6] We filter meaningless samples and select samples for global class balance. To our best knowledge, no other methods are proposed and thereby we only compare ZooPFL with zero-shot models (ZS).

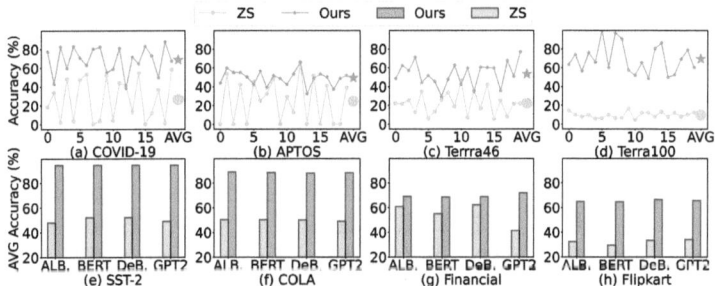

Fig. 3. Results on CV (a–d) and NLP (e–h) tasks.

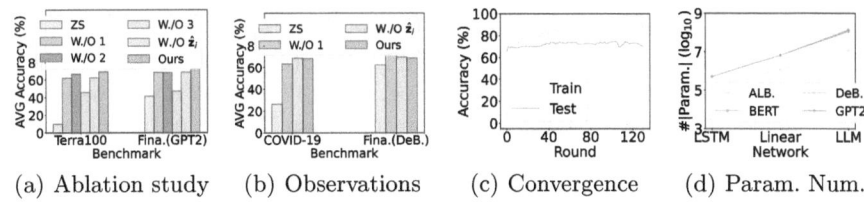

(a) Ablation study   (b) Observations   (c) Convergence   (d) Param. Num.

Fig. 4. Ablation study, convergence, and communication costs.

Implementation Details. For vision tasks, we set g as CLIP [34] with ResNet50 as the image backbone [34]. r is a linear layer with dimension M where

---

[6] We have chosen so many clients because it reflects the typical real-world scenario where there are numerous clients, each with relatively small amounts of data [50].

M is the number of classes. q contains several blocks composed of a convolution layer, a RELU activation layer, a Batch Normalization layer, and a Pooling layer while o contains several blocks composed of a convTranspose layer, a RELU activation layer, and a Batch Normalization layer. We set $d_1 = 6 \times 7 \times 7 = 294$ and $d_2 = 2 \times 7 \times 7 = 98$. We set the learning rate for pretraining as 10^{-4} and set other learning rates as hyperparameters. For simplicity, other learning rates are all the same. We set the local epoch number as 1 and set the global round number $T = 120$. Moreover, we do not tune ρ but set $\rho = 5 \times 10^{-3}$. We select the best results according to accuracy on validation parts.

For language tasks, we select four foundation models, including ALBERT-base [22], BERT-base [12], DeBERTa-base [18], and GPT2 [35]. Note that there are recent large language foundation models such as Llama [42] and Falcon [33], but we can only experiment with the above ones due to constrained computational devices.[7] Our method works for all kinds of foundation models in various sizes. q simply contains several linear layers followed by batch normalization layers. Please note that we transform input embeddings processed by foundation models for NLP instead of original texts. We set $d_1 = 128 - 32 = 96$ and $d_2 = 32$. We set the local epoch number as 1 and set the global round number $T = 130$. Other settings are similar to computer vision.

4.2   Experimental Results

Figure 3 shows the results on all eight benchmarks. And we have the following observations. 1) Our method achieves the best results on average for all benchmarks whatever the backbone is. It significantly outperforms the zero-shot method with remarkable improvements. In computer vision benchmarks, the improvements are about 42%, 25%, 21%, and 59% for COVID-19, Terra100, APTOS, and Terra46 respectively. In natural language processing benchmarks, for SST-2, COLA, and Flipkart, Financial-phrasebank, the improvements are about 43%, 39%, 15%, and 33% respectively. Please note that there only exist a few training data in each client (for COVID-19, each client only has about 50 samples.), which means utilizing foundation models is important. 2) Our method achieves the best accuracy in most clients, demonstrating the necessity of input surgery and semantic re-mapping. As shown in Fig. 3(a)–(d), ZOOPFL only performs slightly worse than ZS in few clients, e.g. client 13 on COVID-19, which can be due to the instability of zeroth-order optimization. 3) For natural language processing, different backbones bring different performance. From Fig. 3(g), we can see that our method based on GPT2 can achieve better results compared to other backbones, although ZS performs the worst with GPT2. However, from Fig. 3(f), we can see that ZOOPFL based on GPT2 does not achieve the best performance. 4) Why large foundation models cannot achieve acceptable performances on these benchmarks? For computer vision, we choose COVID-19,

---

[7] Our hardware is a server with 4 V100 (16G) GPUs, which cannot afford to train larger foundation models.

APTOS, and Terra Incognita and these datasets can be missing during pretraining of CLIP, which leads the failure of CLIP with zero-shot. For natural language processing, although large foundation models can extract remarkable features, they need to be fine-tuned for downstream tasks, which means they may randomly guess without the post-processing. Due to these factors, post-processing to large foundation models is necessary, which is just what we explore in this paper.

4.3   Analysis and Discussion

Ablation Study. Figure 4(a)–4(b) give experiments on ablation study and we have following observations. 1) In most situations, each part of ZooPFL can bring improvements. 2) Step 3 is more significant than Step 2. Since Step 3 remaps outputs, it can offer semantic meanings to foundation models for specific tasks, which is more direct and effective intuitively. Step 2 transforms inputs that still go through foundation models or even random projections, and thereby it is indirect and less effective. However, by combining Step 2 with Step 3, we can achieve further improvements. 3) In some situations, client-specific embeddings do not bring remarkable improvements, which can be induced by two reasons. First, CGE is not stable enough and we cannot ensure ZooPFL finds the best global optimals. Second, to ensure fairness, we offer comparison methods without client-specific embeddings containing larger dimensions and thereby these methods can learn better representations for auto-encoders. 4) Step 1 brings significant improvement for CV while it is less effective for NLP. This can be due to two reasons. We provide better auto-encoders for CV but simple linear layers for NLP. Moreover, the closed pretraining of an auto-encoder without subsequent adjustments to the decoder may not be suitable for NLP. Fortunately, ZooPFL can achieve convincing improvements compared to ZS no matter whether adopting step 1.

Convergence and Communication Cost. We provide convergence analysis and communication cost comparisons in Fig. 4(c) and 4(d), respectively. Figure 4(c) shows that both the average training accuracy and testing accuracy are convergent. There exist slight disturbances due to instability of CGE and the process of federated learning. Moreover, we can find that there exists a divergence between training and testing, which means there could be further improvements if more generalization techniques could be adopted which we leave as our future work. From Fig. 4(d), we can see exchanging in encoders can reduce a significant amount of transmission cost, especially for LSTM, which means our method can be employed in reality.

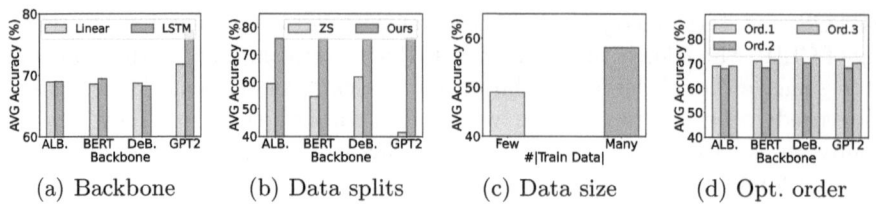

|(a) Backbone | (b) Data splits | (c) Data size | (d) Opt. order |

Fig. 5. Discussions by varying backbones, data splits, etc.

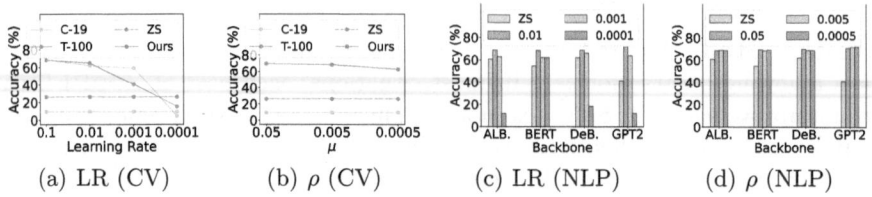

|(a) LR (CV) | (b) ρ (CV) | (c) LR (NLP) | (d) ρ (NLP) |

Fig. 6. Parameter sensitivity of CV and NLP tasks (on finance data).

More Insightful Analysis. 1) **Can stronger backbones bring better performance?** Figure 5(a) and 4(d) show that auto-encoders comprised of LSTM can bring better performance with fewer communications (especially for GPT2), which means more suitable backbones can lead to better performance. 2) **How can data splits influence the performance?** Figure 5(b) shows that ZooPFL still achieves better performance when using a different parameter for Dirichlet distribution (0.1 vs. 0.2) for NLP data split. In this more personalized situation, ZS maintains a similar performance while ours performs better. 3) **More training data, better results?** As shown in Fig. 5(c), we choose the APTOS dataset where our method has the worst performance, to evaluate the influence of training data. We find that more training data can bring further improvements, which is completely consistent with our intuition. 4) **Can optimization order influence performance?** We provide three orders for optimization. Order 1 is what we adopted. Order 2 is to perform step 2 for all rounds and then perform step 3, which means these two steps are split. In order 3, we first optimize the encoder, then client-specific embeddings, and finally semantic re-mapping layers, and these parts are iterative. In Fig. 5(d), Order 1 and Order 3 can perform slightly better than Order 2, which demonstrates the necessity of joint optimization.

Parameter Sensitivity. Figure 6 provides parameter sensitivity and we obtain following observations. 1) Our method is stable for a wide range of parameters although CGE may lead instability. 2) For most situations, larger learning rates with Adam can bring better performance. 3) ZooPFL can achieve further improvement if we finetune hyperparameters more carefully. For example, we can choose larger learning rates, e.g.0.5 or choose more suitable ρ for specific tasks, e.g. 0.05 for CV.

5   Related Work

Federated learning makes it possible to perform distributed multi-party computing without comprising privacy [31,53]. FedAVG is the baseline algorithm for FL by exchanging parameters instead of raw data, which has been used widely [36]. When FedAVG meets non-iid data, it can suffer from low convergence speed and terrible **personalization** performance [10]. [38] proposed PerFedMask that considers the computational capability of different devices while some other work considered utilizing knowledge distillation for personalization [8]. Besides personalization, there exists research focusing on generalization [7]. Our method can deal with situations where distribution shifts exist.

Since deep learning has entered the era of **large foundation models** [4,59], some novel issues, e.g. computation costs and communication costs, are coming into being, leading operations on the whole network impossible [17,58]. Fed-Prompt [57] studied prompt tuning in a model split aggregation way while Fed-CLIP [29] designed an attention-based adapter for CLIP [34]. FwdLLM [50] combined BP-free training with parameter-efficient training methods while pFedPG [52] deployed a personalized prompt generator at the server to produce client-specific visual prompts. These methods all require access to the internals of large models.

Besides data privacy, **model privacy** also raised attention recently [32]. Model suppliers are usually more willing to only provide predictions for given inputs or just provide a product that can only generate predictions [46]. In this paper, we view these protected foundation models as black-box models [16]. Little work paid attention to finetuning or optimizing in this field, but most related work focused on attacks [54]. One related work is FedZO [13] which utilized **zero-order optimization** [15], but it did not consider utilizing large foundation models. Some other work also made use of zero-order optimization for federated learning [24,56], but none of them utilized large black-box foundation models.

Model reprogramming (MR) [44,51] provides a similar solution to ZooPFL. It trains the inserted input transformation and output mapping layers while keeping the source pretrained model inact to enable resource-efficient cross-domain machine learning. The main purpose of model reprogramming is to transfer knowledge to targets and it can be viewed as a sub-field of transfer learning. Recently, [2] proposed the first framework, Reprogrammable-FL, adapting MR to the setting of differentially private federated learning. Reprogrammable-FL learned an input transformation for samples and added learned perturbations to the original samples. It preserved local input transformations and shared output transformation layers, which are totally in contrast to ours. Moreover, ZooPFL is proposed for black-box foundation models and can provide an ideal personalization capability.

6   Conclusion and Discussion

We proposed ZooPFL which can deal with large black-box models in federated learning. ZooPFL mainly consists of two parts, including input surgery and semantic re-mapping. Moreover, with a client-specific embedding, ZooPFL can be more personalized. We demonstrated its effectiveness on both CV and NLP tasks. ZooPFL achieved remarkable performance without large communication costs and high demands of GPUs.

As the first exploration in black-box federated learning for large foundation models, ZooPFL can be more perfect by pursuing the following avenues. 1) Since the stability and speed of CGE influence the performance of step 2, it can be better to seek more stable and efficient optimization algorithms. 2) Foundation models in ZooPFL can be enhanced by other ways, e.g., auxiliary models, to serve as a complement to foundation models. 3) Experiments with larger foundation models can be performed for evaluation when computational resources are enough.

References

1. Achiam, J., et al.: GPT-4 technical report. arXiv preprint arXiv:2303.08774 (2023)
2. Arif, H., Gittens, A., Chen, P.Y.: Reprogrammable-FL: improving utility-privacy tradeoff in federated learning via model reprogramming. In: 2023 IEEE Conference on Secure and Trustworthy Machine Learning (SaTML), pp. 197–209. IEEE (2023)
3. Beery, S., Van Horn, G., Perona, P.: Recognition in terra incognita. In: Proceedings of the European Conference on Computer Vision (ECCV), pp. 456–473 (2018)
4. Bommasani, R., et al.: On the opportunities and risks of foundation models. arXiv preprint arXiv:2108.07258 (2021)
5. Brown, T., et al.: Language models are few-shot learners. Adv. Neural. Inf. Process. Syst. **33**, 1877–1901 (2020)
6. Cai, D., Wu, Y., Wang, S., Lin, F.X., Xu, M.: FedAdapter: efficient federated learning for modern NLP. arXiv preprint arXiv:2205.10162 (2022)
7. Chen, H.Y., Chao, W.L.: On bridging generic and personalized federated learning for image classification. In: International Conference on Learning Representations (2022)
8. Chen, H., Wang, C., Vikalo, H.: The best of both worlds: accurate global and personalized models through federated learning with data-free hyper-knowledge distillation. In: The Eleventh International Conference on Learning Representations (2023)
9. Chen, P.Y.: Model reprogramming: resource-efficient cross-domain machine learning. In: Proceedings of the AAAI Conference on Artificial Intelligence, vol. 38, pp. 22584–22591 (2024)
10. Chen, Y., Vikalo, H., Wang, C.: Fed-QSSL: a framework for personalized federated learning under bitwidth and data heterogeneity. In: Proceedings of the AAAI Conference on Artificial Intelligence, vol. 38, pp. 11443–11452 (2024)
11. DeepMind, G.: Gemini. https://deepmind.google/technologies/gemini/
12. Devlin, J., Chang, M.W., Lee, K., Toutanova, K.: BERT: pre-training of deep bidirectional transformers for language understanding. arXiv preprint arXiv:1810.04805 (2018)
13. Fang, W., Yu, Z., Jiang, Y., Shi, Y., Jones, C.N., Zhou, Y.: Communication-efficient stochastic zeroth-order optimization for federated learning. IEEE Trans. Signal Process. **70**, 5058–5073 (2022)

14. Gao, L., Fu, H., Li, L., Chen, Y., Xu, M., Xu, C.Z.: FedDC: federated learning with non-IID data via local drift decoupling and correction. In: Proceedings of the IEEE/CVF Conference on Computer Vision and Pattern Recognition, pp. 10112–10121 (2022)

15. Ghadimi, S., Lan, G.: Stochastic first-and zeroth-order methods for nonconvex stochastic programming. SIAM J. Optim. **23**(4), 2341–2368 (2013)

16. Guidotti, R., Monreale, A., Ruggieri, S., Turini, F., Giannotti, F., Pedreschi, D.: A survey of methods for explaining black box models. ACM Comput. Surv. (CSUR) **51**(5), 1–42 (2018)

17. Guo, T., Guo, S., Wang, J., Tang, X., Xu, W.: PromptFL: let federated participants cooperatively learn prompts instead of models-federated learning in age of foundation model. IEEE Trans. Mob. Comput. (2023)

18. He, P., Liu, X., Gao, J., Chen, W.: DeBERTa: decoding-enhanced BERT with disentangled attention. In: International Conference on Learning Representations (2021)

19. Hou, B., O'connor, J., Andreas, J., Chang, S., Zhang, Y.: PromptBoosting: black-box text classification with ten forward passes. In: International Conference on Machine Learning, pp. 13309–13324. PMLR (2023)

20. Huang, G., Huang, G.B., Song, S., You, K.: Trends in extreme learning machines: a review. Neural Netw. **61**, 32–48 (2015)

21. Karthik, Maggie, S.D.: APTOS 2019 blindness detection (2019). https://kaggle.com/competitions/aptos2019-blindness-detection

22. Lan, Z., Chen, M., Goodman, S., Gimpel, K., Sharma, P., Soricut, R.: AlBERT: a lite BERT for self-supervised learning of language representations. In: International Conference on Learning Representations (2020)

23. Li, T., Sahu, A.K., Zaheer, M., Sanjabi, M., Talwalkar, A., Smith, V.: Federated optimization in heterogeneous networks. Proc. Mach. Learn. Syst. **2**, 429–450 (2020)

24. Li, Z., Chen, L.: Communication-efficient decentralized zeroth-order method on heterogeneous data. In: 2021 13th International Conference on Wireless Communications and Signal Processing (WCSP), pp. 1–6. IEEE (2021)

25. Liu, P., Yuan, W., Fu, J., Jiang, Z., Hayashi, H., Neubig, G.: Pre-train, prompt, and predict: a systematic survey of prompting methods in natural language processing. ACM Comput. Surv. **55**(9), 1–35 (2023)

26. Liu, S., Chen, P.Y., Kailkhura, B., Zhang, G., Hero III, A.O., Varshney, P.K.: A primer on zeroth-order optimization in signal processing and machine learning: principals, recent advances, and applications. IEEE Signal Process. Mag. **37**(5), 43–54 (2020)

27. Liu, S., Kailkhura, B., Chen, P.Y., Ting, P., Chang, S., Amini, L.: Zeroth-order stochastic variance reduction for nonconvex optimization. In: Advances in Neural Information Processing Systems, vol. 31 (2018)

28. Liu, V., Chilton, L.B.: Design guidelines for prompt engineering text-to-image generative models. In: Proceedings of the 2022 CHI Conference on Human Factors in Computing Systems, pp. 1–23 (2022)

29. Lu, W., Xixu, H., Wang, J., Xie, X.: FedCLIP: fast generalization and personalization for CLIP in federated learning. In: ICLR 2023 Workshop on Trustworthy and Reliable Large-Scale Machine Learning Models (2023)

30. Malo, P., Sinha, A., Korhonen, P., Wallenius, J., Takala, P.: Good debt or bad debt: detecting semantic orientations in economic texts. J. Assoc. Inf. Sci. Technol. **65** (2014)

31. McMahan, B., Moore, E., Ramage, D., Hampson, S., y Arcas, B.A.: Communication-efficient learning of deep networks from decentralized data. In: Artificial Intelligence and Statistics, pp. 1273–1282. PMLR (2017)
32. Mo, F., et al: DarkneTZ: towards model privacy at the edge using trusted execution environments. In: Proceedings of the 18th International Conference on Mobile Systems, Applications, and Services, pp. 161–174 (2020)
33. Penedo, G., et al.: The refinedweb dataset for falcon LLM: outperforming curated corpora with web data only. In: Advances in Neural Information Processing Systems, vol. 36 (2024)
34. Radford, A., et al.: Learning transferable visual models from natural language supervision. In: International Conference on Machine Learning, pp. 8748–8763. PMLR (2021)
35. Radford, A., et al.: Language models are unsupervised multitask learners. OpenAI blog 1(8), 9 (2019)
36. Rodríguez-Barroso, N., Jiménez-López, D., Luzón, M.V., Herrera, F., Martínez-Cámara, E.: Survey on federated learning threats: concepts, taxonomy on attacks and defences, experimental study and challenges. Inf. Fusion 90, 148–173 (2023)
37. Sait, U., et al.: Curated dataset for COVID-19 posterior-anterior chest radiography images (X-rays). Mendeley Data 1 (2020)
38. Setayesh, M., Li, X., Wong, V.W.: PerFedMask: personalized federated learning with optimized masking vectors. In: The Eleventh International Conference on Learning Representations (2023)
39. Socher, R., et al.: Recursive deep models for semantic compositionality over a sentiment treebank. In: Proceedings of the 2013 Conference on Empirical Methods in Natural Language Processing, pp. 1631–1642. Association for Computational Linguistics, Seattle (2013). https://www.aclweb.org/anthology/D13-1170
40. Sun, T., Shao, Y., Qian, H., Huang, X., Qiu, X.: Black-box tuning for language-model-as-a-service. In: International Conference on Machine Learning, pp. 20841–20855. PMLR (2022)
41. Thambiraja, E., Ramesh, G., Umarani, D.R.: A survey on various most common encryption techniques. Int. J. Adv. Res. Comput. Sci. Softw. Eng. 2(7) (2012)
42. Touvron, H., et al.: LLaMA: open and efficient foundation language models. arXiv preprint arXiv:2302.13971 (2023)
43. Tramèr, F., Zhang, F., Juels, A., Reiter, M.K., Ristenpart, T.: Stealing machine learning models via prediction {APIs}. In: 25th USENIX security symposium (USENIX Security 2016), pp. 601–618 (2016)
44. Tsai, Y.Y., Chen, P.Y., Ho, T.Y.: Transfer learning without knowing: reprogramming black-box machine learning models with scarce data and limited resources. In: International Conference on Machine Learning, pp. 9614–9624. PMLR (2020)
45. Vaghani, N., Thummar, M.: Flipkart product reviews with sentiment dataset (2023). https://doi.org/10.34740/KAGGLE/DSV/4940809, https://www.kaggle.com/dsv/4940809
46. Van Dis, E.A., Bollen, J., Zuidema, W., van Rooij, R., Bockting, C.L.: ChatGPT: five priorities for research. Nature 614(7947), 224–226 (2023)
47. Wang, A., Singh, A., Michael, J., Hill, F., Levy, O., Bowman, S.R.: GLUE: a multi-task benchmark and analysis platform for natural language understanding. In: International Conference on Learning Representations (2019)
48. Wang, Y., et al.: Exploring vision-language models for imbalanced learning. Int. J. Comput. Vision (IJCV) (2023)
49. Warstadt, A., Singh, A., Bowman, S.R.: Neural network acceptability judgments. Trans. Assoc. Comput. Linguist. 7, 625–641 (2019)

50. Xu, M., Wu, Y., Cai, D., Li, X., Wang, S.: Federated fine-tuning of billion-sized language models across mobile devices. arXiv preprint arXiv:2308.13894 (2023)

51. Xu, S., et al.: Towards efficient task-driven model reprogramming with foundation models. arXiv preprint arXiv:2304.02263 (2023)

52. Yang, F.E., Wang, C.Y., Wang, Y.C.F.: Efficient model personalization in federated learning via client-specific prompt generation. In: Proceedings of the IEEE/CVF International Conference on Computer Vision, pp. 19159–19168 (2023)

53. Yang, Q., Liu, Y., Chen, T., Tong, Y.: Federated machine learning: concept and applications. ACM Trans. Intell. Syst. Technol. (TIST) **10**(2), 1–19 (2019)

54. Yang, R., Ma, J., Zhang, J., Kumari, S., Kumar, S., Rodrigues, J.J.: Practical feature inference attack in vertical federated learning during prediction in artificial internet of things. IEEE Internet Things J.(2023)

55. Yurochkin, M., Agarwal, M., Ghosh, S., Greenewald, K., Hoang, N., Khazaeni, Y.: Bayesian nonparametric federated learning of neural networks. In: International Conference on Machine Learning, pp. 7252–7261. PMLR (2019)

56. Zelikman, E., Huang, Q., Liang, P., Haber, N., Goodman, N.D.: Just one byte (per gradient): a note on low-bandwidth decentralized language model finetuning using shared randomness. arXiv preprint arXiv:2306.10015 (2023)

57. Zhao, H., Du, W., Li, F., Li, P., Liu, G.: FedPrompt: communication-efficient and privacy-preserving prompt tuning in federated learning. In: ICASSP 2023-2023 IEEE International Conference on Acoustics, Speech and Signal Processing (ICASSP), pp. 1–5. IEEE (2023)

58. Zhou, H., Lan, T., Venkataramani, G.P., Ding, W.: Every parameter matters: ensuring the convergence of federated learning with dynamic heterogeneous models reduction. In: Advances in Neural Information Processing Systems, vol. 36 (2024)

59. Zhuang, W., Chen, C., Lyu, L.: When foundation model meets federated learning: motivations, challenges, and future directions. arXiv preprint arXiv:2306.15546 (2023)

Supercharging Federated Learning with Flower and NVIDIA FLARE

Holger R. Roth[1]([⊠]) [iD], Daniel J. Beutel[2] [iD], Yan Cheng[1] [iD],
Javier Fernandez Marques[2] [iD], Heng Pan[2] [iD], Chester Chen[1] [iD],
Zhihong Zhang[1] [iD], Yuhong Wen[1] [iD], Sean Yang[1] [iD], Isaac Yang[1] [iD],
Yuan-Ting Hsieh[1] [iD], Ziyue Xu[1] [iD], Daguang Xu[1] [iD], Nicholas D. Lane[2] [iD],
and Andrew Feng[1] [iD]

[1] NVIDIA Corporation, Santa Clara, USA
hroth@nvidia.com
[2] Flower Labs, London, UK

Abstract. Several open-source systems, such as Flower and NVIDIA FLARE, have been developed in recent years while focusing on different aspects of federated learning (FL). Flower is dedicated to implementing a cohesive approach to FL, analytics, and evaluation. Over time, Flower has cultivated extensive strategies and algorithms tailored for FL application development, fostering a vibrant FL community in research and industry. Conversely, FLARE has prioritized the creation of an enterprise-ready, resilient runtime environment explicitly designed for FL applications in production environments. In this paper, we describe our initial integration of both frameworks and show how they can work together to supercharge the FL ecosystem as a whole. Through the seamless integration of Flower and FLARE, applications crafted within the Flower framework can effortlessly operate within the FLARE runtime environment without necessitating any modifications. This initial integration streamlines the process, eliminating complexities and ensuring smooth interoperability between the two platforms, thus enhancing the overall efficiency and accessibility of FL applications.

Keywords: Federated learning · Open-source · Framework interoperability · Production deployment

1 Introduction

Federated learning (FL) makes it possible for AI algorithms to gain experience from a vast range of data located at different sites [3,6,7]. The approach enables several organizations to collaborate on the development of models without directly sharing sensitive data. Preserving privacy while still benefiting from diverse datasets across various locations worldwide.

In this paper, we introduce the collaboration between two of the most widely used solutions for FL, NVIDIA FLARE [4] and Flower [1] to establish compatibility between the two frameworks. With this collaboration, NVIDIA will

H. Yu et al. (Eds.): FL 2024 Workshops, LNAI 15501, pp. 36–45, 2025.
https://doi.org/10.1007/978-3-031-82240-7_3

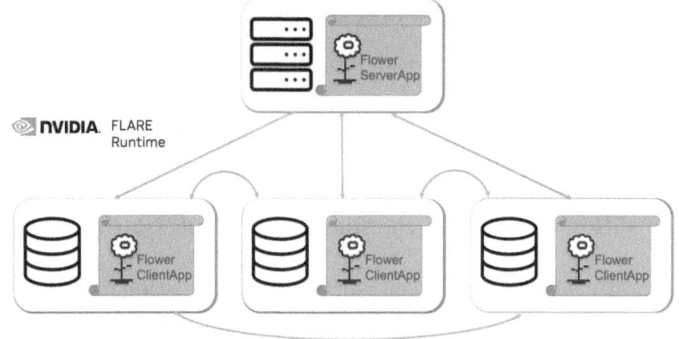

Fig. 1. Flower & NVIDIA FLARE integration.

support running Flower projects on FLARE, thus enabling FLARE developers to access the rich Flower ecosystem, and give Flower developers new options for production deployment through FLARE. The developer communities of both frameworks will be able to build larger-scale consortiums that leverage more data toward training stronger AI models.

Flower is known for its ease of use, mobile device support, and a large, active open-source community of AI developers and researchers that keep Flower at the forefront of new methods. NVIDIA FLARE offers a comprehensive range of FL features, including robust communication, concurrent job scheduling, security, and confidential computing with strong support for industry-leading NVIDIA hardware. Compatibility between the two complementary frameworks will allow developers to combine the strengths of each platform; under this collaboration, users will be able to build varieties of federated AI systems that were not previously possible.

Flower & NVIDIA FLARE integration comes with benefits for both sides. The benefits for FLARE users include using FL algorithms and datasets directly from Flower – reducing the cost of applying new FL algorithms, leveraging rich built-in differential privacy and secure aggregation support, along with the option to mix FLARE APIs or Flower APIs as required. For Flower users, the benefits include a robust communication framework, concurrent jobs, confidential computing on CPU/GPU, and flexible communication patterns such as server-centric or peer-to-peer.

We introduced this initiative between Flower and NVIDIA at the Flower AI Summit 2024 [2]. This event has grown to be the world's largest conference on FL. During the opening AI Industry Day keynote, a live demonstration was provided to the audience of the first working prototype to result from this collaboration. This presentation showed FLARE running an unmodified Flower project that performs FL and federated evaluation over several training rounds. This feature is planned to be released to the public with an upcoming FLARE release. We expect that this initial release will be the first of a series of integrations that provide more comprehensive forms of compatibility between Flower and NVIDIA FLARE in the future.

2   Integration Goals

Our main goal is to enable users to directly deploy Flower `ServerApps` and `ClientsApps` within the FLARE runtime environment. No code changes will be necessary.

Architecturally, Flower uses client/server communication. Flower clients communicate with the server via gRPC[1]. FLARE uses the same architecture and allows multiple jobs to run at the same time (multiple jobs share the same set of clients/servers) without requiring multiple ports to be open on the server host.

Since both frameworks follow the same communication architecture, it is relatively easy to make a Flower application a FLARE job by using FLARE as the communicator for the Flower App, as illustrated in Fig. 1.

In this proposed approach, Flower *SuperNodes* shift away from direct interaction with the Flower *SuperLink*, opting instead for communication through FLARE. This integration offers several distinctive advantages. Firstly, it facilitates the provisioning of startup kits, including certificates, streamlining the setup process. Moreover, it enables the deployment of custom code, allowing for tailored applications to be implemented seamlessly. User authentication and authorization mechanisms enhance security and access control within the system. Additionally, the inclusion of a ReliableMessage mechanism addresses connection stability concerns, ensuring robust communication. Multiple communication schemes, such as gRPC, HTTP, TCP, Redis, among others, offer flexibility in communication protocols. Notably, FLARE supports peer-to-peer (P2P) communication, which allows for diverse topologies, enabling direct interaction between any parties involved. A multi-job system further enhances efficiency by enabling multiple Flower apps to operate simultaneously without necessitating additional ports on the server.

3   Design Principles

The main design principles of FLARE and Flower share some commonalities, which are key to supporting compatibility and are beneficial for the integration of the two frameworks. We detail them below.

3.1   FLARE Multi-Job Architecture

To maximize the utilization of compute resources, FLARE supports multiple jobs running simultaneously, each an independent FL experiment.

As shown in Fig. 2, there is the `Server Control Process` (SCP) on the Server host, and there is a `Client Control Process` (CCP) on each client host.

---

[1] https://grpc.io.

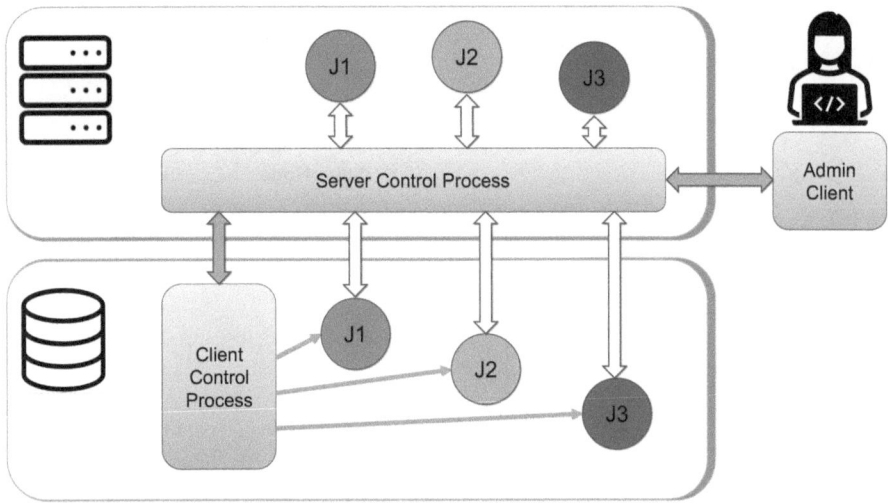

Fig. 2. NVIDIA FLARE Multi-job system architecture.

The SCP communicates with CCPs to manage FLARE jobs (schedule, deploy, monitor, and abort jobs). When the SCP schedules a job, the job is sent to the CCPs of all sites, which create separate processes for the job. These processes form a "Job Network" for the job. This network only exists during the runtime of the job. Figure 2 shows jobs (J1, J2, J3) in different colors on server and client(s). For example, all J1 processes form the Job Network for Job 1.

By default, processes of the same Job Network are not connected directly. Instead, they only connect to the SCP, and all messages between job processes are relayed through the SCP. However, if network policy permits, direct connections could be established automatically between the job processes to obtain maximum communication speed. The underlying communication path is transparent to applications and only requires configuration changes to enable direct communication.

3.2 Flower Next

With the recent introduction of Flower Next[2], Flower enabled multi-run support utilizing long-running server and clients called `SuperLink` and `SuperNodes`, respectively, that allow running multiple Flower Apps as illustrated in Fig. 3. The `SuperLink` and `SuperNode` decouples the communication layer from the Flower `ServerApp` and `ClientApps`. This design is very analogous to FLARE's multi-job architecture (see Sect. 3.1) and allows seamless integration, as discussed in the next section.

---

[2] Flower Next is Flower's new high-level API. All new features (like Flower Mods) will be built on top of it.

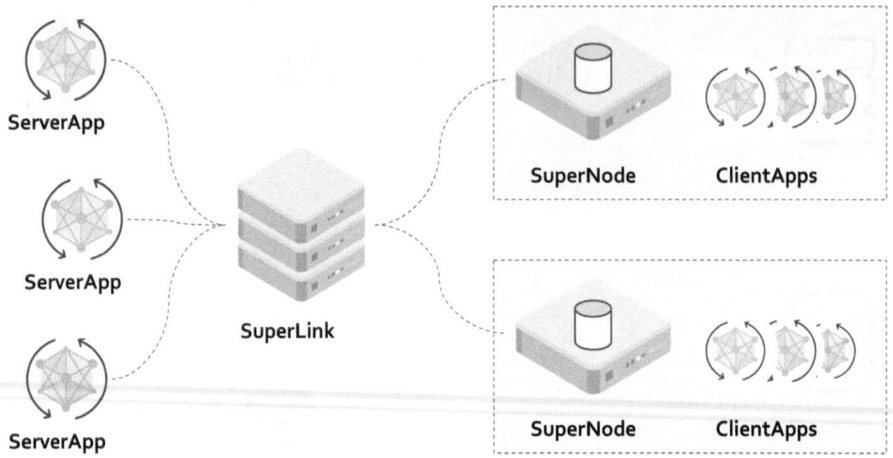

Fig. 3. Flower SuperLink and SuperNodes.

4 Initial Integration

In this first integration, Flower algorithms will be able to utilize the FLARE's reliable messaging system detailed below and other benefits such as metric streaming for experiment tracking.

4.1 FLARE Reliable Messaging

The interaction between the FLARE Clients and Server is through reliable messaging. First, the requester tries to send the request to the peer. If it fails to send it, it will retry a moment later. This process keeps repeating until the request is sent successfully or the amount of time has passed (which will cause the job to abort).

Secondly, once the request is sent, the requester waits for the response. Once the peer finishes processing, the result is sent to the requester immediately (which could be successful or unsuccessful). At the same time, the requester repeatedly sends queries to get the result from the peer until the result is received or the maximum amount of time has passed (which will cause the job to abort). The result could be received in one of the following ways:

1. The result is received from the response message sent by the peer when it finishes the processing.
2. The result is received from the response to the query message of the requester.

4.2 Integration Design

Flower uses gRPC as the communication protocol. To use FLARE as the communicator, we route Flower's gRPC messages through FLARE. To do so, we

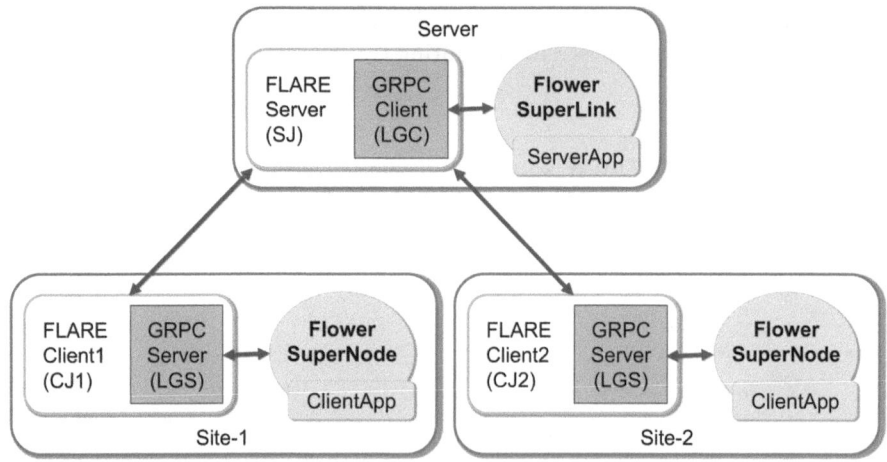

Fig. 4. Integration of Flower Apps within FLARE.

change the server endpoint of each Flower client to a local gRPC server (LGS) within the FLARE client.

As shown in Fig. 4, there is a `Local GRPC server` (LGS) for each site that serves as the server endpoint for the Flower `SuperNode` on the site. Similarly, there is a `Local GRPC Client` (LGC) on the FLARE Server that interacts with the Flower `SuperLink`. The message path between the Flower `SuperNode` and the Flower `SuperLink` is as follows:

1. The Flower `SuperNode` generates a gRPC message and sends it to the LGS in the FLARE Client
2. FLARE Client forwards the message to the FLARE Server – This is a reliable FLARE message.
3. FLARE Server uses the LGC to send the message to the Flower `SuperLink`.
4. The Flower `SuperLink` sends the response back to the LGC in the FLARE Server.
5. FLARE Server sends the response back to the FLARE Client.
6. FLARE Client sends the response back to the Flower `SuperNode` via the LGS.

Note that the Flower `SuperNode` could be running as a separate process or within the same process as the FLARE Client.

This integration design enables users to directly deploy Flower ServerApps and ClientsApps within the FLARE Runtime Environment without requiring any code changes.

5   Experiments

Next, we describe two experiments. First, an integration of running Flower Apps in FLARE's environment without any code changes needed, followed by a tighter integration, allowing a Flower App to utilize some of FLARE's communication features, such as the metric streaming during training used for experiment tracking.

5.1   Integration Without Code Changes

To showcase our integration, we run Flower's PyTorch-Quickstart example directly within FLARE. The Flower creation of Flower ServerApp and ClientApps in shown in Listings 1.1 and 1.2.

```
1 # Define strategy
2 strategy = FedAdam(...)
3
4 # Create Flower ServerApp
5 app = ServerApp(
6     config=ServerConfig(num_rounds=3),
7     strategy=strategy,
8 )
```

Listing 1.1. Creating a Flower ServerApp.

```
1 class FlowerClient(NumPyClient):
2   def fit(self, parameters, config):
3     model.set_weights(parameters)
4     model.fit(x_train, y_train, epochs=1, batch_size=32)
5     return model.get_weights(), len(x_train), {}
6
7   def evaluate(self, parameters, config):
8     model.set_weights(parameters)
9     loss, accuracy = model.evaluate(x_test, y_test)
10     return loss, len(x_test), {"accuracy": accuracy}
11
12
13 def client_fn(cid: str):
14     """Return an instance of Flower 'Client'."""
15     return FlowerClient().to_client()
16
17
18 # Create Flower ClientApp
19 app = ClientApp(
20     client_fn=client_fn,
21 )
```

Listing 1.2. Creating a Flower ClientApp.

With the integration of Flower and FLARE, applications developed with the Flower framework will run seamlessly in FLARE runtime without the user needing to make any changes.

We have two options to deploy a Flower project within the FLARE runtime.

1. Use FLARE's simulator or CLI:
   `nvflare job submit <job_path>`
2. Use Flower Run CLI:
   `flwr run <project_path>`

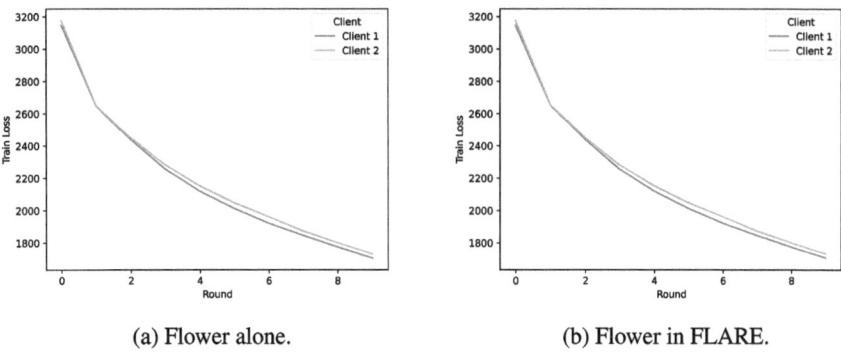

(a) Flower alone.   (b) Flower in FLARE.

Fig. 5. Comparison of running a Flower application natively (a) or within FLARE (b).

Reproducibility: Here, we show that one gets the same results when running a Flower application alone compared to running it within the FLARE environment. We initialize the code using the same random seeds for the clients and plot training curves in Fig. 5. Both graphs will match exactly when overlaid, showing that the messages routed by FLARE do not influence the results.

5.2   Hybrid Integration Using FLARE's Experiment Tracking

By deploying a Flower App within the FLARE runtime, we can now utilize features from both frameworks. For example, we can utilize FLARE's experiment tracking feature within the Flower client code as shown in Listing 1.3.

```
1  from nvflare.client.tracking import SummaryWriter
2  writer = SummaryWriter()
3
4  def train(net, trainloader, epochs):
5      """Train the model on the training set."""
6      criterion = torch.nn.CrossEntropyLoss()
7      optimizer = torch.optim.SGD(net.parameters(), lr=0.001, momentum=0.9)
8
9      global TRAIN_STEP
10     for _ in range(epochs):
11         avg_loss = 0.0
12         for batch in tqdm(trainloader, "Training"):
13             images = batch["img"]
14             labels = batch["label"]
15             optimizer.zero_grad()
16             loss = criterion(net(images.to(DEVICE)), labels.to(DEVICE))
17             loss.backward()
18             optimizer.step()
19             avg_loss += loss.item()
20         writer.add_scalar("train_loss", avg_loss/len(trainloader),
   TRAIN_STEP)
21         TRAIN_STEP += 1
22  ...
```

Listing 1.3. Usage of FLARE's experiment tracking within a Flower ClientApp.

Once the experiment runs, we can see the experiment tracking metrics from each client being streamed to the FLARE server as shown in Fig. 6 in the case of three clients.

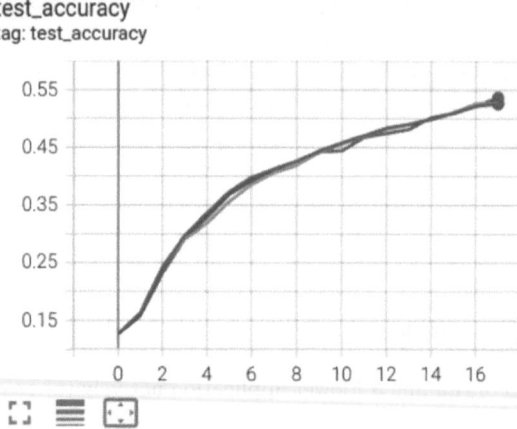

Fig. 6. Flower ClientApps running with FLARE's experiment tracking and visualized using TensorBoard.

6   Discussion

The integration of Flower with NVIDIA FLARE offers mutual benefits to both platforms. For FLARE users, this integration allows for direct utilization of FL algorithms and datasets from Flower, thereby reducing the cost associated with implementing new FL algorithms. Users will also have the flexibility to leverage either FLARE APIs or Flower APIs, providing versatility in their development approach.

On the other hand, Flower users also reap significant advantages from this integration. They gain access to robust communication capabilities, enabling seamless data exchange between Flower and FLARE. Concurrent job execution enhances efficiency by enabling multiple tasks to be processed simultaneously. Furthermore, Flower users benefit from the integration's support for confidential computing on both CPU and GPU, ensuring data security and privacy. The integration also maintains a server-centric architecture while facilitating peer-to-peer communication, offering a comprehensive and versatile solution for FL applications.

Looking ahead, we plan to enable FLARE users to leverage Flower's rich mobile and IoT device support to incorporate these into their federations more seamlessly. Furthermore, the potential for supporting very large messages, up to hundreds of gigabytes, presents an exciting prospect [5]. This would require integration with CellNet in Flower, promising even greater scalability and capability for handling large-scale data processing tasks, which is crucial for building reliable foundation models and is part of our future collaboration plan.

References

1. Beutel, D.J., et al.: Flower: a friendly federated learning research framework. arXiv preprint arXiv:2007.14390 (2020)
2. Roth, H., Beutel, D., Lane, N.: Announcing NVIDIA and flower collaboration (2024). https://flower.ai/blog/2024-03-15-announcing-nvidia-and-flower-collaboration
3. Mammen, P.M.: Federated learning: opportunities and challenges. arXiv preprint arXiv:2101.05428 (2021)
4. Roth, H.R., et al.: NVIDIA flare: federated learning from simulation to real-world. arXiv preprint arXiv:2210.13291 (2022)
5. Roth, H.R., et al.: Empowering federated learning for massive models with NVIDIA flare. arXiv preprint arXiv:2402.07792 (2024)
6. Yang, Q., Liu, Y., Chen, T., Tong, Y.: Federated machine learning: concept and applications. ACM Trans. Intell. Syst. Technol. (TIST) 10(2), 1–19 (2019)
7. Zhang, C., Xie, Y., Bai, H., Yu, B., Li, W., Gao, Y.: A survey on federated learning. Knowl.-Based Syst. 216, 106775 (2021)

Federated Knowledge Transfer Fine-Tuning Large Server Model with Resource-Constrained IoT Clients

Shaoyuan Chen[1,2], Linlin You[1(✉)], Rui Liu[3], Shuo Yu[4], and Ahmed M. Abdelmoniem[5]

[1] School of Intelligent Systems Engineering, Sun Yat-sen University, Shenzhen, China
youllin@mail.sysu.edu.cn
[2] Shenzhen Fangle Technology Co., Ltd., Shenzhen, China
[3] School of Computer Science and Engineering, Nanyang Technological University, Singapore, Singapore
[4] School of Computer Science and Technology, Dalian University of Technology, Dalian, China
[5] School of Electronic Engineering and Computer Science, Queen Mary University of London, London, UK

Abstract. The training of large models, involving fine-tuning, faces the scarcity of high-quality data. Compared to the solutions based on centralized data centers, updating large models in the Internet of Things (IoT) faces challenges in coordinating knowledge from distributed clients by using their private and heterogeneous data. To tackle such a challenge, we propose KOALA (Federated **K**n**o**wledge Tr**a**nsfer Fine-tuning **La**rge Server Model with Resource-Constrained IoT Clients) to impel the training of large models in IoT. Since the resources obtained by IoT clients are limited and restricted, it is infeasible to locally execute large models and also update them in a privacy-preserving manner. Therefore, we leverage federated learning and knowledge distillation to update large models through collaboration with their small models, which can run locally at IoT clients to process their private data separately and enable large-small model knowledge transfer through iterative learning between the server and clients. Moreover, to support clients with similar or different computing capacities, KOALA is designed with two kinds of large-small model joint learning modes, namely to be homogeneous or heterogeneous. Experimental results demonstrate that compared to the conventional approach, our method can not only achieve similar training performance but also significantly reduce the need for local storage and computing power resources.

Keywords: Internet of Things · Federated Learning · Knowledge Transfer · Knowledge Distillation · Large Model Fine-tuning

1 Introduction

Models with ever-growing scale have been introduced, such as BERT [1,2], GPT [3–5], VGG [6], and ViT [7]. To train and adopt them in various Internet of Things scenes, how

H. Yu et al. (Eds.): FL 2024 Workshops, LNAI 15501, pp. 46–60, 2025.
https://doi.org/10.1007/978-3-031-82240-7_4

to utilize distributed data and computing powers becomes crucial. Unfortunately, IoT clients typically exhibit data protection considerations [8,9] and constrained computing capacities [10,11]. These factors impede the use of their data to train complex and large-scale models.

To tackle the challenge of data privacy, solutions based on federated learning (FL) are studied to support the training of large models in a collaborative and privacy-preserving manner, e.g., Yu S et al. [12] propose a method of training the large model alternately in clients with private data and the server with labeled public data; and Wu C et al. [13] introduce a method of federated mutual distillation for training personalized large models, which can significantly reduce communication costs. Even though private knowledge can be shared among distributed clients through FL, the common premise of current methods is to have sufficient local computing capacities to run large models directly on each learning client, making them infeasible to support distributed IoT clients with insufficient local resources.

Therefore, to support the fine-tuning of large models [14,15] and the model adaptation to empower various IoT scenarios, the objective of this study is defined as illustrated in Fig. 1, where 1) the server has sufficient storage and computing powers but lacks high-quality data (only with a limited amount of unlabeled proxy dataset), and 2) IoT clients as a group are rich in sensed data and distributed computing powers, but as for each client, its device and private data are heterogeneous, and its local resources are limited to support the running of large models.

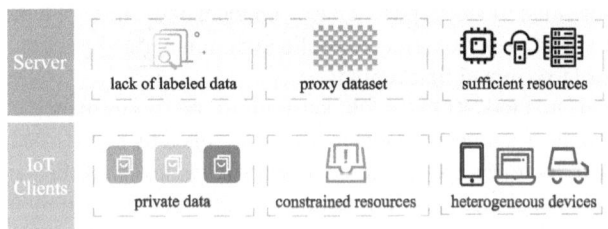

Fig. 1. The situations of the server and IoT clients.

By integrating FL to share private knowledge across IoT clients and knowledge distillation (KD) to transfer encoded knowledge among different models (i.e., between teacher and student models), KOALA is proposed to enable a joint and iterative learning process that allows the IoT clients to run their local small models to extract and share local knowledge, and then the server to update the adapter of the large model based on the local updated small model of each client. Specifically, to implement such a learning process, the forward and reverse distillation techniques are used jointly, to, first, reverse distill trained small models to fine-tune the large model, and then, forward distill the large model to update small models for IoT clients.

Moreover, in conventional FL, the global and local models have the same structure, and the global model can be updated based on the aggregation of local updates directly. However, the large-small model collaborative learning process implemented in KOALA needs to support different models in the server and clients, which makes conventional FL methods infeasible. Hence, according to the difference among small models, KOALA implements two kinds of learning mode to aggregate local knowledge encoded in homogeneous or heterogeneous small models. Specifically, the homogeneous method supports IoT clients to run small models with the same structure, and on the contrary, the heterogeneous method supports each IoT client to run different small models, which are more flexible as they can be created according to the actual computing capacity of the client. After the update of the large model, by using either homogeneous or heterogeneous methods, related small models can distilled from the latest large model and dispatched to their corresponding clients to start a new learning iteration.

Based on standard datasets, the efficiency and effectiveness of KOALA are evaluated. Experimental results show that compared with the baseline, where IoT clients can load and execute the large model with sufficient local resources, our method can approach similar training performance for all tasks, and also significantly reduce the need for local resources.

In general, our main contributions can be summarized as follows:

- We propose a novel large-small model collaborative learning process in data protection and resource-constrained IoT scenarios, through which, FL and KD can work jointly to support the iterative learning of large and small models even though they are cross-scale in model structures;
- We design a reverse knowledge distillation strategy to better handle the outputs of heterogeneous small models updated based on local data, through which, the outputs of local models on proxy datasets are refined and integrated to generate consensus soft labels for large model fine-tuning;
- The proposed method KOALA is verified to be performance-equivalent and resource-efficient. Specifically, large models fine-tuned by KOALA can achieve similar accuracy to the ones updated in conventional methods. At the same time, compared to conventional methods, the storage space needed for loading the local model reduces by about 97.6% (Homo) and 97.2% (Hete), and FLOPs of the local model reduces by about 98.4% (Homo) and 98.6% (Hete).

2   Related Work

2.1   Federated Learning

Federated learning is a privacy-preserving machine learning framework where the server coordinates multiple clients to learn globally shareable models without exchanging local data directly [16]. As the classic method, FedAvg [17] manages each client to train its local model and upload the updated local model to the server. Then, the local models are aggregated to update a global model, which is then downloaded by active clients in the next round. However, the issue of non-identically and independently distributed (Non-IID) data among clients degrades the performance of federated learning [18], prompting numerous methods that aim to alleviate this problem. Accordingly, FedProx [19] introduces a proximal term to the loss function in local training, to constrain the updating of model parameters. SCAFFOLD [20] introduces control variables to reduce "client drift". MOON [21] combines federated learning and contrastive learning to make the local model updating closer to the global model and farther away from the previous local model. Since highly heterogeneous data may prevent the model from converging, and a common global model fails to meet the individual needs of different clients, personalized federated learning is essential [22]. FedClassAvg [23] conducts federated learning on heterogeneous models through classifier aggregation. Per-FedAvg [24] incorporates the classic meta-learning framework, MAML [25], to train personalized models based on the global meta-model. Differently, PFedMe [26] does not utilize the global model directly, but instead concurrently trains the global model and personalized models.

2.2 Knowledge Distillation

Hinton et al. have first introduced knowledge distillation [27]. Their work employs a weighted sum of the hard and soft loss as the complete loss. The soft loss is the loss between the soft outputs of the student model and the soft labels generated by the teacher model, and the hard loss is the loss between the hard outputs of the student model and the real labels. Adriana Romero et al. [28] introduce knowledge distillation based on hidden layer knowledge features (hints). Zhang et al. [29] propose mutual distillation, enabling different models to mutually distill knowledge from one another.

2.3 Federated Knowledge Distillation

Knowledge Distillation has gained increasing attention to integrating with Federated Learning [30]. FedMD [31] makes the integration based on a shared dataset to calculate mean scores that guide the knowledge distillation of each client. Instead, FD [32] eliminates the need for a shared dataset and allows clients to calculate prediction scores for each label on their local dataset, and the server to calculate the global mean prediction score per label, which serves as soft labels during the local distillation. FedGKT [33] combines federated learning with split learning (SL) [34]. FedDKC [35] is similar to FedGKT and can reduce the gap between knowledge distributions of the heterogeneous models. Although FedGKT and FedDKC can support resource-constrained clients, both methods require local real labels to be uploaded, which compromises client privacy. Moreover, their target is to train the small model under the guidance of large models, instead of considering how to integrate knowledge extracted from different clients to update the large model efficiently and effectively.

3 Methodology

3.1 Problem Statement

Suppose there are N clients i $(i = 1, 2, \ldots, N)$, each of which has its private dataset with labels $j = 1, 2, \ldots, C$. The sample size of client i is n_i. To support the classification tasks, the key goal, defined in Eq. 1, is to minimize the loss difference between the large model updated by our method suppose constrained local resources and the conventional one suppose sufficient local resources, where Ω and Ω_{Conv} are the large model trained by our method and the conventional one, respectively, $\mathcal{L}()$ is the loss function and D is the test dataset.

$$\arg\min_{\Omega} F(\Omega) = \frac{\mathcal{L}(\Omega, D) - \mathcal{L}(\Omega_{Conv}, D)}{|D|} \tag{1}$$

3.2   Motivation

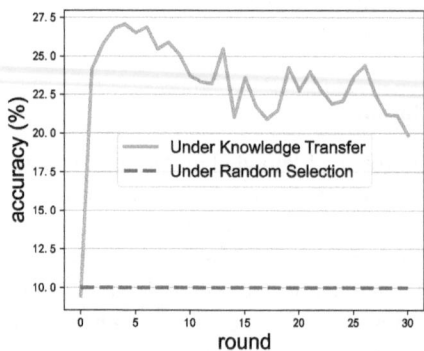

Fig. 2. Accuracy (%) under knowledge transfer and random selection.

Our method is based on this intuition: the small model can be viewed as the local private knowledge extractor that can be used at the server to transfer knowledge embedded within private data to the large model.

To verify our intuition, we design a simple experiment where in each round, the small model is trained by a labeled dataset, and then a large model is fine-tuned based on a proxy dataset through knowledge distillation with the small model as the teacher model and the large model as the student model. Note that CIFAR-10 is used for small model training and its test dataset is used for evaluating the performance of the large model. Moreover, the small and large models are MobileNet V3 Small and VGG19, respectively.

According to the result shown in Fig. 2, we can observe that the accuracy of large models can be improved significantly, even though it only processes the unlabelled proxy dataset. Therefore, the small model can share local private knowledge with the large model based on the knowledge extraction and transfer process, which motivates us to design KOALA that can integrate federated learning and knowledge distillation to implement a large-small model collaborative learning process.

3.3   The Proposed Method: KOALA

In KOALA, we implement a large-small model collaborative learning process, through which, small models serve as local knowledge extractors and the large model is fine-tuned according to the distilled knowledge from small models. Specifically, in each

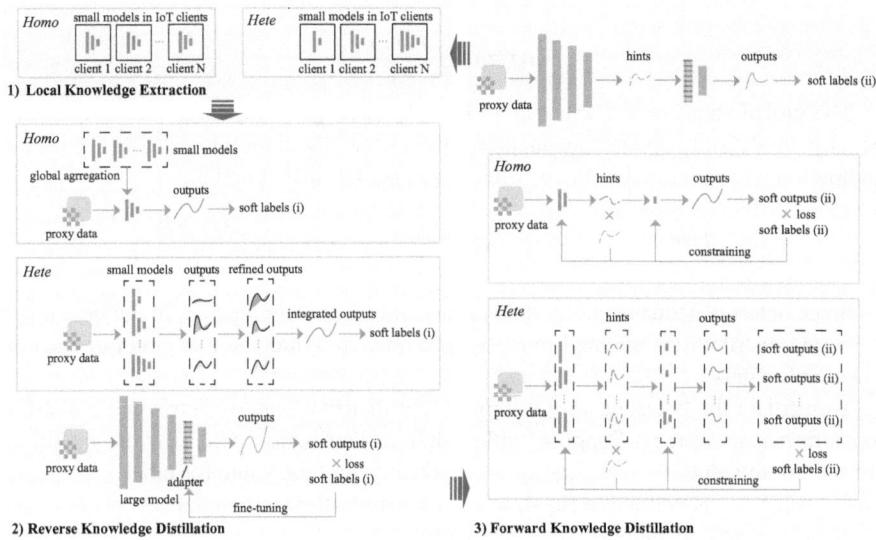

Fig. 3. The framework of KOALA, which consists of 1) local knowledge extraction, 2) reverse knowledge distillation, and 3) forward knowledge distillation.

IoT client, the corresponding small model is downloaded from the server and trained locally based on its private data. In the server, a bi-directional knowledge distillation mechanism is introduced, which supports 1) the reverse distillation to fine-tune the large model based on small models, and 2) the forward distillation to update small models based on the large model.

As shown in Fig. 3, KOALA consists of three steps, namely 1) Local Knowledge Extraction, 2) Reverse Knowledge Distillation, and 3) Forward Knowledge Distillation. Since the IoT clients can be heterogeneous in not only their data but also their computing capacities, KOALA is designed with two kinds of learning modes, namely one for homogeneous small models (denoted as homo), and the other one for heterogeneous small models (denoted as hete).

Local Knowledge Extraction. In this step, small models either homo or hete are updated according to the private data of corresponding IoT clients. After the extraction of local knowledge, small models are uploaded to the server.

Reverse Knowledge Distillation. After all the local updated small models are collected, the server starts the reverse distillation, in which, the large model serves as the student model, and the small model serves as the teacher model.

Specifically, in the homo mode, the small models are aggregated to first generate the global small model ω, and then used to produce soft labels as defined in Eq. 2 based on the proxy data x, where T is distillation temperature.

$$softmax(\frac{f(x,\omega)}{T}) \tag{2}$$

The global small model ω transfers local knowledge to the large model Ω, where the large model only updates its adapter. The reverse distillation loss $loss_r^{homo}$ used in the homo mode is defined in Eq. 3, where $l_{KL}()$ is KL loss function.

$$loss_r^{homo} = l_{KL}(softmax(\frac{f(x,\omega)}{T}), softmax(\frac{f(x,\Omega)}{T})) \tag{3}$$

Since heterogeneous small models cannot directly be aggregated, in the hete mode, the output distributions of small models are refined and integrated to generate the consensus soft labels.

To mediate the heterogeneity within output distributions, we introduce a distribution refinement strategy. Suppose within output distribution $f(x,\omega_i)$, the maximum and minimum value is $z_{i,max}$, $z_{i,min}$, respectively, and the value for label j is $z_{i,j}$, the refined value $\hat{z}_{i,j}$ is defined in Eq. 4, where ω_i is the i-th small model (for client i), and k is the coefficient to support the refinement.

$$\hat{z}_{i,j} = k\frac{z_{i,j} - z_{i,min}}{z_{i,max} - z_{i,min}} \tag{4}$$

To sum up the refined values for all labels, we can get

$$\sum_{j=1}^{C} \hat{z}_{i,j} = k\frac{\sum_{j=1}^{C}(z_{i,j} - z_{i,min})}{z_{i,max} - z_{i,min}} = k\frac{C(\overline{z}_i - z_{i,min})}{z_{i,max} - z_{i,min}} \tag{5}$$

In Eq. 5, $\overline{z}_i$ is the mean value of output distribution $f(x,\omega_i)$. Suppose the mean values of refined distributions of all the small models are equal to A (which is a constant), and therefore,

$$A = \frac{\sum_{j=1}^{C}\hat{z}_{i,j}}{C} = k\frac{\overline{z}_i - z_{i,min}}{z_{i,max} - z_{i,min}} \tag{6}$$

Then, the coefficient k can be calculated.

$$k = A\frac{z_{i,max} - z_{i,min}}{\overline{z}_i - z_{i,min}} \tag{7}$$

We substitute it to Eq. 4, and get the distribution refinement strategy as

$$\hat{z}_{i,j} = A\frac{z_{i,j} - z_{i,min}}{\overline{z}_i - z_{i,min}} \tag{8}$$

According to Eq. 8, we get the refined output distributions $\hat{z}_i = \{\hat{z}_{i,1}, \hat{z}_{i,2}, ..., \hat{z}_{i,C}\}$. Then, we obtain the integrated output distributions among small models through Eq. 9, donated as $\tilde{z}$. Suppose set of active clients is S in this round.

$$\tilde{z} = \sum_{i \in S} \frac{n_i}{\sum_{i \in S} n_i} \hat{z}_i \tag{9}$$

Based on $\tilde{z}$, the consensus soft labels are calculated.

$$softmax(\frac{\tilde{z}}{T}) \tag{10}$$

Then, we fine-tune the large model Ω based on the reverse distillation loss $loss_r^{hete}$ as defined in Eq. 11.

$$loss_r^{hete} = l_{KL}(softmax(\frac{\tilde{z}}{T}), softmax(\frac{f(x, \Omega)}{T})) \tag{11}$$

Forward Knowledge Distillation. Following the reverse distillation, we implement the forward distillation to update the small model according to the updated large model, where the large model serves as the teacher model, and the small model serves as the student model.

To calculate the forward distillation loss, the output feature loss (the loss between the output layers) and the hidden feature loss (the loss between the hidden layers) need to be calculated.

In the homo mode, the global small model ω is the student model to be updated. Ω^h represents the first h layers within the larger model, whereas ω^g represents first g layers within the global small model. Accordingly, the output feature loss $loss_{out}^{homo}$ and hidden feature loss $loss_{hid}^{homo}$ are computed according to Eqs. 12 and 13, respectively, where W is the bridging matrix and $l_{MSE}()$ is MSE loss function.

$$loss_{out}^{homo} = l_{KL}(softmax(\frac{f(x, \Omega)}{T}), softmax(\frac{f(x, \omega)}{T})) \tag{12}$$

$$loss_{hid}^{homo} = l_{MSE}(f(x, \Omega^h), f(x, \omega^g)W) \tag{13}$$

Therefore, the sum of $loss_{out}^{homo}$ and $loss_{hid}^{homo}$ forms the forward distillation loss $loss_f^{homo}$ as defined in Eq. 14, where λ is a constant.

$$loss_f^{homo} = loss_{out}^{homo} + \lambda loss_{hid}^{homo} \tag{14}$$

In the hete mode, each small model $\omega_i(i \in S)$ serves as the student model undergoing knowledge distillation for the update. Suppose the i-th small model ω_i is the student model, ω_i^g represents first g layers within ω_i and W_i is the bridging matrix for ω_i, the output feature loss $loss_{out,i}^{hete}$ and hidden feature loss $loss_{hid,i}^{hete}$ for the i-th small model ω_i can be calculated according to Eqs. 15 and 16, respectively.

$$loss_{out,i}^{hete} = l_{KL}(softmax(\frac{f(x, \Omega)}{T}), softmax(\frac{f(x, \omega_i)}{T})) \tag{15}$$

$$loss_{hid,i}^{hete} = l_{MSE}(f(x, \Omega^h), f(x, \omega_i^g)W_i) \tag{16}$$

Accordingly, the forward distillation loss for the i-th small model $loss_{f,i}^{hete}$ is

$$loss_{f,i}^{hete} = loss_{out,i}^{hete} + \lambda loss_{hid,i}^{hete} \tag{17}$$

Algorithm 1. KOALA

Input: large model Ω, global small model ω, local small model ω_i (for client i), learning rate η_0, η_1, η_2, number of rounds R, current round r, set of active clients S, proxy data x, local data (x_0, y_0), $l_{CE}()$ is Cross-Entropy loss function

1: Let $r = 0$.
2: **while** $r \leq R$ **do**
3:    $r \leftarrow r + 1$
      $S \leftarrow$ Sampling
      Client $i \in S$ executes:
      $\omega_i \leftarrow \omega_i - \eta_0 \nabla l_{CE}(y_0, f(x_0, \omega_i))$
      uploading ω_i to the Server
      Server executes:
4:    **if** Homo **then**
5:       $\omega \leftarrow \sum_{i \in S} \frac{n_i}{\sum_{i \in S} n_i} \omega_i$
         soft labels of ω are represented as (2)
         fine-tuning the large model:
         $loss_r^{homo}$ is computed as (3)
         $\Omega \leftarrow \Omega - \eta_1 \nabla loss_r^{homo}$
         constraining the global small model:
         $loss_f^{homo}$ is computed as (12)(13)(14)
         $\omega \leftarrow \omega - \eta_2 \nabla loss_f^{homo}$
6:    **end if**
7:    **if** Hete **then**
8:       output distributions are refined as (8)
         integrated output distributions are computed as (9)
         consensus soft labels are represented as (10)
         fine-tuning the large model:
         $loss_r^{hete}$ is computed as (11)
         $\Omega \leftarrow \Omega - \eta_1 \nabla loss_r^{hete}$
         constraining the small models:
         $loss_{f,i}^{hete}$ is computed as (15)(16)(17)
         $\omega_i \leftarrow \omega_i - \eta_2 \nabla loss_{f,i}^{hete}$
9:    **end if**
10: **end while**

Finally, either in homo or hete mode, the small model is updated based on its forward distillation loss and after the update, it is dispatched to the related client to start a new learning round until certain criteria are met (e.g., the model converges or the maximum learning round is reached).

To better illustrate the overall workflow of KOALA, its pseudo-code is given in Algorithm 1.

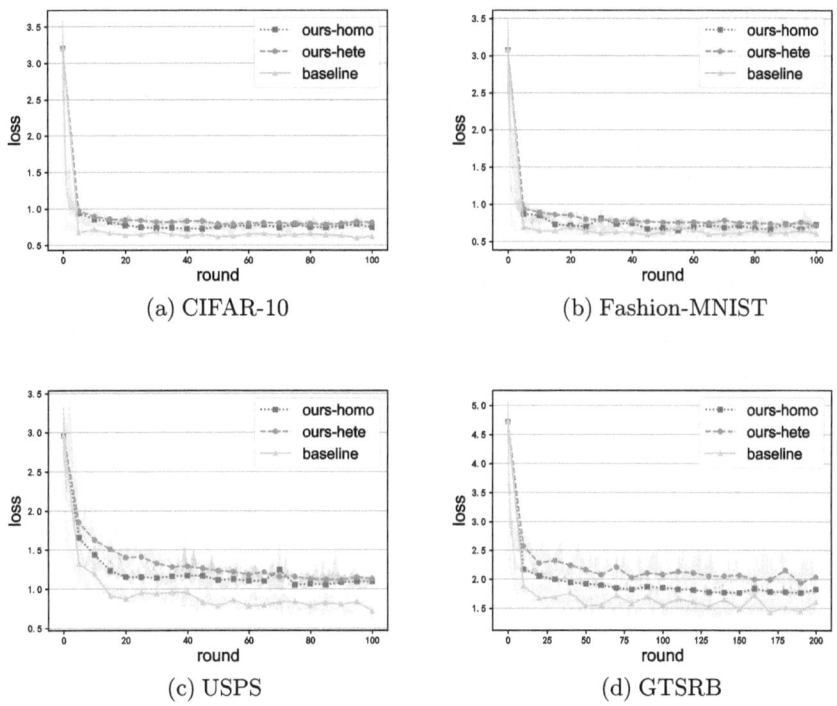

(a) CIFAR-10   (b) Fashion-MNIST

(c) USPS   (d) GTSRB

Fig. 4. Loss reduction. The loss value represents the mean loss over 3 trials. The shadows indicate the range of losses across the 3 trials.

4   Experimental Results

4.1   Setup

We introduce the experimental setup in 4 key aspects: models, datasets, baseline, and hyperparameters.

Models. We select TorchVision backbones[1] and append the classifier onto the last layer of each backbone to form the large model and small models used in our experiments. The classifier of the large model is viewed as the adapter. The backbone for the large model is VGG19. In our homo mode, the small model is MobileNet V2. In our hete mode, the small models are MobileNet V2, MobileNet V3 Small, EfficientNet B0, ShuffleNet V2 X0_5, and ShuffleNet V2 X2_0, respectively. Moreover, we implement additional experiments to count the model FLOPs, where we use 64×64 randomly generated "image" as the input.

Datasets. We select 4 datasets: CIFAR-10 [36], Fashion-MNIST [37], USPS [38], and GTSRB [39]. The entire test set of each dataset is used to evaluate the large model, recording its performance before training (round 0) and at the end of each learning

---

[1] https://pytorch.org/vision/0.13/models.html.

Table 1. Accuracy (%). We run 3 trials and report the mean and standard derivation of the best accuracy in each trial.

method	CIFAR-10	Fashion-MNIST	USPS	GTSRB
ours-homo	76.02 ± 0.55	77.53 ± 0.33	77.76 ± 2.01	51.99 ± 1.08
ours-hete	75.97 ± 0.33	77.89 ± 0.08	76.20 ± 0.68	52.32 ± 0.93
baseline	79.35 ± 0.12	80.44 ± 0.32	81.48 ± 0.88	58.84 ± 0.14

Table 2. Model Params and FLOPs. The ID 0 and ID 1∼5 respectively refers to the large model and the small models. The model of ID 3 is used for local loading and execution in ours-homo, and models of ID 1∼5 are used for those in ours-hete. The large model is used for local loading and execution in baseline. In 'Params' and 'FLOPs' columns, the delimiter characters are used to separate the value of the model for CIFAR-10/Fashion-MNIST/USPS tasks (left) from that for GTSRB task (right).

Model ID	Backbone Name	PARAMS	FLOPs	Model Type
0	VGG19	143.68M/143.71M	3.43G/3.43G	large model
1	ShuffleNet V2 X2_0	7.40M/7.44M	101.45M/101.52M	small model
2	EfficientNet B0	5.30M/5.33M	71.32M/71.39M	
3	MobileNet V2	3.51M/3.55M	55.84M/55.90M	
4	MobileNet V3 Small	2.55M/2.59M	14.03M/14.10M	
5	ShuffleNet V2 X0_5	1.38M/1.41M	9.18M/9.24M	

round. The proxy dataset is a subset of the original train set by removing the labels. The local datasets of clients are obtained by Dirichlet Distribution, with the concentration parameter of 1.0. In addition, there is no overlap between the proxy dataset and private client datasets.

Baseline. We set a baseline under the assumption that all IoT clients have sufficient local resources to run the large model directly, and Federated Averaging (FedAvg) [17] is used to update the global model. Specifically, the workflow of the baseline to update the global model consists of three steps, namely: 1) clients download the global large model; 2) the large model is fine-tuned locally; and 3) the large model parameters are uploaded to the server for the global aggregation. During client-server interactions, the adapter instead of the entire model is exchanged between the server and clients, except for the first download of the large model from the server to the clients.

Hyperparameters. We consider a scenario involving 5 clients and 1 server. Adam is selected as the optimizer and the distillation temperature is set to 7 in all the experiments. For the baseline, the learning rate for local fine-tuning is 0.001, and weight decay is 0.000001. In KOALA, for reverse distillation, the learning rate is 0.001, and the weight decay is 0.000001; and for forward distillation, the learning rate is 0.0001, and the weight decay is 0.000001. For the output distribution refinement in the hete mode, the mean value A is set to 2.

4.2   Loss and Accuracy

The loss curves are illustrated in Fig. 4, and the accuracy of different methods is listed in Table 1. It is remarkable fact that our method demonstrates optimal performance in the CIFAR-10 and Fashion-MNIST tasks, closely approaching the baseline both in loss reduction and model accuracy.

4.3   Ablation in Bi-directional Distillation

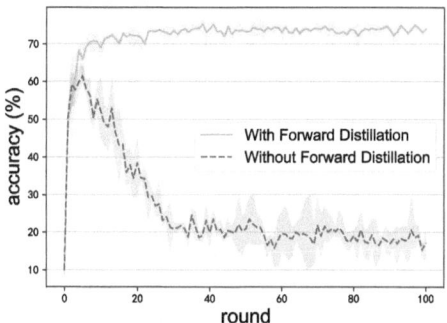

Fig. 5. Accuracy (%) with and without Forward Distillation. The acc is the mean value of accuracies in 3 trials and the shadows demonstrate the variability range under different random seeds.

During the bi-directional distillation in the server, the small model transfers local knowledge to the large model in reverse distillation, and the large model updates the small model in forward distillation. Reverse distillation is indispensable for fine-tuning the large model, and forward distillation also matters for the update of small models, which work jointly making the iterative learning between large and small models workable.

   To reveal the necessity and efficacy of forward distillation, we implement an additional experiment with or without forward distillation in the homo mode to support the CIFAR-10 task. The experiment runs for 3 trials by using the same seed setups as the previous experiments. As illustrated in Fig. 5, it shows that forward distillation plays a significant role in the bi-directional distillation to enable the extraction of private knowledge from local clients to continuously update the large model.

4.4   Demands for Storage and Computing Power

Table 2 shows the Params and FLOPs of the models during the experiments. The classifiers for different tasks may have a slight difference. When we demonstrate the Params and FLOPs, we use the delimiters to separate the value of the model for the CIFAR-10, Fashion-MNIST, and USPS tasks from that for the GTSRB task. In addition, Fig. 6 shows the storage space needed to load related models to be trained.

Since the small models have much fewer parameters than the large model, the mean storage space for all clients reduces by 97.6% (Homo) and 97.2% (Hete). We can also observe that FLOPs of the large model is significantly higher than that of each small model. The mean FLOPs of the local models of all clients (calculated according to models for CIFAR-10/Fashion-MNIST/USPS tasks) reduces by 98.4% (Homo) and 98.6% (Hete).

In summary, the storage and computing power required for the model to be loaded and executed locally are much lower than the ones needed for the baseline, which proofs the efficiency and effectiveness of KOALA in supporting various IoT scenarios consisting of large amount of heterogeneous IoT clients.

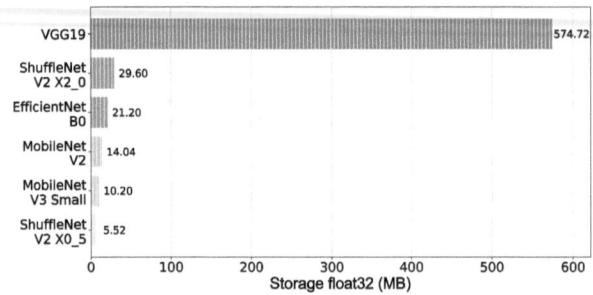

Fig. 6. Storage for model local-loading in float32. The storage data in the figure is calculated according to model Params (for the CIFAR-10/Fashion-MNIST/USPS tasks) as listed in Table 2.

5   Conclusion

To fine-tune large models by orchestrating distributed IoT clients with limited storage space or computing capabilities, we propose KOALA, a privacy-preserving and resource-efficient method that integrates federated learning and knowledge distillation by implementing a novel large-small model collaborative learning process. In general, it uses small models to extract private knowledge without having large models running on IoT clients. Moreover, it also supports the knowledge transfer between the large model and small models by implementing a bi-directional distillation, in which, small models can be updated according to the large model through the common forward distillation, and also the large model can be fine-tuned by reverse distillation by aggregating knowledge from either homogeneous or heterogeneous small models. Experimental results show that compared to the conventional method, KOALA can significantly reduce the demands for local storage space and computing power to fine-tune large models with competitive performance.

Acknowledgments. This work was supported in part by the Guangdong Basic and Applied Basic Research Foundation under Grant 2023A1515012895, in part by the National Key Research and Development Program of China under Grant 2023YFB4301900, and in part by Department of Science and Technology of Guangdong Province (Project No. 2021QN02S161).

References

1. Devlin, J., Chang, M.-W., Lee, K., Toutanova, K.: BERT: pre-training of deep bidirectional transformers for language understanding. arXiv preprint arXiv:1810.04805 (2018)
2. Liu, Y., et al.: RoBERTa: a robustly optimized BERT pretraining approach. arXiv preprint arXiv:1907.11692 (2019)
3. Radford, A., Narasimhan, K., Salimans, T., Sutskever, I.: Improving language understanding by generative pre-training. Technical report, OpenAI (2018)
4. Radford, A., Wu, J., Child, R., Luan, D., Amodei, D., Sutskever, I.: Language models are unsupervised multitask learners. OpenAI Blog 1(8), 9 (2019)
5. Brown, T., et al.: Language models are few-shot learners. In: 33rd Advances in Neural Information Processing Systems, pp. 1877–1901 (2020)
6. Simonyan, K., Zisserman, A.: Very deep convolutional networks for large-scale image recognition. arXiv preprint arXiv:1409.1556 (2014)
7. Dosovitskiy, A., et al.: An image is worth 16×16 words: transformers for image recognition at scale. arXiv preprint arXiv:2010.11929 (2020)
8. Chen, C., Feng, X., Zhou, J., Yin, J., Zheng, X.: Federated large language model: a position paper. arXiv preprint arXiv:2307.08925 (2023)
9. Zhuang, W., Chen, C., Lyu, L.: When foundation model meets federated learning: motivations, challenges, and future directions. arXiv preprint arXiv:2306.15546 (2023)
10. Wang, X., Han, Y., Wang, C., Zhao, Q., Chen, X., Chen, M.: In-edge AI: intelligentizing mobile edge computing, caching and communication by federated learning. IEEE Netw. 33(5), 156–165 (2019)
11. Imteaj, A., Thakker, U., Wang, S., Li, J., Amini, M.H.: A survey on federated learning for resource-constrained IoT devices. IEEE Internet Things J. 9(1), 1–24 (2021)
12. Yu, S., Munoz, J.P., Jannesari, A.: Federated foundation models: privacy-preserving and collaborative learning for large models. arXiv preprint arXiv:2305.11414 (2023)
13. Wu, C., Wu, F., Lyu, L., Huang, Y., Xie, X.: Communication-efficient federated learning via knowledge distillation. Nat. Commun. 13(1), 2032 (2022)
14. Houlsby, N., et al.: Parameter-efficient transfer learning for NLP. In: International Conference on Machine Learning, pp. 2790–2799 (2019)
15. Han, Z., Gao, C., Liu, J., Zhang, S.Q.: Parameter-efficient fine-tuning for large models: a comprehensive survey. arXiv preprint arXiv:2403.14608 (2024)
16. Zhang, C., Xie, Y., Bai, H., Yu, B., Li, W., Gao, Y.: A survey on federated learning. Knowl. Based Syst. 216, 106775 (2021)
17. McMahan, B., Moore, E., Ramage, D., Hampson, S., Arcas, B.: Communication-efficient learning of deep networks from decentralized data. In: Artificial Intelligence and Statistics, pp. 1273–1282 (2017)
18. Mora, A., Fantini, D., Bellavista, P.: Federated learning algorithms with heterogeneous data distributions: an empirical evaluation. In: IEEE/ACM 7th Symposium on Edge Computing (SEC), pp. 336–341 (2022)
19. Li, T., Sahu, A.K., Zaheer, M., Sanjabi, M., Talwalkar, A., Smith, V.: Federated optimization in heterogeneous networks. In: 2nd Proceedings of Machine Learning and Systems, pp. 429–450 (2020)
20. Karimireddy, S.P., Kale, S., Mohri, M., Reddi, S.J., Stich, S., Suresh, A.T.: SCAFFOLD: stochastic controlled averaging for federated learning. In: International Conference on Machine Learning, pp. 5132–5143 (2020)
21. Li, Q., He, B., Song, D.: Model-contrastive federated learning. In: Proceedings of the IEEE/CVF Conference on Computer Vision and Pattern Recognition, pp. 10713–10722 (2021)

22. Tan, A.Z., Yu, H., Cui, L., Yang, Q.: Towards personalized federated learning. IEEE Trans. Neural Netw. Learn. Syst. (2022)

23. Jang, J., Ha, H., Jung, D., Yoon, S.: FedClassAvg: local representation learning for personalized federated learning on heterogeneous neural networks. In: Proceedings of the 51st International Conference on Parallel Processing, pp. 1–10 (2022)

24. Fallah, A., Mokhtari, A., Ozdaglar, A.: Personalized federated learning: a meta-learning approach. arXiv preprint arXiv:2002.07948 (2020)

25. Finn, C., Abbeel, P., Levine, S.: Model-agnostic meta-learning for fast adaptation of deep networks. In: International Conference on Machine Learning, pp. 1126–1135 (2017)

26. Dinh, C., Tran, N., Nguyen, J.: Personalized federated learning with Moreau envelopes. In: 33rd Advances in Neural Information Processing Systems, pp. 21394–21405 (2020)

27. Hinton, G., Vinyals, O., Dean, J.: Distilling the knowledge in a neural network. arXiv preprint arXiv:1503.02531 (2015)

28. Romero, A., Ballas, N., Ebrahimi, K.S., Chassang, A., Gatta, C., Bengio, Y.: FitNets: hints for thin deep nets. In: Proceedings of the ICLR (2015)

29. Zhang, Y., Xiang, T., Hospedales, T.M., Lu, H.: Deep mutual learning. In: Proceedings of the IEEE Conference on Computer Vision and Pattern Recognition, pp. 4320–4328 (2018)

30. Mora, A., Tenison, I., Bellavista, P., Rish, I.: Knowledge distillation for federated learning: a practical guide. arXiv preprint arXiv:2211.04742 (2022)

31. Li, D., Wang, J.: FedMD: heterogenous federated learning via model distillation. arXiv preprint arXiv:1910.03581 (2019)

32. Jeong, E., Oh, S., Kim, H., Park, J., Bennis, M., Kim, S.L.: Communication-efficient on-device machine learning: federated distillation and augmentation under non-IID private data. arXiv preprint arXiv:1811.11479 (2018)

33. He, C., Annavaram, M., Avestimehr, S.: Group knowledge transfer: federated learning of large CNNs at the edge. In: 33rd Advances in Neural Information Processing Systems, pp. 14068–14080 (2020)

34. Gupta, O., Raskar, R.: Distributed learning of deep neural network over multiple agents. J. Netw. Comput. Appl. **116**, 1–8 (2018)

35. Wu, Z., et al.: Exploring the distributed knowledge congruence in proxy-data-free federated distillation. ACM Trans. Intell. Syst. Technol. **15**(2), 1–34 (2024)

36. Krizhevsky, A., Hinton, G.: Learning multiple layers of features from tiny images. Technical report, University of Toronto (2009)

37. Xiao, H., Rasul, K., Vollgraf, R.: Fashion-MNIST: a novel image dataset for benchmarking machine learning algorithms. arXiv preprint arXiv:1708.07747 (2017)

38. Hull, J.J.: A database for handwritten text recognition research. IEEE Trans. Pattern Anal. Mach. Intell. **16**(5), 550–554 (1994)

39. Stallkamp, J., Schlipsing, M., Salmen, J., Igel, C.: Man vs. computer: benchmarking machine learning algorithms for traffic sign recognition. Neural Netw. **32**, 323–332 (2012)

Federated Incomplete Multi-view Clustering with Heterogeneous Graph Neural Networks

Xueming Yan[1,3], Ziqi Wang[2], and Yaochu Jin[3(✉)]

[1] Guangdong University of Foreign Studies, Guangzhou, China
`yanxm@gdufs.edu.cn`
[2] East China University of Science and Technology, Shanghai, China
[3] School of Engineering, Westlake University, Hangzhou, China
`jinyaochu@westlake.edu.cn`

Abstract. Federated multi-view clustering offers the potential to develop a global clustering model using data distributed across multiple devices. However, current methods face challenges due to the absence of label information and the paramount importance of data privacy. A significant issue is the feature heterogeneity across multi-view data, which complicates the effective mining of complementary clustering information. Additionally, the inherent incompleteness of multi-view data in a distributed setting can further complicate the clustering process. To address these challenges, we introduce a federated incomplete multi-view clustering framework with heterogeneous graph neural networks (FIM-GNNs). In the proposed FIM-GNNs, autoencoders built on heterogeneous graph neural network models are employed for feature extraction of multi-view data at each client site. At the server level, heterogeneous features from overlapping samples of each client are aggregated into a global feature representation. Global pseudo-labels are generated at the server to enhance the handling of incomplete view data, where these labels serve as a guide for integrating and refining the clustering process across different data views. Comprehensive experiments have been conducted on public benchmark datasets to verify the performance of the proposed FIM-GNNs in comparison with state-of-the-art algorithms.

Keywords: Incomplete multi-view clustering · Federated learning · Heterogeneous graph neural networks

1 Introduction

Multi-view clustering is a fundamental machine learning task aiming to improve clustering performance by leveraging the consistency and complementary information from different views [1, 24, 29]. Traditional multi-view clustering methods typically process raw data directly or through basic feature transformations, but the performance of these approaches tend to deteriorate on high-dimensional

H. Yu et al. (Eds.): FL 2024 Workshops, LNAI 15501, pp. 61–76, 2025.
https://doi.org/10.1007/978-3-031-82240-7_5

data [33,34]. To overcome these limitations, deep learning technologies have been introduced into multi-view clustering. By utilizing neural networks to extract complex and abstract features from views, deep multi-view clustering methods are capable of handling more complex data structures and relationships [9,30].

Despite significant achievements of deep multi-view clustering methods in dealing with traditional Euclidean space data [15,25], real-world data often naturally exists in graph forms, such as social networks and knowledge graphs, presenting new challenges for clustering tasks. In particular, the complexity of graph structures makes it difficult for traditional clustering methods to be effective [28]. Graph neural networks (GNNs) have gained widespread attention for their ability to capture structural information effectively [19]. In multi-view clustering applications [3,18], GNNs can utilize the relationships between views as well as structural and feature information to obtain node features suited for clustering, effectively integrating multi-view data and enhancing clustering performance. However, existing methods based on GNNs often overlook the heterogeneity of data across different views, and the node features obtained may be unsuited for clustering outcomes [4]. Additionally, these methods typically employ centralized training, which can raise privacy concerns of multi-view data [5].

Federated learning, as a distributed learning model, offers a solution to address data heterogeneity issues while protecting data privacy [11]. By combining federated learning with graph neural networks, it is possible to capture graph structures and node features while ensuring data privacy [32]. However, federated GNN-based methods face dual challenges in solving clustering problems: inconsistency and heterogeneity of data across different views [7,8]. Data from different views are not always perfectly overlapping and vary in data features and sizes. Moreover, due to various uncontrollable factors in practical applications, as shown in Fig. 1, multi-view data may be incomplete, further complicating clustering tasks [2,14].

To address these challenges, this paper proposes a federated incomplete multi-view clustering framework based on heterogeneous graph neural networks (FIM-GNNs). This framework aims to capture node features with heterogeneous GNNs from different views, and the global aggregation is designed to merge the complementary information from various views. Additionally, with the help of global pseudo labels, we merge feature extraction and clustering into a unified process, and use these labels to assist client training to achieve consistency in incomplete multi-view data. The main contributions of this paper can be summarized as follows:

- We propose a federated incomplete multi-view clustering framework utilizing heterogeneous GNNs. Local training with heterogeneous GNNs and a global aggregation are introduced to effectively harness the complementary information in multi-view data, significantly enhancing the clustering performance.
- A global pseudo-label mechanism is designed with heterogeneous aggregation in a federated environment, enhancing the ability of the FIM-GNNs to handle incomplete view data and improving the consistency of features as well as the performance of the clustering results.

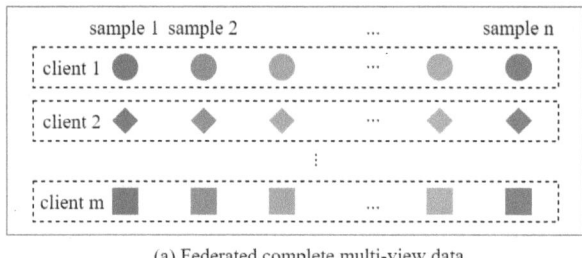

(a) Federated complete multi-view data

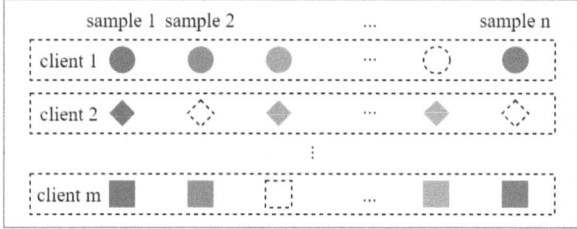

(b) Federated incomplete multi-view data

Fig. 1. The disparity between complete and incomplete multi-view federated data. (a) Federated complete multi-view clustering, where different clients possess complete, distinct sets of sample features. (b) Federated incomplete multi-view clustering, where different clients possess different sets of sample features. Each client may have missing samples, but each sample exists in at least one client.

- Comprehensive experiments demonstrate the competitive performance of the FIM-GNNs in handling data heterogeneity and incompleteness compared to four state-of-the-art incomplete multi-view clustering methods across three public datasets.

2 Related Work

This section provides the problem formulation of federated incomplete multi-view clustering and a short overview of existing multi-view clustering techniques. The notations in this study are listed in Table 1.

2.1 Problem Formulation

For a multi-view dataset with N samples, where $X_c = \{X_c^1, \ldots, X_c^i, \ldots, X_c^m\}$, $X_c^i \in \mathbb{R}^{N \times D_m}$ represents the feature set of the nodes, and the sample features D_i of different views exhibit differences. In practice, some views may have missing sample data. Therefore, the description of an incomplete multi-view clustering dataset is as follows:

$$X^i = (M^i \otimes \mathbf{1}) \odot X_c^i \tag{1}$$

which is subject to the following constraint:

$$\sum_{i=1}^{N} M_j^i \geq 1 \tag{2}$$

Here, $M = \{M^1, \ldots, M^i, \ldots, M^m\}$ represents a set of binary selection matrices, with $M^i \in \{0,1\}^{N\times 1}$. The entries of $M^i = 1$ indicate that the corresponding features are retained, whereas $M^i = 0$ means that the features are discarded. $\mathbf{1} \in \mathbb{R}^{1\times N}$, and $M^i \otimes \mathbf{1}$ indicates that either all sample features are missing or all are present, meaning that partial missing features within the samples are not considered. $\odot$ represents the Hadamard product. $\sum_{j=1}^{N} M_j^i \geq 1$ ensures that each sample retains at least one feature, and no sample is completely devoid of features.

In this study, we consider the problem of incomplete multi-view clustering under a federated framework, as shown in Fig. 1. Assume there is an incomplete multi-view dataset $X = \{X_1, \ldots, X_m\}$ and $A = \{A_1, \ldots, A_m\}$ distributed across m clients. For client i, $X_i \in \mathbb{R}^{N_i \times D_i}$ represents the node features, and $A_i \in \mathbb{R}^{N_i \times N_i}$ represents the graph structure. Due to the data heterogeneity in a federated setting, both the sample dimensions D_i and the number of samples N_i vary across clients. Additionally, due to missing data, $N_i < N$. The incomplete multi-view clustering problem involves extracting features from the incomplete node features and graph structures of each view, followed by an aggregation to produce the final clustering results.

Table 1. Summary of the main notations.

Symbols	Descriptions
m	Number of clients
N	Number of samples
D_i	Feature dimension of the i-th client
N_i	Number of samples in the i-th client
X^i	Node features of the i-th client
A^i	The graph structure matrix of the i-th client
Z^i	Features extracted from the i-th client
Z_j^i	Features of sample j extracted by the i-th client
Z_C^i	Features extracted based on overlapping data from the i-th client
U^m	Cluster centers of the m-th view
Z	Global features of overlapping samples
C	Global cluster center
P	Global pseudo-labels
R_i	The missing rate of the i-th view

2.2   Multi-view Clustering

Recently, GNNs have emerged as effective tools for graph clustering tasks [16] to deal with multi-view data. GNN-based graph clustering techniques combine GNNs with autoencoders to perform clustering tasks in an unsupervised manner. For example, O2MAC [4] captures features using a shared multilayer graph convolutional encoder across different views and performs graph reconstruction with a multilayer graph convolutional decoder in each view. DAEGC [18] utilizes a graph attention-based autoencoder that considers both node attributes and the structural information of the graph. MAGCN [3] extends this approach to multi-view graph clustering, taking into account the geometric relationships and probabilistic distribution consistency between multi-view data to further enhance clustering tasks. GC-VAE [5] combines variational graph autoencoders with graph convolutional networks, clustering nodes based on graph topology and node features. However, these methods utilize centralized training and overlook the importance of data privacy protection.

GNNs-based multi-view clustering aims to enhance clustering performance by leveraging consistent and complementary information across multiple views [6]. Meanwhile, federated multi-view clustering provides a promising solution for protecting data privacy in various distributed devices/silos, as discussed in [13]. For example, a distributed multi-view spectral clustering method called FMSC [20] employs homomorphic encryption and differential privacy techniques to protect data privacy. However, the time-consuming encryption and decryption processes reduce the efficiency of the model. By considering the communication issues, FedMVL [8] proposes a vertically federated learning framework based on nonnegative orthogonal decomposition, effectively reducing the cost of the model. However, these shallow methods struggle to effectively extract node information, limiting model performance. FL-MV-DSSM [7] utilizes a deep structured semantic model to construct a multi-perspective recommendation framework. However, these federated learning multi-view clustering methods overlook the incompleteness of data across different views and are limited by their clustering approaches, which constrains model performance.

Recently, some researchers [10,22,27] have started paying attention to incomplete clustering algorithms, which employ the complete views to predict the missing data. For example, EE-IMVC [12] imputed each incomplete base matrix generated by incomplete views with a learned consensus clustering matrix. Moreover, IMVC-CBG [21] reconstructed missing views with a consensus bipartite graph by minimizing the conditional entropy of multiple views using dual prediction. After that, IMVC [26] learns the features for each view by autoencoders and utilizes an adaptive feature projection to avoid the imputation for missing data. Fed-DMVC [2] addresses the incompleteness issue in federated multi-view clustering with an autoencoder model. However, these methods do not simultaneously consider both data heterogeneity and data incompleteness issues in the process of multi-view clustering.

3   Proposed Method

In this section, we present the federated incomplete multi-view clustering with heterogeneous graph neural networks (FIM-GNNs), illustrated in Fig. 2. Heterogeneous graph neural networks, such as GCN [31] and GAT [17], are utilized to extract features and tailored for local client-side training. These incomplete multi-view features are then combined at the server to generate global pseudo-labels. Following this, clustering results are derived through the algorithm optimization. Lastly, we provide an analysis of the time complexity for the proposed FIM-GNNs.

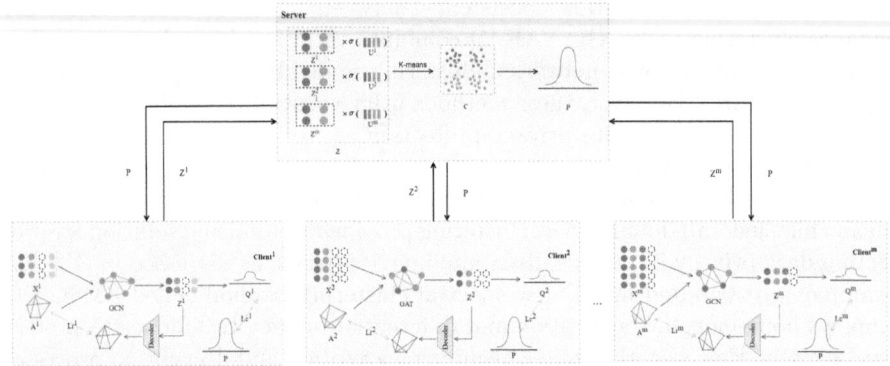

Fig. 2. Overview of FIM-GNNs. There are m clients and one server. Initially, the clients perform feature extraction using GAT or GCN based on local features. We employ a decoder for graph reconstruction and the global pseudo-label P as auxiliary training information.

3.1   Local Training with Heterogeneous GNNs

Based on the heterogeneity of the multi-view data at each client side, we utilize the different GNNs as graph autoencoders for feature extraction in different view data. In addition, we introduce global pseudo-labels P acquired from the server as labels to assist client-side training. In the graph autoencoder process, we extract low-dimensional features from the client side, aiming to capture the latent features of the multi-view data while preserving data privacy. For the ith client's data X^i and graph structure A^i, we use the GNN-based encoder method to project them into low-dimensional features Z^i, and utilize a decoder to reconstruct the graph structure A^i. Considering the differences in sample quantity and dimension across different views (clients), we adopt two types of GNN models, GCN and GAT, to construct graph autoencoders for feature extraction. When the missing rate of the i-th view data is not too low, we construct a two-layer GCN as the encoder for feature extraction:

$$Z = f(X, A) = \text{softmax}\left(\hat{A}\text{ReLU}\left(\hat{A}XW^{(0)}\right)W^{(1)}\right) \tag{3}$$

where $\hat{A} = \tilde{D}^{-1/2}\tilde{A}\tilde{D}^{-1/2}$, and $W^{(0)}$, $W^{(1)}$ are the parameters for the first and second layers of the GCN, respectively. When the missing rate of the i-th view data is low, we use a two-layer GAT as the encoder for feature extraction:

$$z_j^{(1)} = \sigma \left(\sum_{k \in N_j} \alpha_{jk} W^{(0)} x_k \right) \tag{4}$$

$$z_j^{(2)} = \sigma \left(\sum_{k \in N_j} \alpha_{jk} W^{(1)} z_k^{(1)} \right) \tag{5}$$

where $W^{(0)}$ and $W^{(1)}$ are the parameters for the first and second layers of the GAT, respectively. The attention coefficients α_{jk} are computed as follows:

$$\alpha_{jk} = \frac{\exp(\sigma(\boldsymbol{a}^T[W x_{ij} \| W x_k]))}{\sum_{r \in N_j} \exp(\sigma(\boldsymbol{a}^T[W x_j \| W x_r]))} \tag{6}$$

where $z_j^{(1)}$ and $z_j^{(2)}$ are the features of vertex j obtained from the first layer GAT and the second layer GAT, respectively. For updating the adjacency matrix, it is defined as:

$$\hat{A} = \text{sigmoid}(Z^T \bullet Z). \tag{7}$$

Next, for updating the loss function, it is defined as:

$$L_r^i = \text{loss}(A^i, \hat{A}^i) \tag{8}$$

After feature extraction, a self-supervised clustering layer is introduced for each client. The cluster membership matrix $U^i = [u_1^i, \ldots, u_k^i] \in \mathbb{R}^{K \times d_v}$ determines the soft cluster assignments Q^i, which are calculated as follows:

$$q_{ij}^i = \frac{(1 + \|z_j^m - u_k^m\|^2)^{-1}}{\sum_k (1 + \|z_j^m - u_k^m\|^2)^{-1}} \tag{9}$$

where q_{ij}^i represents the probability that sample j from the i-th client is assigned to cluster k. Next, for client i, we use the global pseudo-labels P and the soft cluster assignments Q^i to compute the KL divergence loss:

$$L_c^i = \text{KL}(P \| Q^i) = \sum_j \sum_k p_{jk} \log \frac{p_{jk}}{q_{jk}^i} \tag{10}$$

Then, the total loss function is defined as:

$$L = L_r + \gamma L_c \tag{11}$$

Here, L_r is the reconstruction loss, and L_c is the clustering loss, where γ is a hyper-parameter that balances the importance of the reconstruction loss relative to the clustering loss.

3.2   Global Aggregation

After obtaining the features Z^i of different clients and the clustering centers U^i, the server uses heterogeneous aggregation on the overlapping sample features Z_C^i to obtain the global feature Z, and then updates the global pseudo-labels P based on Z.

To leverage the consistency and complementarity of different views, we perform heterogeneous aggregation on the overlapping sample features of different clients. Due to the heterogeneity of client data, the feature dimensions obtained are different, making direct aggregation challenging. Therefore, we assign different weights W_i to the features of different clients based on U^i. Then, we concatenate the weighted overlapping sample features Z_C^i for each sample obtained from different clients to produce the high-dimensional feature Z:

$$Z = [w_1 Z_C^1, w_2 Z_C^2, \ldots, w_m Z_C^m] \tag{12}$$

where w_i is calculated by:

$$w_i = 1 + \log\left(1 + \frac{\sigma(U^i)}{\sum_v \sigma(U^i)}\right) \tag{13}$$

where $Z \in \mathbb{R}^{N \times \sum d_i}$ represents the global feature, Z_C^i indicats the overlapping sample features of the i-th view, and $\sigma(.)$ represents the variance. Clearly, a higher variance indicates better clustering results. Therefore, by performing weighted aggregation through W_i, it is possible to enhance the influence of features from views with better clustering results and reduce the influence of features from views with poorer clustering results.

The optimal cluster assignment C is then obtained using the K-means algorithm by minimizing:

$$\min_C \sum_{j=1}^{N_c} \sum_{k=1}^{K} \|z_j - c_k\|^2 \tag{14}$$

where A is the adjustment matrix used to align the two instances of S. The server sends the global pseudo-label P to the clients as global information to integrate the complementary features of different views. The final global pseudo-labels P is obtained through the following calculation:

$$P = \varepsilon(s_j)A, \tag{15}$$

$$s_{jk} = \frac{(1 + \|z_j - c_k\|^2)^{-1}}{\sum_j (1 + \|z_j - c_k\|^2)^{-1}}, s_{jk} \in S \tag{16}$$

and

$$\varepsilon(s_i) = \frac{\left(\frac{s_{jk}}{\sum_j s_{jk}}\right)^2}{\sum_j \left(\frac{s_{jk}}{\sum_j s_{jk}}\right)^2} \tag{17}$$

Due to differences in the cluster centers in each round of aggregation, the Hungarian algorithm is used to introduce A to align S across different communication rounds. Finally, the most likely cluster assignment for each data point is determined by:

$$y_j = \arg\max_{jk} \left(\frac{1}{m} \sum_m q_{jk}^i \right) \tag{18}$$

3.3 Algorithm Optimization

As shown in Algorithm 1, the optimization in the proposed FIM-GNNs primarily consists of the client and server components. Firstly, we carry out the pre-training of the heterogeneous GNNs at the client side. We use all the data X^i from each view, and train the encoder and decoder only using the reconstruction loss to enhance the model's capability in feature extraction. In the proposed FIM-GNNs, we initialize k cluster centers using the K-means algorithm. Subsequently, we train the FIM-GNNs using the holistic federated framework, where the server aggregates the heterogeneous features Z_C^i of overlapping samples from each client into a global feature Z, based on which global pseudo-labels P are generated and sent back to the clients. Each client then uses the overlapping sample data X_C^i and the global pseudo-labels P to train the model in parallel for T rounds, obtaining features Z_C^i and cluster centers U_i. The server and clients update alternately over E communication rounds.

Algorithm 1. Optimization process in the proposed FIM-GNNs

1: **Input:** Datasets $X = \{X^1, \ldots, X^m\}$, adjacency matrices $A = \{A^1, \ldots, A^m\}$, number of clusters K, number of communication rounds E, number of training rounds T.

2: **Output:** Cluster results

3: **while** not reaching E **do**

4:     **for** $m = 1$ to M in parallel **do**

5:         **if** $E = 1$ then

6:             Pretrain the autoencoders by Eq. (8).

7:         **else**

8:             **while** not reach T **do**

9:                 Update Z_m, U_m by optimizing Eq. (11)

10:             **end while**

11:         **end if**

12:         Upload Z_m and U_m to the server.

13:     **end for**

14:     Update Z by Eq. (13).

15:     Update C by Eq. (14).

16:     Obtain P by Eq. (15).

17:     Distribute P to each client.

18: **end while**

19: Calculate the clustering predictions based on Eq. (13).

3.4   Complexity Analysis

Algorithm 1 consists of two main phases, which together determines its computational complexity. The algorithm begins with training each view separately. This step has a complexity of $O(N(dd_1 + d_1d_2))$, where N and d represent the sample size and sample dimension, respectively. d_1 and d_2 are the feature dimensions of the views. Next, in the aggregation phase, each client contributes to the global model by calculating the feature matrix P and cluster centers C, resulting in a complexity of $O(NDK)$, where D is the feature dimension, and K is the number of clusters. For updating P, the complexity is $O(K^3 + NK)$. Therefore, the proposed FIM-GNNs is with a complexity of $O(K^3 + NDK + N(dd_1 + d_1d_2))$.

4   Experiments

4.1   Experimental Setup

Based on the differences in sample features across various views within the federated framework, we conducted training on two widely used datasets, Caltech-7 and BDGP, to validate the performance of our proposed FIM-GNNs. Table 2 show the description of the datasets. In the experiments, we construct the graph structure information as in [25]. Taking into account the differences in dimensionality and quantity of data across different clients, we select partial views as the dataset. Simultaneously, based on the specific missing rates R_i of each view, parts of the samples are missing, but we ensure that each sample exists in at least one view.

Table 2. Dataset Description.

Datasets	C	N	D_i
Caltech-7	7	1474	928,512,254
BDGP	5	2000	1,000,500,250

We firstly use two standard clustering metrics, namely accuracy (ACC) and Normalized Mutual Information (NMI) for evaluations. Additionally, we use the Adjusted Rand Index (ARI) to assess the quality of clustering. We compared the proposed FIM-GNNs with four state-of-the-art incomplete multi-view clustering methods. CDIMC-NET [23] is a method that integrates deep encoders and graph embedding strategies, and introduces a self-paced strategy to select optimal samples for model training. COMPLETER [10] is a contrastive learning-based method that achieves cross-view data recovery from an information-theoretic perspective. APADC [26] is an adaptive feature projection-based incomplete multi-view clustering method, which introduces distribution-aligned feature learning. IMVC-CBG [21] is an anchor-based multi-view learning method, introducing a bipartite graph framework to address incomplete multi-view clustering.

In our experiments, we set the number of epochs to 10, with a learning rate initialized at 0.005 and reduced by half every 50 epochs. We use Adam optimizer. For both the GAT and GCN frameworks, the Adam optimizer is used, with a pre-training learning rate of 0.005 and a training learning rate of 0.001. For the GAT framework, on the BDGP dataset, the dimensions of the two GAT layers are [128, 16], and on the Caltech-7 dataset, the dimensions of the two layers are [512, 32]. For the GCN framework, the dimensions of the two GCN layers are [128, 16]. When the missing rate β does not exceed 0.1, the GCN framework is used; when the missing rate exceeds 0.1, the GAT framework is used. The hyperparameter γ is set to 1.

Table 3. Performance comparison of different missing rates on Caltech-7 and BDGP Datasets.

Datasets	$[R_1, R_2, R_3]$	[0.2, 0.05, 0.05]			[0.2, 0.2, 0.1]			[0.3, 0.3, 0.1]		
	Metrics	ACC	NMI	ARI	ACC	NMI	ARI	ACC	NMI	ARI
Caltech-7	CDIMC-NET	0.532	**0.564**	**0.419**	0.362	0.114	0.084	0.509	**0.512**	0.371
	COMPLETER	0.476	0.342	0.348	0.579	0.469	0.332	0.476	0.345	0.342
	APADC	0.544	0.542	0.403	0.462	0.413	0.232	0.534	0.411	0.384
	IMVC-CBG	0.502	0.351	0.284	0.513	0.298	0.224	0.521	0.291	0.203
	FIM-GNNs	**0.604**	0.426	0.348	**0.582**	**0.489**	**0.397**	**0.565**	0.479	**0.391**
BDGP	CDIMC-NET	0.369	0.107	0.008	0.368	0.161	0.113	0.367	0.101	0.009
	COMPLETER	0.341	0.105	0.103	0.357	0.113	0.084	0.345	0.106	0.104
	APADC	0.291	0.135	0.041	0.283	0.032	0.031	0.266	0.091	0.021
	IMVC-CBG	0.521	0.303	0.268	0.501	0.293	0.258	0.491	0.287	0.261
	FIM-GNNs	**0.614**	**0.426**	**0.399**	**0.625**	**0.470**	**0.435**	**0.580**	**0.368**	**0.331**

4.2 Performance Evaluation

Table 3 summarizes the experimental results on two datasets, where $[R_1, R_2, R_3]$ means the missing rates on different clients. It can be observed that our method basically achieves the best results in five incomplete multi-view clustering methods, demonstrating the effectiveness of our approach. Compared with three deep neural network-based methods (CDIMC-NET, COMPLETER and APADC), the FIM-GNNs achieves better results, indicating that the introduction of heterogeneous graph structure as auxiliary information can effectively improve model performance.

In addition, to visually observe the clustering results more intuitively, we utilized t-SNE for visualization of the results with a missing rate of [0.2, 0.2, 0.1] on the BDGP dataset. Figure 3 presents the visualization results after reducing the features of complete samples to two-dimensional, where different colors represent different clusters. It can be observed that initially, the nodes are relatively scattered, and the boundaries between different clusters are not distinct. As the communication rounds increase, nodes within the same cluster gradually aggregate, and the boundaries between different clusters become clearer. This is because a global pseudo-label mechanism with heterogeneous aggregation is beneficial for obtaining the accuracy of the federated incomplete multi-view clustering results.

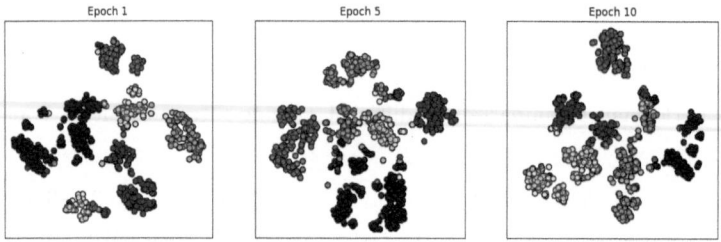

Fig. 3. The *t*-SNE visualization results for different communication epochs on the BDGP dataset.

4.3   Effect of Heterogeneous GNNs

To evaluate the impact of heterogeneous GNNs, we assessed the performance of FIM-GNNs with GAT, GCN, and a combination of GCN and GAT, respectively. As shown in Fig. 4, the experiments across two datasets indicated that the combination of GCN and GAT generally yields better results, while the individual models (GAT and GCN) also perform well. The performance of the combination of GCN and GAT demonstrates the effectiveness of heterogeneous GNNs in dealing with the incompleteness of performance across different views.

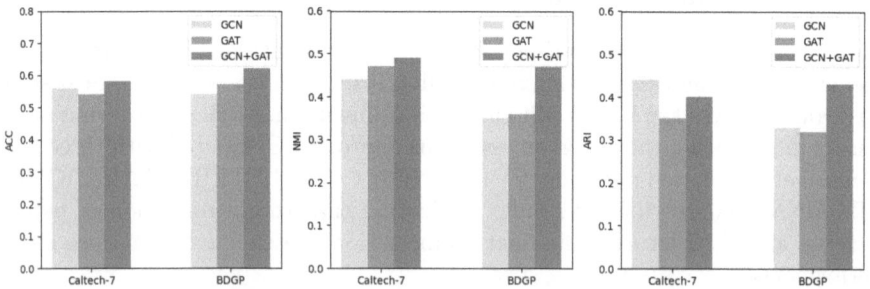

Fig. 4. Experimental results of the FIM-GNNs with GAT, GCN, and a combination of GCN and GAT, respectively.

4.4   Parameter Sensitivity

We determine the model for each client based on the missing rate threshold β in the each view. When the view missing rate does not exceed β, we use GCN; otherwise we use GAT. To verify the effectiveness of β, we run the FIM-GNNs with β set at [0.05, 0.10, 0.15, 0.20, 0.25, 0.30], and the results are shown in the Fig. 5. We can see from the observations that $\beta = 0.1$ yields the best performance on Caltech-7 and BDGP datasets.

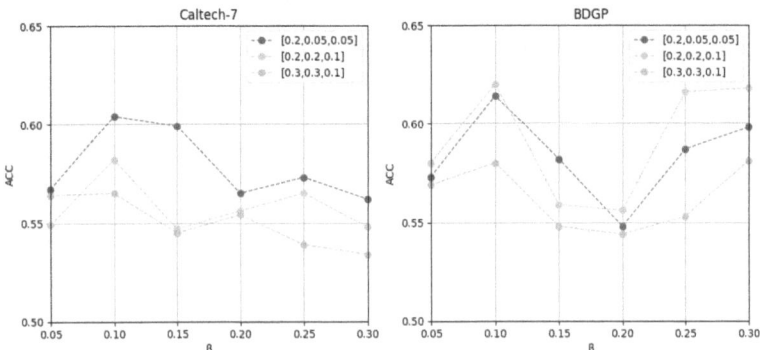

Fig. 5. Accuracy results were obtained by using different β values on the Caltech-7 and BDGP datasets.

During local training on the client side, a hyperparameter γ is used to balance the clustering loss and reconstruction loss. We conducted experiments on the BDGP dataset by varying the values of the hyperparameter γ from 10^{-3}, 10^{-2}, ..., 10^{2}, 10^{3} to test parameter sensitivity, as shown in Fig. 6. It can be observed that different clients exhibit varying sensitivities to γ, but overall, the performance is optimal when $\gamma = 1$, so we set $\gamma = 1$ in this study.

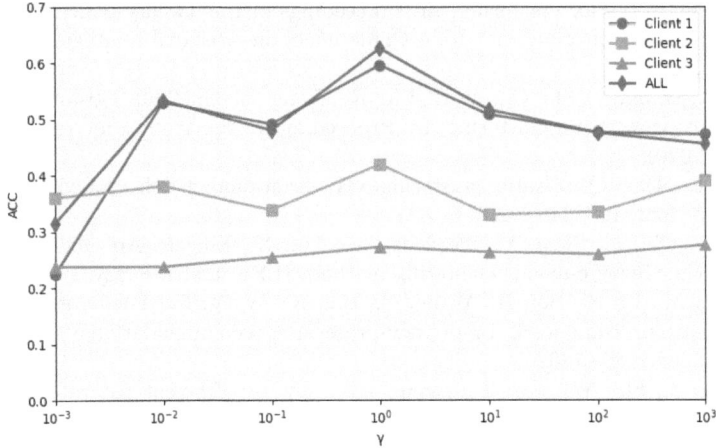

Fig. 6. Accuracy results obtained using different γ values on the BDGP dataset, ranging from 10^{-3} to 10^{3}.

5   Conclusion

In this study, we present a federated incomplete multi-view clustering framework with heterogeneous GNNs. Local client-side training and global heterogeneous aggregation are introduced to effectively enhance the performance of federated incomplete multi-view clustering. Moreover, we employ a global pseudo-label mechanism with heterogeneous aggregation to deal with incomplete view data. The effectiveness of FIM-GNNs is evaluated on public datasets compared to state-of-the-art incomplete multi-view clustering methods. Although BGNAS can obtain effective and efficient clustering results for incomplete multi-view data, it is still worth considering its applicability to extremely imbalanced multi-view data or other complex clustering tasks. In the future, the proposed FIM-GNNs can potentially be integrated with heterogeneous GNNs for incomplete multi-modal clustering tasks or specific domains.

Acknowledgments. This work was supported in part by the National Natural Science Foundation of China under Grant No. 62136003, and in part by the Guangdong Basic and Applied Basic Research Foundation under Grant No. 2024A1515011729 and No. 2023A1515012534.

Disclosure of Interests. There are no ethical issues.

References

1. Cai, H., Wang, Y., Qi, F., Wang, Z., Cheung, Y.: Multiview tensor spectral clustering via co-regularization. IEEE Trans. Pattern Anal. Mach. Intell. (2024)
2. Chen, X., et al.: Federated deep multi-view clustering with global self-supervision. In: Proceedings of the 31st ACM International Conference on Multimedia, pp. 3498–3506 (2023)
3. Cheng, J., Wang, Q., Tao, Z., Xie, D., Gao, Q.: Multi-view attribute graph convolution networks for clustering. In: Proceedings of the Twenty-Ninth International Conference on International Joint Conferences on Artificial Intelligence, pp. 2973–2979 (2021)
4. Fan, S., Wang, X., Shi, C., Lu, E., Lin, K., Wang, B.: One2multi graph autoencoder for multi-view graph clustering. In: Proceedings of the Web Conference, pp. 3070–3076 (2020)
5. Guo, L., Dai, Q.: Graph clustering via variational graph embedding. Pattern Recogn. **122**, 108334 (2022)
6. Hu, X., Qin, J., Shen, Y., Pedrycz, W., Liu, X., Liu, J.: An efficient federated multi-view fuzzy c-means clustering method. IEEE Trans. Fuzzy Syst. (2023)
7. Huang, M., Li, H., Bai, B., Wang, C., Bai, K., Wang, F.: A federated multi-view deep learning framework for privacy-preserving recommendations. arXiv preprint arXiv:2008.10808 (2020)
8. Huang, S., Shi, W., Xu, Z., Tsang, I.W., Lv, J.: Efficient federated multi-view learning. Pattern Recogn. **131**, 108817 (2022)
9. Li, Q., An, S., Li, L., Liu, W., Shao, Y.: Multi-view diffusion process for spectral clustering and image retrieval. IEEE Trans. Image Process. (2023)

10. Lin, Y., Gou, Y., Liu, Z., Li, B., Lv, J., Peng, X.: Completer: incomplete multi-view clustering via contrastive prediction. In: Proceedings of the IEEE/CVF Conference on Computer Vision and Pattern Recognition, pp. 11174–11183 (2021)
11. Liu, Q., et al.: Secure federated evolutionary optimization-a survey. Engineering (2023)
12. Liu, X., et al.: Efficient and effective regularized incomplete multi-view clustering. IEEE Trans. Pattern Anal. Mach. Intell. **43**(8), 2634–2646 (2020)
13. Qiao, D., Ding, C., Fan, J.: Federated spectral clustering via secure similarity reconstruction. In: Advances in Neural Information Processing Systems, vol. 36 (2024)
14. Ren, Y., et al.: A novel federated multi-view clustering method for unaligned and incomplete data fusion. Inf. Fusion **108**, 102357 (2024)
15. Ren, Y., et al.: Deep clustering: a comprehensive survey. arXiv preprint arXiv:2210.04142 (2022)
16. Tsitsulin, A., Palowitch, J., Perozzi, B., Müller, E.: Graph clustering with graph neural networks. J. Mach. Learn. Res. **24**(127), 1–21 (2023)
17. Veličković, P., Cucurull, G., Casanova, A., Romero, A., Lio, P., Bengio, Y.: Graph attention networks. arXiv preprint arXiv:1710.10903 (2017)
18. Wang, C., Pan, S., Hu, R., Long, G., Jiang, J., Zhang, C.: Attributed graph clustering: a deep attentional embedding approach. arXiv preprint arXiv:1906.06532 (2019)
19. Wang, H., Yang, Y., Liu, B.: GMC: graph-based multi-view clustering. IEEE Trans. Knowl. Data Eng. **32**(6), 1116–1129 (2019)
20. Wang, H., Li, A., Shen, B., Sun, Y., Wang, H.: Federated multi-view spectral clustering. IEEE Access **8**, 202249–202259 (2020)
21. Wang, S., et al.: Highly-efficient incomplete large-scale multi-view clustering with consensus bipartite graph. In: Proceedings of the IEEE/CVF Conference on Computer Vision and Pattern Recognition, pp. 9776–9785 (2022)
22. Wen, J., Wu, Z., Zhang, Z., Fei, L., Zhang, B., Xu, Y.: Structural deep incomplete multi-view clustering network. In: Proceedings of the 30th ACM International Conference on Information & Knowledge Management, pp. 3538–3542 (2021)
23. Wen, J., Zhang, Z., Xu, Y., Zhang, B., Fei, L., Xie, G.S.: CDIMC-net: cognitive deep incomplete multi-view clustering network. In: Proceedings of the Twenty-Ninth International Conference on International Joint Conferences on Artificial Intelligence, pp. 3230–3236 (2020)
24. Wen, J., Zhang, Z., Zhang, Z., Fei, L., Wang, M.: Generalized incomplete multiview clustering with flexible locality structure diffusion. IEEE Trans. Cybern. **51**(1), 101–114 (2020)
25. Xiao, S., Du, S., Chen, Z., Zhang, Y., Wang, S.: Dual fusion-propagation graph neural network for multi-view clustering. IEEE Trans. Multimed. (2023)
26. Xu, J., et al.: Adaptive feature projection with distribution alignment for deep incomplete multi-view clustering. IEEE Trans. Image Process. **32**, 1354–1366 (2023)
27. Xu, J., et al.: Deep incomplete multi-view clustering via mining cluster complementarity. In: Proceedings of the AAAI Conference on Artificial Intelligence, vol. 36, pp. 8761–8769 (2022)
28. Yan, X., Huang, H., Hao, Z., Wang, J.: A graph-based fuzzy evolutionary algorithm for solving two-echelon vehicle routing problems. IEEE Trans. Evol. Comput. **24**(1), 129–141 (2019)

29. Yan, X., Xue, H., Jiang, S., Liu, Z.: Multimodal sentiment analysis using multi-tensor fusion network with cross-modal modeling. Appl. Artif. Intell. **36**(1), 2000688 (2022)

30. Yan, X., Zhong, G., Jin, Y., Ke, X., Xie, F., Huang, G.: Binary spectral clustering for multi-view data. Inf. Sci. (2024)

31. Zhang, S., Tong, H., Xu, J., Maciejewski, R.: Graph convolutional networks: a comprehensive review. Comput. Soc. Netw. **6**(1), 1–23 (2019). https://doi.org/10.1186/s40649-019-0069-y

32. Zheng, Z., Wang, Z., Yan, X., Jin, Y., Liu, S., Liu, Q.: Federated graph neural networks with bipartite embedding for multi-objective facility location. In: 2023 5th International Conference on Data-driven Optimization of Complex Systems (DOCS), pp. 1–8. IEEE (2023)

33. Zhong, G., Pun, C.M.: Improved normalized cut for multi-view clustering. IEEE Trans. Pattern Anal. Mach. Intell. **44**(12), 10244–10251 (2021)

34. Zhong, G., Shu, T., Huang, G., Yan, X.: Multi-view spectral clustering by simultaneous consensus graph learning and discretization. Knowl.-Based Syst. **235**, 107632 (2022)

Benchmarking Data Heterogeneity Evaluation Approaches for Personalized Federated Learning

Zhilong Li[1], Xiaohu Wu[1(✉)], Xiaoli Tang[2], Tiantian He[3,4], Yew-Soon Ong[2,3,4], Mengmeng Chen[1], Qiqi Liu[5], Qicheng Lao[1], and Han Yu[4]

[1] Beijing University of Posts and Telecommunications, Beijing, China
`xiaohu.wu@bupt.edu.cn`
[2] College of Computing and Data Science, Nanyang Technological University, Singapore, Singapore
[3] Institute of High Performance Computing, Agency for Science, Technology and Research, Singapore, Singapore
[4] Centre for Frontier AI Research, Agency for Science, Technology and Research, Singapore, Singapore
[5] School of Engineering, Westlake University, Hangzhou, China

Abstract. There is growing research interest in measuring the statistical heterogeneity of clients' local datasets. Such measurements are used to estimate the suitability for collaborative training of personalized federated learning (PFL) models. Currently, these research endeavors are taking place in silos and there is a lack of a unified benchmark to provide a fair and convenient comparison among various approaches in common settings. We aim to bridge this important gap in this paper. The proposed benchmarking framework currently includes six representative approaches. Extensive experiments have been conducted to compare these approaches under five standard non-IID FL settings, providing much needed insights into which approaches are advantageous under which settings. The proposed framework offers useful guidance on the suitability of various data divergence measures in FL systems. It is beneficial for keeping related research activities on the right track in terms of: (1) designing PFL schemes, (2) selecting appropriate data heterogeneity evaluation approaches for specific FL application scenarios, and (3) addressing fairness issues in collaborative model training. The code is available at https://github.com/Xiaoni-61/DH-Benchmark.

Keywords: Federated learning · data heterogeneity · collaboration benefit · divergence

1 Introduction

Federated learning (FL) is a promising privacy-preserving collaborative machine learning (ML) paradigm [12,28,55]. Under FL, multiple FL clients train a shared model with their own datasets and upload their local model updates to a FL

H. Yu et al. (Eds.): FL 2024 Workshops, LNAI 15501, pp. 77–92, 2025.
https://doi.org/10.1007/978-3-031-82240-7_6

server for aggregation and redistribution [32]. One key challenge of FL is that the data distributions across different clients can be heterogeneous (i.e., non-independently and identically distributed (non-IID)) [10,56]. This has inspired the field of personalized federated learning (PFL) [37] to build more powerful ML models, better realizing the final goal of FL.

The non-IIDness of clients' local data entails evaluating data complementarity/similarity between clients and building a personalized ML model for each client. A FL system itself is a collaborative network of clients where a client i may be complemented by other clients j with different weights, which measure the data heterogeneity. The basic way that FL works is to aggregate the clients' local model updates according to their weights, e.g., the vanilla FedAvg framework [32]. In the context of PFL, we believe that it is still of fundamental importance to obtain a personalized model for each client by aggregating the clients' local model updates according to the weights. Measuring statistical heterogeneity of data is one way to understand the data complementarity and potential collaboration advantages among clients. Recently, there has been growing interest in measuring data heterogeneity. These techniques are either divergence-based measures (e.g., Jensen-Shannon (JS) divergence [20,43], $\mathcal{C}$-divergence [44,45], hash function-based distribution sketches [41]), or model-based approaches (e.g., Shapley Value [46,47], Hypernetworks [14,54], cosine similarity [48]). Although important, current research endeavors take place in silos and some are even not specifically designed for PFL. A comprehensive study is needed to simultaneously compare all the schemes in common settings of PFL.

To this end, we develop a comprehensive benchmark to study the various approaches mentioned above. The main contributions of this paper are as follows.

1. We summarize the six techniques (JS divergence, $\mathcal{C}$-divergence, distribution sketch-based euclidean distance, Shapley Value, Hypernetworks, cosine similarity) into a unified framework to understand their application in FL settings. The unified framework clarifies the ways of quantifying the collaboration advantages among clients and the theoretical development of using collaboration advantages or data similarity for PFL.
2. We evaluate all six approaches under five standard Non-IID settings summarized in [56] across eight widely-adopted benchmark datasets. We assess the performance of each approach in terms of computation cost, communication overhead and scalability. The results provide insights into which approaches are advantageous under which settings.
3. The unified framework and the experimental results identify scenarios where the current approaches perform relatively poorly, highlighting promising future research directions for collaborative PFL.

2   Preliminary

2.1   FL Notation

Consider a FL setting with N clients. Each client $i \in \{1, 2, \ldots, N\}$ has a dataset $\hat{D}_i = \{(x_k^{(i)}, y_k^{(i)})\}_{k=1}^{m_i}$ consisting of m_i samples drawn from an underlying data distribution $\mathcal{D}_i$, where $x_k^{(i)} \in \mathcal{X}$ denotes the feature while $y_k^{(i)} \in \mathcal{Y}$ denotes the label. The total number of samples across all clients is $m = \sum_{i=1}^{N} m_i$. Let $\beta_i = m_i/m$ denote the proportion of data samples held by client i, and $\beta = [\beta_1, \ldots, \beta_N]$ represent the quantity distribution of data samples across clients. Given a machine learning model (hypothesis) h and a risk function ℓ, the local expected risk of client i is defined as $\mathcal{L}_i(h) = \mathbb{E}_{(x,y) \in \mathcal{D}_i} \ell(h(x), y)$ and its local empirical risk is given by $\hat{\mathcal{L}}_i(h) = \frac{1}{m_i} \sum_{k=1}^{m_i} \ell(h(x_k^{(i)}), y_k^{(i)})$. The goal of each client i is to find a model h within the hypothesis space $\mathcal{H}$ that minimizes its local expected risk, denoted as $h_i^* = \arg\min_{h \in \mathcal{H}} \mathcal{L}_i(h)$, based on its finite local dataset $\hat{\mathcal{D}}_i$.

We denote w_i^t as the model parameters of client i at the beginning of the training round t. Let $\alpha_i^t = (\alpha_{i,1}^t, \ldots \alpha_{i,N}^t)$ denote the weighted collaboration vector of client i in the training round t, where $\sum_{j=1}^{N} \alpha_{i,j}^t = 1$ and $\alpha_{i,j}^t \geq 0$. Except the scheme in [41], the central server performs a weighted aggregation of the model parameters from all clients for each client i. As a result, the model parameters of i become $w_j^{t+1} = \sum_{j=1}^{N} \alpha_{i,j}^t w_j^t$. The weight $\alpha_{i,j}^t$ can be viewed as a quantification of the collaboration advantage that client j brings to client i in the training round t. Let α^t be a $N \times N$ matrix whose i-th row is α_i^t. α^t defines a directed benefit graph among the N clients. In the schemes of [47,48], the value of $\alpha_{i,j}^t$ changes in each round of training. In the schemes of [42–44], the value of $\alpha_{i,j}^t$ is independent of the round t and is precomputed before the FL training process starts; thus, $\alpha_{i,j}^t$, α_i^t and α^t are also simply denoted as $\alpha_{i,j}$, α_i and α. The way that the scheme in [41] works will be introduced in Sect. 3.4.

2.2 Typical Non-IID Data Settings

From a probability distribution perspective, the local data distribution $P(x_i, y_i)$ of client i can be represented by a conditional probability $P(x_i|y_i)P(y_i)$ or $P(y_i|x_i)P(x_i)$. There are three typical non-IID data settings in the FL context [37,55,56]: (1) label distribution skew, where $P(y_i)$ differs among clients; (2) feature distribution skew, where $P(x_i)$ differs among clients; and (3) quantity skew, where $P(x_i, y_i)$ is the same for all clients i, but the amount of data varies across clients.

The label distribution skew can be categorized into two settings. Firstly, in the quantity-based label imbalance setting, each client is randomly allocated k different label IDs. For each label, the samples are randomly and equally divided among the clients assigned to that label. We denote this setting as $\#C = k$. Secondly, in the distribution-based label imbalance setting, a Dirichlet distribution $Dir_N(\epsilon)$ is used. For each label c, a vector $q_c \in \mathbb{R}^N$ is drawn from the distribution $Dir_N(\epsilon)$ and client i is allocated a $q_{c,i}$ proportion of the data samples for label c. We denote this setting as $p_k \sim Dir(\epsilon)$. The feature distribution skew mainly has two settings. Firstly, in the noise-based feature imbalance setting, the entire dataset is randomly and equally divided among N clients [31]. Given a noise level σ, noises $\hat{x} \sim Gau(\sigma \cdot i/n)$ are added to the (local) dataset of each client i, where $Gau(\sigma \cdot i/n)$ is a Gaussian distribution with mean 0 and variance

$\sigma \cdot i/n$. We denote this setting as $\hat{\mathbf{x}} \sim Gau(\sigma)$. Secondly, in the *real-world feature imbalance* setting, the entire dataset is randomly and evenly partitioned among different clients [17], with each client receiving data sharing the same real-world characteristics, such as being from the same writers. In the *quantity skew* setting, a vector $q \in \mathbb{R}^N$ is drawn from the distribution $Dir_N(\epsilon)$, and each client i is allocated a q_i proportion of the total data samples of a dataset. We denote this setting as $q \sim Dir(\epsilon)$.

3 Data Heterogeneity Evaluation Benchmark

Existing methods for evaluating data heterogeneity can be roughly grouped into two main categories: those based on statistical divergence of data distributions [41,43,44] and those based on model performance [42,47,48]. In this section, we will detail these two categories of methods and their applications in PFL.

3.1 Preliminaries for Statistical Divergence-Based Approaches

Methods in this category are based on the divergence, a kind of statistical distance measure. It is a function that takes two probability distributions as input and returns a numerical value quantifying the difference between them [34]. In FL, the local model updates are uploaded to the central server, which performs a weighted aggregation of these updates to produce either a global model or a personalized models for each client. The divergence of data distributions among clients can guide more informed decisions on the choice of the aggregation weights [20,43,44] or clustering clients with similar data distributions [41,44,45].

A Unified Theoretical Framework. Some works in this category [43,44] have some features in common. In these methods, the weighted empirical risk $\hat{\mathcal{L}}_{\alpha_i}(h)$ for client i is defined as $\hat{\mathcal{L}}_{\alpha_i}(h) = \sum_{j=1}^{N} \alpha_{i,j} \hat{\mathcal{L}}_j(h)$. The model of i can be learned by minimizing $\hat{\mathcal{L}}_{\alpha_i}(h)$. Let $\hat{h}_{\alpha_i} = \arg\min_{h \in \mathcal{H}} \hat{\mathcal{L}}_{\alpha_i}(h)$ be the hypothesis that minimizes the weighted empirical risk $\hat{\mathcal{L}}_{\alpha_i}(h)$. The following bound is used by both [43] and [44]:

$$\mathcal{L}_i(\hat{h}_{\alpha_i}) - \mathcal{L}_i(\hat{h}_i^*) \leqslant Q_{\gamma,1}\sqrt{\sum_{j=1}^{N} \alpha_{i,j}^2/m_j} + Q_{\gamma,2}\sum_{j=1}^{N} \alpha_{i,j} \cdot D(\mathcal{D}_i, \mathcal{D}_j) \quad (1)$$

where $Q_{\gamma,1}$ and $Q_{\gamma,2}$ are parameters related to the type of divergence used in [43, 44]. Equation (1) shows that for client i the gap between $\hat{h}_{\alpha_i}$ and $\hat{h}^*$ depends on the weight α_i, the number of samples m_i and the divergence $D(\mathcal{D}_i, \mathcal{D}_j)$ between two data distributions. The optimal model for i can be obtained by choosing appropriate decision variables to minimize the right-hand side of Eq. (1). These methods are based on two statistical divergences, Jensen-Shannon Divergence and $\mathcal{C}$-Divergence.

3.2 Jensen-Shannon Divergence [43]

The Jensen-Shannon (JS) divergence between two distributions P and Q is denoted as $\text{JSD}(P,Q)$ [39]. It is based on the Kullback-Leibler (KL) divergence, denoted as $\text{KLD}(P,Q)$. For two discrete probability distributions on the same space $\mathcal{Z}$, we have $\text{KLD}(P,Q) = \sum_{z \in \mathcal{Z}} P(z) \log \frac{P(z)}{Q(z)}$ and $\text{JSD}(P,Q) = \frac{1}{2}\text{KLD}(P,M) + \frac{1}{2}\text{KLD}(Q,M)$ where $M = \frac{1}{2}(P+Q)$ denotes the mixture distribution of P and Q. The JS divergence has desirable properties, such as being symmetric and always having a finite value.

Application. Ding et al. [43] use the JS divergence to estimate the Integral Probability Metrics (IPM), which are another type of statistical distance with desirable theoretical properties for analytical tractability. The IPM between two distributions $\mathcal{D}_i$ and $\mathcal{D}_j$ are denoted as $d_{\mathcal{H}}(\mathcal{D}_i, \mathcal{D}_j)$, which is used by [43] to instantiate the divergence term $D(\mathcal{D}_i, \mathcal{D}_j)$ on the right-hand side of Eq. (1). Furthermore, Ding et al. [43] provide an optimal solution α_i to the corresponding optimal problem. The resulting PFL scheme is called **pFedJS**.

3.3 $\mathcal{C}$-Divergence [44]

$\mathcal{C}$-divergence is defined as [33, 35, 36]: $D_c(\mathcal{D}_i, \mathcal{D}_j) = \max_{h \in \mathcal{H}} |\mathcal{L}_i(h) - \mathcal{L}_j(h)|$. In the hypothesis space $\mathcal{H}$, $D_c(\mathcal{D}_i, \mathcal{D}_j)$ indicates the maximum difference between the local expected risks of two data distributions $\mathcal{D}_i$ and $\mathcal{D}_j$. Suppose ℓ is the 0–1 loss function. The definition of $\mathcal{C}$-divergence guarantees that its divergence value will be as close to one as possible if two distributions are distinctly different. Thus, it can be used to cluster clients into groups with similar data distributions.

Application. In the FL context, $\mathcal{C}$-divergence has been used to partition all clients into K coalitions $\{\mathcal{C}_1, \cdots, \mathcal{C}_k\}$, each with similar data distributions [44, 45]. The function $\ell(m(x), y)$ is also denoted as $f(x,y)$, mapping from $\mathcal{X} \times \mathcal{Y}$ to $\{0,1\}$. Bao et al. [44] transform the $\mathcal{C}$-divergence into the following form: $D_{i,j} = \max_{f \in \mathcal{F}} |\Pr_{(x,y) \in D_i}[f(x,y) = 1] + \Pr_{(x,y) \in D_j}[f(x,y) = 0] - 1|$. A client classifier $f \in \mathcal{F}$ can be trained to predict the distribution similarity. If the estimated distance $D_{i,j}$ is approximately 100%, then the two distributions being compared are significantly different. Unlike in [43], α_i is a dependent variable here, and the weight $\alpha_{i,j}$ of j to i is predefined as the proportion of the data quantity of j to the coalition's data quantity. Specifically, for any $i \in \mathcal{C}_k$, $\alpha_{i,j} = \beta_j / \sum_{l \in \mathcal{C}_k} \beta_l$ if $j \in \mathcal{C}_k$ and $\alpha_{i,j} = 0$ otherwise. Here, $D_c(\mathcal{D}_i, \mathcal{D}_j)$ is used to instantiate the divergence term $D(\mathcal{D}_i, \mathcal{D}_j)$ on the right-hand side of Eq. (1). Bao et al. [44] provide an efficient optimizer to optimize the coalition structure. Once $\{\mathcal{C}_1, \cdots, \mathcal{C}_k\}$ is determined, $\{\alpha_i\}_{i=1}^N$ will be determined accordingly. The corresponding PFL scheme is called **FedCollab**.

3.4 Distribution Sketch-Based Euclidean Distance [41]

Let $\mathbf{z_i} = (z_{i,1}, \ldots, z_{i,d})$, where $i \in \{1, 2\}$. The distance of two vectors is defined as $\sqrt{\sum_{l=1}^{d} (z_{1,l} - z_{2,l})^2}$. On the other hand, efficient computation of statistical divergences of high-dimensional data is challenging. To address this, Liu et al. [41] proposes a one-pass distribution sketch algorithm to represent the client data distributions. Then, the divergence is measured by the Euclidean distance of such distribution sketches. Central to their algorithm is Locality Sensitive Hashing (LSH), which uses hash functions to map data samples from high-dimensional space to low-dimensional buckets, ensuring that samples close to each other have a high probability of having the same hash value. Building on this, the Repeated Array of Count Estimators (RACE) is adopted [21–24]. Let $z = (x, y)$ denote a data sample. RACE uses R LSH functions to construct a matrix $A \in \mathbb{R}^{R \times B}$. Each LSH function g_i maps a data vector into B hash bins. For a given dataset $\hat{\mathcal{D}}$, any data sample $z \in \hat{\mathcal{D}}$ is mapped to R different hash values, denoted as $\{g_i(z) \mid i \in [1, R]\}$. The corresponding positions in matrix A are then incremented by 1. In this way, RACE can characterize the data distribution of $\hat{\mathcal{D}}_i$ for each client i using the corresponding A, referred to as the client data sketch CS_i.

Application. Liu et al. [41] show that an average of all client sketches can effectively approximate the sketch GS of the global data distribution across clients. The central server calculates the Euclidean distance between GS and CS_i before the FL training process starts. The inverses of these distances serve as the probabilities for selecting K clients, denoted as $\mathcal{C}$ for local training in round t. Specifically, clients with CS_i closer to GS are prioritized for collaboration. The local updates from $\mathcal{C}$ are aggregated by the central server, resulting in a global model $w^{t+1} = \sum_{j \in \mathcal{C}} w_j^t$. Finally, each client builds a personalized model based on the global model and its local data. We refer to the PFL approach in [41] as **RACE**.

3.5 Shapley Value [47]

Shapley Value (SV) is a classic approach to quantifying individual contributions within a group under the Cooperative Game Theory [1]. Let $\mathcal{N} = \{1, \ldots, N\}$. In machine learning, the data Shapley value of client i is defined as $\varphi_i(\mathcal{N}, V) = \sum_{S \subseteq \mathcal{N} - \{i\}} \frac{V(S \cup \{i\}) - V(S)}{\binom{N-1}{|S|}}$, where $V(\cdot)$ denotes the utility evaluation function [5, 11, 46]. In FL, the utility evaluation function $V(S)$ is based on the model performance achieved by the participation of S. Let M_S denote the global FL model trained with S on a separate test dataset $\mathcal{D}_S$. Then, $V(S) = V(M_S) = V\big(\mathcal{A}(M^{(0)}, \mathcal{D}_S)\big)$, where $\mathcal{A}$ is the learning algorithm and $M^{(0)}$ denotes the initial model [46].

Application. Wu et al. [47] apply the SV technique for PFL. For each client i, there is an N-dimensional relevance vector $\phi^{i,t} = [\phi_1^{i,t}, \ldots, \phi_N^{i,t}]$, where $\phi_j^{i,t}$ denotes the relevance score of client j to i in round t. In each round t, the models of clients with the top-K relevance score are downloaded, forming a coalition $S_{i,k}^t$ for client i; then, the SV φ_j^t of each client $j \in S_{i,k}^t$ is calculated and used to update the corresponding elements of $\phi^{i,t}$: $\phi_j^{i,t+1} = \eta \phi_j^{i,t} + (1 - \eta)\varphi_j^t$. For client i, the weighted collaboration vector α_i is also set according to the

SVs: $\alpha_{i,j}^t = \max\{\varphi_j^t, 0\}/\|w_i^t - w_j^t\|$ if $j \in \mathcal{S}_{i,k}^t$ and $\alpha_{i,j}^t = 0$ otherwise, where $\|\cdot\|$ denotes the Euclidean distance. The PFL scheme in [47] is called **pFedSV**.

3.6   Cosine Similarity [48]

Let $\mathbf{z_i} = (z_{i,1}, \ldots, z_{i,d})$, where $i \in \{1, 2\}$. The cosine similarity of two non-zero vectors is defined as $cos(\mathbf{z_1}, \mathbf{z_2}) = \frac{\mathbf{z_1} \cdot \mathbf{z_2}}{\|\mathbf{z_1}\|\|\mathbf{z_2}\|}$, where $\mathbf{z_1} \cdot \mathbf{z_2}$ is the inner product and $\|\cdot\|$ denotes the Euclidean norm. Intuitively, the closer the two vectors are, the smaller the angle between them, and thus the cosine value will be closer to one. Let us consider the personalized models $\mathbf{h_i}$ and $\mathbf{h_j}$ of clients i and j. Their cosine similarity is $cos(\mathbf{h_i}, \mathbf{h_j})$.

Application. Intuitively, when the data distribution of two clients i and j are more similar, their models are more similar, and their collaboration strength (i.e., $\alpha_{i,j}$) should be larger [13,16]. In practice, data distributions are inaccessible, so the similarity between model parameters is used to guide the collaboration strength. In each training round t, Ye et al. [48] propose minimizing the following function in a privacy-preserving manner while adhering to the standard FL training process: $\sum_{i=1}^N \beta_i \left(\mathcal{L}_i \left(\sum_{j=1}^N \alpha_{i,j}^t w_j^t \right) - \frac{\lambda}{2} \sum_{j=1}^N \alpha_{i,j}^t cos(w_i^t, w_j^t) \right)$, where the decision variables are $\{w_i^t\}_{i=1}^N$ and α^t, and λ is a hyperparameter to balance the individual utilities and the collaboration necessity.

3.7   Hypernetworks [42]

Each client i has a risk/loss function $\ell_i: \mathbb{R}^N \to \mathbb{R}_+$. Given a learned hypothesis $h \in \mathcal{H}$, let the loss vector $\ell(h) = [\ell_1, \ldots, \ell_N]$ represent the utility loss of the N clients under the hypothesis h. The hypothesis h is considered a Pareto solution if there is no other hypothesis h' that dominates h, i.e., $\nexists h' \subset \mathcal{H}$, s. t. $\forall i : \ell_i(h') \leqslant \ell_i(h)$ and $\exists j : \ell_j(h') < \ell_j(h)$. Let $r = (r_1, \ldots, r_N) \in \mathbb{R}^N$ denote a preference vector where $\sum_{k=1}^N r_k = 1$ and $r_k \geq 0, \forall k \in \{1, \ldots, N\}$. The hypernetwork HN takes r as input and outputs a Pareto solution h, i.e., $h \leftarrow HN(\phi, r)$, where ϕ denotes the parameters of the hypernetwork [14].

Application. For each client i, linear scalarization can be used. Cui et al. [42] determine an optimal preference vector r_i^* to generate the hypothesis h_i^* that minimizes the loss with the data $\hat{\mathcal{D}}_i$. This is expressed as $h_i^* = HN(\phi, r_i^*)$, where $r_i^* = \arg\min_r \hat{\mathcal{L}}_i(HN(\phi, r))$. For each client i, the value of r_i^* is assigned to α_i. In [42], collaboration equilibrium (CE) is sought with additional considerations. We refer to the PFL scheme here as **CE** due to its origin in [42].

4   Experimental Studies

To investigate the effectiveness of existing FL schemes in studying the statistical heterogeneity of data, we conducted extensive experiments on eight public datasets. These included five image datasets (i.e., *MNIST, CIFAR-10, FMNIST,*

SVHN, *FEMNIST*), and three tabular datasets (i.e., *adult*, *rcv1*, and *covtype*). For specific experimental procedures, we followed the protocol outlined in [56]. By default, the framework involves ten clients, each performing training over 10 epochs per communication round with a batch size of 64, across a total of 50 communication rounds. We use top-1 accuracy to indicate the differences in test case accuracy of various schemes under different non-IID conditions. Unless otherwise specified, the value in the tables represent the average test case results across all clients using their personalized models. For the full details of the experimental setup and results, please refer to [19]. The main insights of this paper are highlighted in *italic text*.

4.1 Analysis of the Accuracy Obtained by Collaboration

The accuracy of the six methods under the five standard non-IID settings and the IID data setting is shown in Table 1. Non-IID data can degrade the FL

Table 1. Comparison of various schemes under different conditions

Category	Dataset	Partitioning	pFedGraph	pFedSV	pFedJS	FedCollab	RACE	CE
Label distribution skew	MNIST	$p_k \sim Dir(0.5)$	**98.90%±0.10%**	91.18%±3.84%	98.54%±0.40%	79.66%±3.59%	**98.90%±0.27%**	98.82%±0.15%
		#C=1	**10.65%±0.70%**	10.24%±0.08%	10.09%±0.00%	10.00%±0.00%	10.09%±0.00%	10.30%±0.02%
		#C=2	**95.60%±0.43%**	35.52%±6.90%	10.17%±0.15%	19.93%±0.47%	10.17%±0.15%	84.65%±7.36%
		#C=3	**97.34%±0.81%**	52.95%±16.93%	9.84%±0.92%	27.96%±1.67%	12.73%±6.26%	93.52%±2.34%
	FMNIST	$p_k \sim Dir(0.5)$	**87.54%±0.44%**	80.74%±2.25%	85.34%±1.53%	69.10%±2.01%	85.68%±1.51%	86.93%±0.83%
		#C=1	**10.67%±1.33%**	10.05%±0.09%	10.00%±0.00%	10.00%±0.00%	10.00%±0.00%	10.00%±0.00%
		#C=2	**71.37%±8.10%**	26.94%±1.29%	10.00%±0.00%	18.81%±1.19%	10.00%±0.00%	58.44%±6.91%
		#C=3	**80.96%±2.21%**	34.44%±5.55%	10.00%±0.00%	26.56%±1.03%	25.45%±30.90%	74.11%±1.79%
	CIFAR-10	$p_k \sim Dir(0.5)$	**64.69%±0.92%**	44.87%±1.48%	45.80%±1.68%	36.10%±0.51%	49.32%±3.52%	62.65%±3.00%
		#C=1	10.00%±0.00%	**10.08%±0.16%**	10.00%±0.00%	10.00%±0.00%	10.00%±0.00%	10.00%±0.00%
		#C=2	39.77%±7.50%	17.53%±6.53%	10.00%±0.00%	17.20%±0.98%	10.00%±0.00%	**42.87%±6.35%**
		#C=3	**56.00%±0.03%**	26.33%±4.99%	10.00%±0.00%	23.78%±0.19%	10.00%±0.00%	49.27%±1.03%
	SVHN	$p_k \sim Dir(0.5)$	86.59%±0.39%	63.23%±6.19%	71.11%±7.10%	54.93%±3.96%	74.85%±5.48%	**87.64%±2.33%**
		#C=1	**18.37%±2.43%**	11.29%±0.00%	6.13%±0.00%	10.00%±0.00%	6.13%±0.00%	9.03%±1.55%
		#C=2	**69.35%±6.51%**	27.63%±5.98%	15.53%±4.46%	18.59%±3.01%	15.53%±4.46%	52.22%±12.74%
		#C=3	70.29%±2.32%	51.56%±4.39%	10.95%±4.99%	23.11%±1.88%	10.95%±4.99%	**70.47%±1.77%**
	adult	$p_k \sim Dir(0.5)$	**80.83%±0.83%**	78.97%±3.57%	76.40%±0.05%	72.89%±5.35%	77.57%±2.29%	74.86%±5.15%
		#C=1	**67.58%±17.58%**	39.45%±0.00%	23.62%±0.00%	50.00%±0.00%	23.62%±0.00%	50.00%±0.00%
	rcv1	$p_k \sim Dir(0.5)$	49.66%±0.82%	61.02%±10.36%	49.35%±1.81%	62.00%±10.27%	49.59%±2.06%	**79.55%±5.58%**
		#C=1	**51.16%±0.00%**	50.28%±0.05%	**51.16%±0.00%**	50.00%±0.00%	51.16%±0.00%	50.00%±0.00%
	covtype	$p_k \sim Dir(0.5)$	50.72%±0.48%	50.96%±0.24%	50.00%±1.20%	50.24%±0.00%	**51.16%±0.00%**	50.58%±0.58%
		#C=1	**50.00%±0.00%**	49.28%±0.48%	48.80%±0.00%	**50.00%±0.00%**	48.80%±0.00%	**50.00%±0.01%**
Number of times that performs the best			16	1	1	1	1	5
Feature distribution skew	MNIST	$\bar{x} \sim Gau(0.1)$	98.78%±0.22%	98.87%±0.25%	99.02%±0.10%	98.61%±0.06%	**99.11%±0.01%**	98.98%±0.06%
	FMNIST		88.50%±0.01%	84.13%±0.79%	**88.61%±0.00%**	87.37%±0.40%	87.77%±0.01%	88.43%±0.41%
	CIFAR-10		69.18%±0.80%	62.24%±0.06%	70.09%±0.54%	65.82%±3.41%	**70.96%±0.17%**	67.44%±1.93%
	SVHN		87.18%±2.71%	85.65%±0.09%	87.34%±0.57%	86.29%±0.00%	86.57%±0.28%	**87.61%±0.03%**
	FEMNIST	real-world	99.27%±0.04%	97.80%±1.15%	99.23%±0.00%	98.93%±0.20%	**99.28%±0.01%**	99.26%±0.01%
Number of times that performs the best			0	0	1	0	3	1
Quantity skew	MNIST	$q \sim Dir(0.5)$	99.04%±0.06%	98.29%±0.67%	99.12%±0.12%	96.61%±3.43%	**99.14%±0.08%**	98.99%±0.04%
	FMNIST		**88.85%±0.29%**	84.78%±3.92%	88.31%±0.30%	87.10%±1.12%	87.90%±0.28%	88.48%±0.20%
	CIFAR-10		**72.19%±0.03%**	61.68%±0.98%	71.70%±0.40%	62.51%±2.91%	71.86%±0.35%	70.12%±0.70%
	SVHN		88.16%±0.17%	76.63%±1.52%	85.05%±0.72%	85.14%±0.44%	84.54%±0.26%	**88.52%±0.39%**
	adult		**82.34%±0.04%**	82.24%±1.26%	82.23%±0.08%	82.15%±0.18%	82.25%±0.29%	82.07%±0.10%
	rcv1		51.16%±0.00%	51.40%±0.25%	**96.31%±0.17%**	95.44%±0.31%	95.73%±0.57%	96.25%±0.22%
	covtype		**51.20%±0.00%**	**51.20%±0.00%**	51.20%±0.10%	**51.20%±0.00%**	**51.20%±0.00%**	51.20%±0.05%
Number of times that performs the best			4	1	2	1	2	1
Homogeneous partition	MNIST	IID	98.96%±0.04%	98.63%±0.07%	99.06%±0.12%	98.60%±0.00%	**99.13%±0.00%**	98.97%±0.04%
	FMNIST		**88.91%±0.03%**	82.36%±0.71%	87.77%±0.07%	87.30%±0.41%	88.16%±0.04%	88.36%±0.42%
	CIFAR-10		68.10%±0.44%	62.18%±0.57%	69.59%±0.57%	63.28%±0.88%	**70.39%±0.17%**	66.54%±1.81%
	FEMNIST		**99.33%±0.01%**	97.64%±1.36%	99.24%±0.03%	99.12%±0.06%	99.28%±0.02%	99.25%±0.00%
	SVHN		**88.41%±0.14%**	85.71%±0.04%	86.07%±0.35%	87.25%±1.24%	86.82%±0.23%	87.84%±0.35%
	adult		82.22%±0.29%	81.37%±0.55%	81.91%±1.09%	82.53%±0.47%	81.76%±0.39%	**83.87%±2.04%**
	rcv1		51.40%±0.25%	95.28%±0.21%	**96.15%±0.38%**	51.40%±0.25%	95.88%±0.32%	81.11%±29.95%
	covtype		**51.23%±0.06%**	51.20%±0.01%	**51.23%±0.06%**	51.25%±0.05%	49.95%±1.25%	**51.23%±0.06%**
Number of times that performs the best			4	0	2	0	2	2

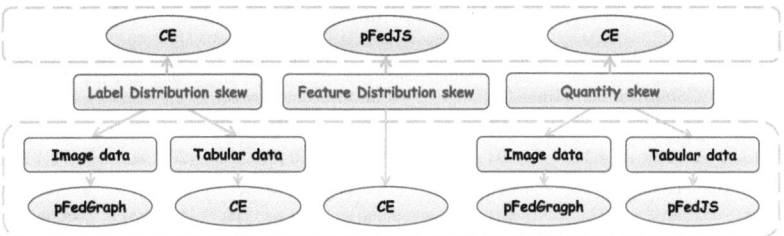

Fig. 1. The decision tree for identifying the optimal FL scheme under different non-IID setting.

performance to some extent. The results under the IID setting is used as a baseline to evaluate the performance of the six methods under non-IID settings.

Performance Comparison. Figure 1 summarizes the results in Table 1, with the blue ovals at the bottom illustrating which schemes are advantageous under each setting. There is no universally best scheme; the choice depends on the specific setting. In the label distribution skew setting, *pFedGraph* significantly outperforms other schemes on image data, while *CE* performs best on average for tabular data. For feature distribution skew, *RACE* usually achieves the highest accuracy. In the quantity skew setting, *pFedGraph* continues to excel on image data, while *pFedJS* achieves the highest accuracy on tabular data. Our observation is as follows: *as illustrated by the bottom blue ovals of Fig. 1, each non-IID setting has a corresponding technique that maximizes the collaboration advantages and personalized model accuracy.*

The pairwise collaboration advantages of clients can be measured by the matrix α^t or α, which defines a benefit graph of clients. In the line of research [15, 38, 42, 50], some desired properties (i.e., additional constraints) need to be maintained in the collaboration relationships of clients to address the issues with fairness, collaboration and competition [3, 18, 49, 53, 57, 58]; then, the final collaboration relationships of clients will form a subgraph of the benefit graph. Currently, only the hypernetwork technique is used to estimate α^t, without considering whether other techniques might be more advantageous. As identified by this paper, the matrix α^t can in fact be estimated by the *pFedJS, FedCollab, pFedSV, pFedGraph,* and *hypernetwork* techniques, where hypernetwork is used in the CE scheme. In the case of [42], the matrix α^t needs to be computed and the collaboration relationships of clients are determined before the FL training process starts; once these relationships are established, they remain fixed during the entire training process; thus, a fixed matrix α is required, and only the *pFedJS, FedCollab,* and *Hypernetwork* techniques can be applied. In the case of [15], both the matrix α^t and the collaboration relationships of clients can be updated in each round of FL training, as long as it does not create conflicts of interest among clients; thus, all five techniques mentioned above can be used to compute the matrix α^t. Regarding the choice of proper techniques for generating the benefit graph, the better technique is the one achieving higher overall accu-

Table 2. The computation time (seconds) and communication size (MBs) of different schemes.

	Computation Time				Communication Size			
	MNIST	CIFAR-10	adult	rcv1	MNIST	CIFAR-10	adult	rcv1
pFedJS	23.69 s	124.1 s	1.591 s	30.87 s	170.1 MB	240.1 MB	20.1 MB	5770.1 MB
pFedGraph	9.410 s	6.340 s	4.870 s	27.02 s	170 MB	240 MB	20 MB	5770 MB
pFedSV	1258 s	5444 s	149.1 s	244.5 s	850 MB	1200 MB	100 MB	28850 MB
FedCollab	305.9 s	1312 s	48.88 s	63.69 s	215.9 MB	304.8 MB	25.4 MB	7327.9 MB
RACE	4.169 s	27.26 s	2.003 s	3.017 s	105.9 MB	145.2 MB	13.3 MB	3462.6 MB
CE	391.8 s	1740 s	142.4 s	166.5 s	33330.1 MB	47020.1 MB	3490.1 MB	925820.1 MB

racy. From Table 1, we make the following observations: (1) *In the case where the benefit graph (i.e., the matrix α^t) can be updated in each round of FL training, it is desirable that under each non-IID setting, the matrix α^t is generated by the corresponding technique illustrated by the blue ovals at the bottom of Fig. 1. (2) In the case where the benefit graph (i.e., the matrix α) needs to be fixed and computed before the FL training process starts, it is desirable that under each non-IID setting, the matrix α is generated by the corresponding technique illustrated by the blue ovals at the top of Fig. 1.*

Effect of Different Non-IID Settings. It can be observed from Table 1 that: 1) for the feature distribution and quantity skew settings, existing schemes achieve accuracy close to the IID setting; 2) among all non-IID settings, the label distribution skew is the most challenging. Notably, in the quantity-based label imbalance setting, as the number of classes C decreases from three to one, the degree of data heterogeneity increases, leading to a decrease in accuracy. In the future, *there is still room to improve existing schemes for the label distribution skew setting.*

Effect of Different Tasks. CIFAR-10 is the most complex dataset, and its accuracy varies significantly across different schemes and non-IID settings. For other, simpler image datasets, the accuracy differences are relatively small across all cases. Tabular data also presents significant challenges, with accuracy consistently low across all six schemes (e.g., $\leqslant 52\%$ for covtype in all cases). These observations suggest that *more challenging tasks like CIFAR-10 and tabular datasets should be included in future benchmarks to better study the complementarity among clients.*

Finally, as generalized in Eq. (1), the difference between the weighted empirical risk and the optimal expected risk can be well bounded when two types of divergences are applied, respectively. *An interesting direction for future research is to explore whether such a bound exists for other divergence measures, such as the earth mover distance [2] and the Fréchet distance [4], which are mentioned in [41].*

4.2 Efficiency

Schemes except for [41] compute a matrix α only once before the FL training process starts [42–44] or a matrix α^t in each round of FL training [47,48] to quantify the collaboration advantages of clients. Liu et al. [41] perform a one-time computation of the distance/divergence between the client and global data distribution sketches before the FL training process starts. We evaluated (1) the time required to compute the matrix (α^t or α) or the divergence in each scheme under the noise-based feature imbalance setting, and (2) the communication overhead with the server (i.e., the amount of data communicated with the server over 50 communication rounds). Table 2 shows the experimental results.

The computational overhead of pFedSV is the highest across all datasets, followed closely by CE and FedCollab. The high computational overhead of these schemes is due to their use of neural networks to compute α [51,52]. In pFedJS, the JS divergence is computed in the joint feature and label space, whose dimension can be high; we note that the implementation in [43] considers only the label distribution skew case, where only the label space is concerned. In pFedGraph, the optimization of personalized models is performed locally. RACE and pFedJS execute simple binary operations, resulting in significantly faster computation. For the CE scheme, all clients train a Hypernetwork, resulting in a large amount of data exchanged with the server during the preparation of α. The communication overhead for pFedGraph, pFedJS, FedCollab and RACE is similar, as they typically require uploading the local model and downloading the personalized model during training. However, pFedSV has a relatively higher communication overhead because it needs to compute the Shapley Value locally using other clients' models.

Recently, there has been growing interest in measuring collaboration advantages to establish collaboration relationships among clients in the Internet of Things (IoT) field [8,20,25–27]. In these works, the JS divergence is commonly used. As pointed out in [41], divergence estimation can be difficult in high-dimensional spaces and require expensive computation [2,29]. In IoTscenarios, clients are typically resource-constrained devices with limited hardware resources (energy, bandwidth, computation). With these considerations, Liu et al. [41] propose a one-time distribution sketch technique to estimate data distribution divergence using lightweight computation. However, in their scheme, Liu et al. [41] don't need to generate the matrix α or α^t to quantify the collaboration advantages of clients. As shown in Table 2, using distribution sketches to measure divergence is much faster than using JS divergence. On the other hand, FL is often studied from a game theory perspective [6,7,9], where each client in the collaborative FL network aims to maximize its utility by collaborating with others [30]. Thus, the collaboration advantages (i.e., α or α^t) of clients need to be well understood and quantified in a lightweight way for the IoTsapplications. For example, Lu et al. [20] consider applying FL to IoTs and assume that the collaboration advantage (i.e., the utility) is linearly proportional to the JS divergence, which may be a simplistic assumption. Thus, *to make the existing technical development in literature more practical, it may be promising to study* *how to use the lightweight one-time distribution sketch technique to generate the matrix α or α^t, which lays a practical foundation for the FL collaboration establishment in the IoTs field.*

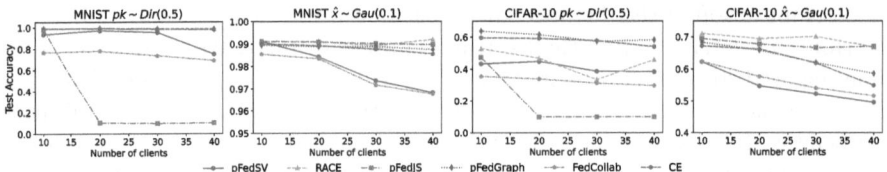

Fig. 2. The change of test accuracy with the number of clients: the first (resp. last) two plots are for CIFAR-10 (resp. MNIST).

4.3   Scalability

From Fig. 2, it can be observed that the accuracy of schemes may vary, and in many cases, their accuracy decreases as the number of clients increases. Among the six schemes, no scheme dominates the other schemes across all cases. The sensitivity of these schemes' performance to the number of clients implies that scalability should be an important aspect to consider when evaluating a FL scheme in the related research.

5   Concluding Remarks

In this paper, we summarize the six major techniques (JS divergence, $\mathcal{C}$-divergence, distribution sketch, Shapley Value, Hypernetworks, cosine similarity) to quantify data heterogeneity in FL settings into a first-of-its-kind unified framework to understand their effects in-depth. Extensive experiments over eight popular datasets have been conducted to compare these schemes under five standard non-IID FL settings, providing much-needed insight into which schemes are advantageous under which settings. The unified framework and the experimental results identify the scenarios, under which the current schemes perform relatively poorly, and future research problems for PFL. It is useful for identifying the right techniques for quantifying the collaboration advantages among clients, guiding the related research on collaboration, fairness, and competition in FL settings. The findings suggest that lightweight FL schemes based on techniques such as the distribution sketch are worth studying in the future.

Acknowledgments. This research is supported in part by the National Key Research and Development Program of China (No. 2024YFE0200503). This research is also supported in part by the National Natural Science Foundation of China under 62327801.

References

1. Shapley, L.S.: A Value for N-Person Games. Princeton University Press, Princeton (1953)
2. Andoni, A., Indyk, P., Krauthgamer, R.: Earth mover distance over high-dimensional spaces. In: Proceedings of the Nineteenth Annual ACM-SIAM Symposium on Discrete Algorithms, pp. 343–352. Society for Industrial and Applied Mathematics, USA (2008)
3. Lyu, L., Xu, X., Wang, Q., Yu, H.: Collaborative fairness in federated learning. In: Federated Learning: Privacy and Incentive, pp. 189–204. Springer, Cham (2020)
4. Heusel, M., Ramsauer, H., Unterthiner, T., Nessler, B., Hochreiter, S.: GANs trained by a two time-scale update rule converge to a local Nash equilibrium. In: Advances in Neural Information Processing Systems, vol. 30 (2017)
5. Huang, C.-Y., Lei, Q., Li, X.: Efficient medical image assessment via self-supervised learning. In: MICCAI Workshop on Data Augmentation, Labelling, and Imperfections, pp. 102–111. Springer, Cham (2022)
6. Khan, L.U., Saad, W., Han, Z., Hossain, E., Hong, C.S.: Federated learning for internet of things: recent advances, taxonomy, and open challenges. IEEE Commun. Surv. Tutor. **23**(3), 1759–1799 (2021)
7. Gupta, R., Gupta, J.: Federated learning using game strategies: state-of-the-art and future trends. Comput. Netw. **225**, 109650 (2023)
8. Arisdakessian, S., Wahab, O.A., Mourad, A., Otrok, H.: Coalitional federated learning: improving communication and training on non-IID data with selfish clients. IEEE Trans. Serv. Comput. **16**(4), 2462–2476 (2023)
9. Tu, X., Zhu, K., Luong, N.C., Niyato, D., Zhang, Y., Li, J.: Incentive mechanisms for federated learning: from economic and game theoretic perspective. IEEE Trans. Cogn. Commun. Netw. **8**(3), 1566–1593 (2022)
10. Li, X., Jiang, M., Zhang, X., Kamp, M., Dou, Q.: FedBN: federated learning on non-IID features via local batch normalization. In: International Conference on Learning Representations (2020)
11. Ghorbani, A., Zou, J.: Data Shapley: equitable valuation of data for machine learning. In: International Conference on Machine Learning, pp. 2242–2251. PMLR (2019)
12. Guo, S., Zhang, T., Xu, G., Yu, H., Xiang, T., Liu, Y.: Byzantine-resilient decentralized stochastic gradient descent. IEEE Trans. Circuits Syst. Video Technol. **32**(6), 4096–4106 (2021)
13. Luo, M., Chen, F., Hu, D., Zhang, Y., Liang, J., Feng, J.: No fear of heterogeneity: classifier calibration for federated learning with non-IID data. Adv. Neural. Inf. Process. Syst. **34**, 5972–5984 (2021)
14. Navon, A., Shamsian, A., Fetaya, E., Chechik, G.: Learning the pareto front with hypernetworks. In: International Conference on Learning Representations (2020)
15. Tan, S., et al.: FedCompetitors: harmonious collaboration in federated learning with competing participants. In: Proceedings of the AAAI Conference on Artificial Intelligence, vol. 38, no. 14, pp. 15231–15239 (2024)
16. Li, T., Sahu, A.K., Zaheer, M., Sanjabi, M., Talwalkar, A., Smith, V.: Federated optimization in heterogeneous networks. In: Proceedings of Machine Learning and Systems, vol. 2, pp. 429–450 (2020)
17. Caldas, S., et al.: Leaf: a benchmark for federated settings. arXiv preprint arXiv:1812.01097 (2018)

18. Huang, C., Ke, S., Liu, X.: Duopoly business competition in cross-silo federated learning. IEEE Trans. Netw. Sci. Eng. **11**(1), 340–351 (2024)
19. Li, Z., et al.: Benchmarking data heterogeneity evaluation approaches for personalized federated learning. arXiv preprint arXiv:2410.07286 (2024)
20. Lu, J., Chen, Y., Cao, S., Chen, L., Wang, W., Xin, Y.: LEAP: optimization hierarchical federated learning on non-IID data with coalition formation game. In: Proceedings of the 33rd International Joint Conference on Artificial Intelligence (2024, to appear)
21. Luo, C., Shrivastava, A.: Arrays of (locality-sensitive) count estimators (ACE): anomaly detection on the edge. In: Proceedings of the 2018 World Wide Web Conference, pp. 1439–1448. ACM (2018)
22. Liu, Z., Coleman, B., Zhang, T., Shrivastava, A.: Retaining knowledge for learning with dynamic definition. Adv. Neural. Inf. Process. Syst. **35**, 14944–14958 (2022)
23. Coleman, B., Geordie, B., Chou, L., Elworth, R.A.L., Treangen, T., Shrivastava, A.: One-pass diversified sampling with application to terabyte-scale genomic sequence streams. In: International Conference on Machine Learning, pp. 4202–4218. PMLR (2022)
24. Coleman, B., Baraniuk, R., Shrivastava, A.: Sub-linear memory sketches for near neighbor search on streaming data. In: International Conference on Machine Learning, pp. 2089–2099. PMLR (2020)
25. Zhang, N., Ma, Q., Mao, W., Chen, X.: Coalitional FL: coalition formation and selection in federated learning with heterogeneous data. IEEE Trans. Mob. Comput. 1–15 (2024)
26. Zhang, J., Guo, S., Guo, J., Zeng, D., Zhou, J., Zomaya, A.Y.: Towards data-independent knowledge transfer in model-heterogeneous federated learning. IEEE Trans. Comput. **72**(10), 2888–2901 (2023)
27. Zhu, R., Yang, M., Wang, Q.: ShuffleFL: addressing heterogeneity in multi-device federated learning. Proc. ACM Interact. Mob. Wearable Ubiquit. Technol. **8**(2), 1–34 (2024)
28. Yang, Q., Liu, Y., Chen, T., Tong, Y.: Federated machine learning: concept and applications. ACM Trans. Intell. Syst. Technol. **10**(2), 12:1–12:19 (2019)
29. Huang, J., Zhang, R., Buyya, R., Chen, J., Wu, Y.: Heads-join: efficient earth mover's distance similarity joins on Hadoop. IEEE Trans. Parallel Distrib. Syst. **27**(6), 1660–1673 (2015)
30. Donahue, K., Kleinberg, J.: Model-sharing games: analyzing federated learning under voluntary participation. In: Proceedings of the AAAI Conference on Artificial Intelligence, vol. 35, no. 6, pp. 5303–5311 (2021)
31. Zhang, K., Zuo, W., Chen, Y., Meng, D., Zhang, L.: Beyond a Gaussian denoiser: residual learning of deep CNN for image denoising. IEEE Trans. Image Process. **26**(7), 3142–3155 (2017)
32. McMahan, B., Moore, E., Ramage, D., Hampson, S., Arcas, B.A.: Communication-efficient learning of deep networks from decentralized data. In: Proceedings of the 20th International Conference on Artificial Intelligence and Statistics (AISTATS 2017), pp. 1273–1282 (2017)
33. Wu, J., He, J.: Continuous transfer learning with label-informed distribution alignment. arXiv preprint arXiv:2006.03230 (2020)
34. Rezende, D.J.: Short notes on divergence measures (2018)
35. Mohri, M., Muñoz Medina, A.: New analysis and algorithm for learning with drifting distributions. In: Bshouty, N.H., Stoltz, G., Vayatis, N., Zeugmann, T. (eds.) ALT 2012. LNCS (LNAI), vol. 7568, pp. 124–138. Springer, Heidelberg (2012). https://doi.org/10.1007/978-3-642-34106-9_13

36. Ben-David, S., Blitzer, J., Crammer, K., Kulesza, A., Pereira, F., Vaughan, J.W.: A theory of learning from different domains. Mach. Learn. **79**, 151–175 (2010)
37. Tan, A.Z., Yu, H., Cui, L., Yang, Q.: Towards personalized federated learning. IEEE Trans. Neural Netw. Learn. Syst. **34**(12), 9587–9603 (2022)
38. Chen, M., et al.: Free-rider and conflict aware collaboration formation for cross-silo federated learning. In: The 38th Annual Conference on Neural Information Processing Systems, pp. 1–10 (2024)
39. Caticha, A.: Relative entropy and inductive inference. In: AIP Conference Proceedings, vol. 707, no. 1, pp. 75–96. American Institute of Physics (2004)
40. Liu, R.W., et al.: Intelligent edge-enabled efficient multi-source data fusion for autonomous surface vehicles in maritime Internet of Things. IEEE Trans. Green Commun. Netw. **6**(3), 1574–1587 (2022)
41. Liu, Z., Xu, Z., Coleman, B., Shrivastava, A.: One-pass distribution sketch for measuring data heterogeneity in federated learning. Adv. Neural. Inf. Process. Syst. **36**, 15660–15679 (2023)
42. Cui, S., Liang, J., Pan, W., Chen, K., Zhang, C., Wang, F.: Collaboration equilibrium in federated learning. In: Proceedings of the 28th ACM SIGKDD Conference on Knowledge Discovery and Data Mining, pp. 241–251 (2022)
43. Ding, S., Wang, W.: Collaborative learning by detecting collaboration partners. Adv. Neural. Inf. Process. Syst. **35**, 15629–15641 (2022)
44. Bao, W., Wang, H., Wu, J., He, J.: Optimizing the collaboration structure in cross-silo federated learning. In: Proceedings of the 40th International Conference on Machine Learning, pp. 1718–1736. PMLR (2023)
45. Long, G., Xie, M., Shen, T., Zhou, T., Wang, X., Jiang, J.: Multi-center federated learning: clients clustering for better personalization. World Wide Web **26**(1), 481–500 (2023)
46. Liu, Z., Chen, Y., Yu, H., Liu, Y., Cui, L.: GTG-Shapley: efficient and accurate participant contribution evaluation in federated learning. ACM Trans. Intell. Syst. Technol. **13**(4), 21, Article no. 60 (2022)
47. Wu, L., et al.: Rethinking personalized client collaboration in federated learning. IEEE Trans. Mob. Comput. 1–13 (2024)
48. Ye, R., Ni, Z., Wu, F., Chen, S., Wang, Y.: Personalized federated learning with inferred collaboration graphs. In: Proceedings of the 40th International Conference on Machine Learning, pp. 39801–39817. PMLR (2023)
49. Lyu, L., et al.: Towards fair and privacy-preserving federated deep models. IEEE Trans. Parallel Distrib. Syst. **31**(11), 2524–2541 (2020)
50. Wu, X., Yu, H.: MarS-FL: enabling competitors to collaborate in federated learning. IEEE Trans. Big Data (2022). https://doi.org/10.1109/TBDATA.2022.3186991
51. He, T., Liu, Y., Ong, Y.S., Wu, X., Luo, X.: Polarized message-passing in graph neural networks. Artif. Intell. **331**, 104129 (2024)
52. He, T., Ong, Y.S., Bai, L.: Learning conjoint attentions for graph neural nets. Adv. Neural. Inf. Process. Syst. **34**, 2641–2653 (2021)
53. Guo, X., Yi, L., Wu, X., Yu, K., Wang, G.: Enhancing causal discovery in federated settings with limited local samples. In: International Workshop on Federated Foundation Models in Conjunction with NeurIPS 2024 (2024)
54. Shamsian, A., Navon, A., Fetaya, E., Chechik, G.: Personalized federated learning using hypernetworks. In: Proceedings of the 38th International Conference on Machine Learning, pp. 9489–9502. PMLR (2021)
55. Kairouz, P., McMahan, H.B., Avent, B., et al.: Advances and open problems in federated learning. Found. Trends Mach. Learn. **14**(1–2), 1–210 (2021)

56. Li, Q., Diao, Y., Chen, Q., He, B.: Federated learning on non-IID data silos: an experimental study. In: Proceedings of the 2022 IEEE 38th International Conference on Data Engineering (ICDE), pp. 965–978 (2022)
57. Yu, H., Miao, C., An, B., Shen, Z., Leung, C.: Federated learning on non-IID data silos: an experimental study. In: Proceedings of the 13th International Conference on Autonomous Agents and Multi-Agent Systems (AAMAS 2014), pp. 357–364 (2014)
58. Yu, H., et al.: Mitigating herding in hierarchical crowdsourcing networks. Sci. Rep. **6**(4) (2016)

Heterogeneous Federated Learning with Convolutional and Spiking Neural Networks

Yingchao Yu[1], Yuping Yan[2], Jisong Cai[3], and Yaochu Jin[2(✉)]

[1] Donghua University, Shanghai 201620, China
[2] Westlake University, Hangzhou 310030, China
{yanyuping,jinyaochu}@westlake.edu.cn
[3] Wuhan University, Wuhan 430072, China
2021302181110@whu.edu.cn

Abstract. Federated learning (FL) has emerged as a promising paradigm for training models on decentralized data while safeguarding data privacy. Most existing FL systems, however, assume that all machine learning models are of the same type, although it becomes more likely that different edge devices adopt different types of AI models, including both conventional analogue artificial neural networks (ANNs) and biologically more plausible spiking neural networks (SNNs). This diversity empowers the efficient handling of specific tasks and requirements, showcasing the adaptability and versatility of edge computing platforms. One main challenge of such heterogeneous FL system lies in effectively aggregating models from the local devices in a privacy-preserving manner. To address the above issue, this work benchmarks FL systems containing both convoluntional neural networks (CNNs) and SNNs by comparing various aggregation approaches, including federated CNNs, federated SNNs, federated CNNs for SNNs, federated SNNs for CNNs, and federated CNNs with SNN fusion. Experimental results demonstrate that the CNN-SNN fusion framework exhibits the best performance among the above settings on the MNIST dataset. Additionally, intriguing phenomena of competitive suppression are noted during the convergence process of multi-model FL.

Keywords: CNN-SNN fusion · Federated learning · Competitive suppression

1 Introduction

Embedded artificial intelligence and heterogeneous edge devices will be in increasing demand in various industrial and IoT systems. Alongside devices incorporating traditional convolutional neural networks (CNNs) [14,15], those utilizing spiking neural networks (SNNs) [9,20] will also emerge as strong contenders due to their advantage of low power consumption. Effectively and

H. Yu et al. (Eds.): FL 2024 Workshops, LNAI 15501, pp. 93–105, 2025.
https://doi.org/10.1007/978-3-031-82240-7_7

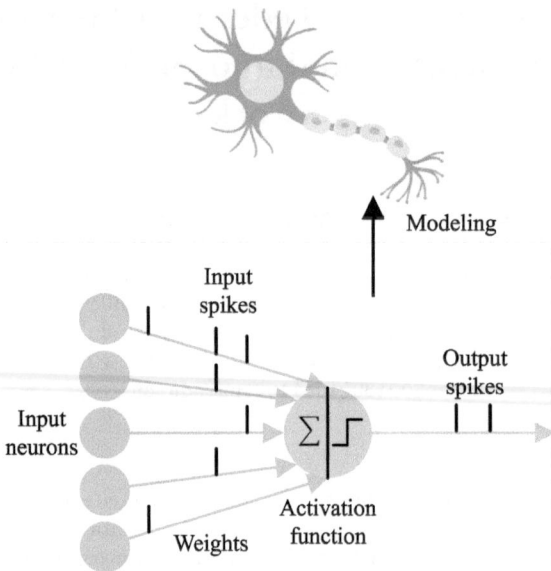

Fig. 1. An illustration of behavior of a spiking neuron.

securely leveraging data from these heterogeneous devices will be key to this scenario.

Both CNNs and SNNs are artificial neural networks that can be used to solve various AI tasks, however, they have distinct architectures and operate in different ways. CNNs [4] are primarily used for tasks involving grid-structured data, such as images, videos, and signals. They are composed of multiple layers, including convolutional layers, pooling layers, and fully connected layers. CNNs are widely used in image recognition, object detection, image segmentation, and other computer vision tasks due to their ability to capture spatial dependencies in data efficiently.

SNNs [3] are a type of neural network model inspired by biological neurons, particularly in their use of spikes or action potentials for information processing. Unlike CNNs, SNNs operate in discrete time steps, with neurons firing spikes in response to input stimuli. SNNs can process temporal information efficiently and are well-suited for tasks involving spatiotemporal data, such as time series prediction, speech recognition, and sensor data processing. Due to its event-driven and energy-efficient nature, SNNs are more suitable for mobile and edge devices.

Given the distinct suitability of CNNs and SNNs for different scenarios, exploring the potential of combining their capabilities across various modalities presents a practical challenge for addressing their individual limitations. By integrating the diverse modal data processed by CNNs and SNNs into joint learning frameworks, we can leverage the complementary strengths of each architecture to enhance overall model performance and robustness. However, the establish-

---

Algorithm 1: FedAvg

Input: The K clients are indexed by k, B is the local mini batch-size, E is number of local epochs, and η is the learning rate

Output: Updated model

1 Server Side: weights initialization w_o
2 **do**
3   Select $S_t \leftarrow m \leftarrow (C * K, 1)$ clients randomly.
4   **for** each client $k \in S_t$ **in parallel do**
5        $w_{t+1}^k \leftarrow ClientUpdate(k, w_t)$
6          $w_{t+1} \leftarrow \sum_{k=1}^{K} \frac{n_k}{n} w_{t+1}^k$
7   **end for**
8 **end for**
9 **Return** w_{t+1}
10 Local update(k, w)
11 $\mathcal{B} \leftarrow$ split d_k into batches of size B
12 **for** each local epoch e from 1 to E **do**
13   **for** $b \in \mathcal{B}$ **do**
14        $w \leftarrow w - \eta \nabla(w, b)$
15   **end for**
16 **end for**
17 **Return** w

---

ment of a secure and privacy-preserving environment for CNN-SNN interaction is another critical challenge.

Federated learning (FL) [7,13] has emerged as a promising solution to this problem, offering a decentralized approach to model training that respects data privacy and security. While existing federated CNN [12] and federated SNN [16,17,19] frameworks enable training within a single modality, the exploration of multi-modal learning techniques that leverage both SNN and CNN capabilities remains unclear. By bridging this gap and developing novel approaches for multi-modal learning, we can unlock the full potential of CNN-SNN fusion in federated environment.

In this paper, we present a novel approach to multi-modal federated learning, leveraging the fusion of CNNs and SNNs. The contributions of this study are as follows:

- This paper pioneers the integration of CNN-SNN models within an FL framework.
- To elucidate the efficacy of our proposed framework, we conduct a thorough comparative analysis against various federated learning approaches. Specifically, we compare our CNN-SNN fusion framework with federated CNNs, federated SNNs, federated CNNs for SNNs, and federated SNNs for CNNs.
- Our CNN-SNN fusion outperforms the CNN for SNN and SNN for CNN frameworks and we observe interesting competitive suppression phenomena during the training process of CNN-SNN fusion.

2   Preliminaries

In this section, we introduce the preliminaries relevant to our work, namely FL and SNNs.

2.1   Federated Learning

FL is a distributed machine learning paradigm in which each of the participants trains a model on local data and uploads the parameters of the updated model to the server. Then the server aggregates the local models to obtain a global model. Compared with traditional machine learning techniques, FL cannot only improve learning efficiency but also solve the problem of data silos and protect local data privacy [1].

In horizontal FL (HFL) [21,22], the feature space is shared across all parties, but each party may have a distinct sample space in their datasets, representing one of the most prevalent frameworks in federated learning. Initially, the server initializes a model with random parameters θ_0 and distributes it to all participating clients. Subsequently, a subset of k out of n clients receive the model and compute training gradients locally based on their respective datasets. These updated models are then transmitted back to the server, which aggregates the gradients from all participating clients to compute the global parameters:

$$\theta_r = \sum_{i=1}^{k} \theta_i / k \tag{1}$$

Federated Averaging (FedAvg) [13,18] is one of the most widely adopted methods in FL. Its pseudocode is delineated in Algorithm 1.

In this method, stochastic gradient descent (SGD) [8] is utilized to minimize the global dropout and accuracy function f_{FL}. In Federated Stochastic Gradient Descent (FedSGD) [13], all clients are involved ($C = 1$), and each client k updates its local parameters as follows:

$$w_{t+1}^k \leftarrow w_t - \nabla g_k. \tag{2}$$

Subsequently, the server aggregates these updated parameters into a global parameter w_{t+1} using weighted averaging:

$$w_{t+1} \leftarrow \sum_{k=1}^{K} \frac{n_k}{n} w_{t+1}^k \tag{3}$$

If clients conduct multiple updates within their local datasets, the local parameters are iteratively updated by:

$$w^k \leftarrow w^k - \eta \nabla F_k(w_k). \tag{4}$$

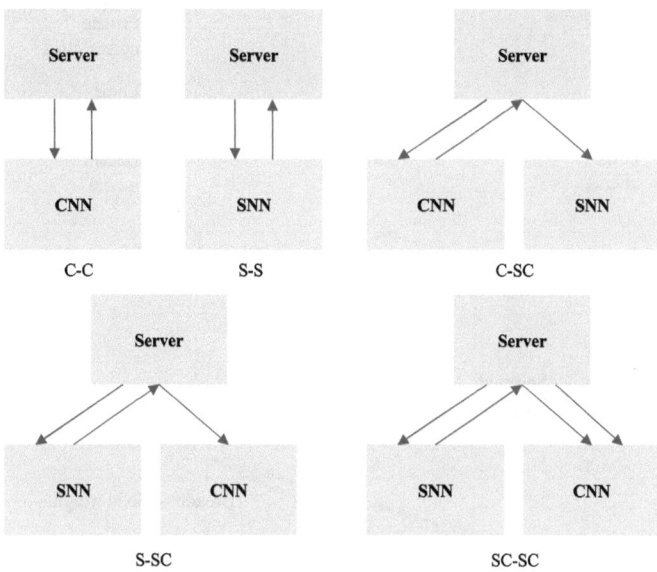

Fig. 2. Five experimental frameworks.

2.2 Spiking Neural Networks

In an SNN, information is encoded in the timing of these spikes [11]. The Leaky Integrate-and-Fire (LIF) [6,10] neuron model is one of the simplest and most commonly used neuron models in SNNs. It captures the basic behavior of biological neurons by integrating incoming input signals over time and emitting an output spike when a certain threshold is reached.

An LIF neuron in layer l with index i can formally be described in differential form:

$$\tau_{\text{mem}} \frac{dU_i^{(l)}}{dt} = -\left(U_i^{(l)} - U_{\text{rest}}\right) + RI_i^{(l)}, \tag{5}$$

where $U_i(t)$ is the membrane potential, U_{rest} is the resting potential, τ_{mem} is the membrane time constant, R is the input resistance, and $I_i(t)$ is the input current.

Figure 1 describes the basic calculation process of the SNN. Considering a neuron i receiving input from a set of neurons N, the incoming spikes from these input neurons are weighted by the parameters w_{ij} for all j belonging to N and are accumulated to form the neuron. Upon reaching a predefined threshold v, the neuron generates an output spike. Following this spike, the membrane potential undergoes a reset process.

In SNNs, the input current is typically generated by synaptic currents induced by the arrival of presynaptic spikes $S_j^{(l)}(t)$. When working with differential equations, a spike train $S_j^{(l)}(t)$ as a sum of Dirac delta functions

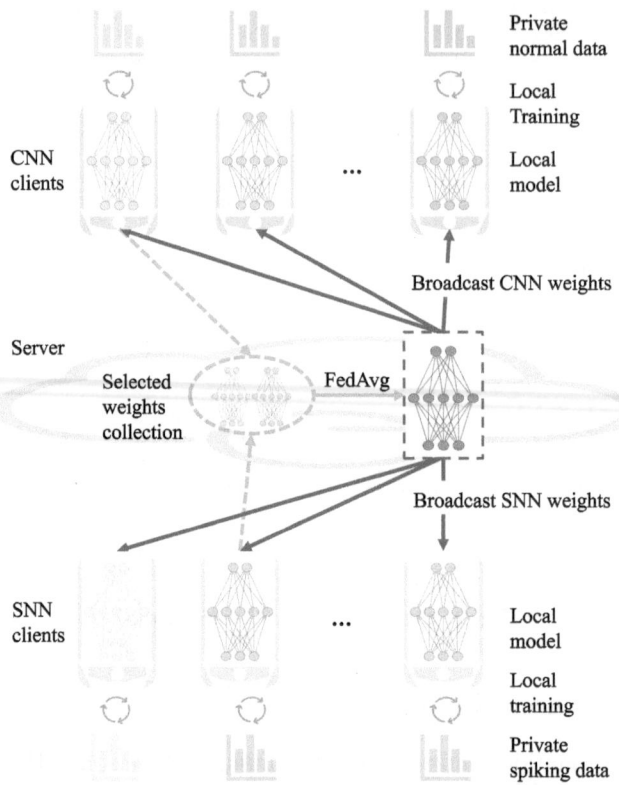

Fig. 3. The federated CNN-SNN fusion framework.

$S_j^{(l)}(t) = \sum_{s \in C_j^{(l)}} \delta(t - s)$ is denoted, where s iterates over the firing times $C_j^{(l)}$ of neuron j in layer l.

Synaptic currents exhibit distinct temporal dynamics. A common simplification is to model their time evolution as an exponentially decaying current following each presynaptic spike. Additionally, we assume linearity in the summation of synaptic currents. The dynamics of these operations can be encapsulated by the following expression:

$$\frac{\mathrm{d}I_i^{(l)}}{\mathrm{d}t} = -\underbrace{\frac{I_i^{(l)}(t)}{\tau_{\mathrm{syn}}}}_{\text{exp. decay}} + \underbrace{\sum_j W_{ij}^{(l)} S_j^{(l-1)}(t)}_{\text{feed-forward}} + \underbrace{\sum_j V_{ij}^{(l)} S_j^{(l)}(t)}_{\text{recurrent}}. \tag{6}$$

Here, the summation extends over all presynaptic neurons j, with $W_{i,j}^{(l)}$ representing the corresponding afferent weights from the layer below. Additionally, $V_{i,j}^{(l)}$ denotes explicit recurrent connections ij within each layer. We can represent a single LIF neuron through two linear differential equations, where the initial conditions undergo instantaneous modification upon each spike occurrence.

Table 1. Model architectures of CNN and SNN.

CNN			SNN		
Layer name	Param shape	Output shape	Layer name	Param shape	Output shape
Input	-	None×1×32×32	Input	-	None×T×1×32×32
Conv2d	Weights: 32×1×3×3	None×32×32×32	Conv2d	Weights: 32×1×3×3	None×T×32×32×32
BatchNorm2d	Weights: 32 Bias: 32	None×32×32×32	BatchNorm2d	Weights: 32 Bias: 32	None×T×32×32×32
Sigmoid	-	None×32×32×32	IFNode	-	None×T×32×32×32
MaxPool2d	-	None×32×16×16	MaxPool2d	-	None×T×32×16×16
Conv2d	Weights: 32×1×3×3	None×32×16×16	Conv2d	Weights: 32×1×3×3	None×T×32×16×16
BatchNorm2d	Weights: 32 Bias: 32	None×32×16×16	BatchNorm2d	Weights: 32 Bias: 32	None×T×32×16×16
Sigmoid	-	None×32×16×16	IFNode	-	None×T×32×16×16
MaxPool2d	-	None×32×8×8	MaxPool2d	-	None×T×32×8×8
Linear	Weights: 512×2048	None×512	Linear	Weights: 512×2048	None×T×512
Sigmoid	-	None×512	IFNode	-	None×T×512
Linear	Weights: 10×512	None×10	Linear	Weights: 10×512	None×T×10
Sigmoid	-	None×10	IFNode	-	None×T×10
-			Surrogate function of IFNode: sigmoid		

Leveraging this property, we can introduce a reset term via an additional factor that immediately decreases the membrane potential by $(\vartheta - U_{\text{rest}})$ whenever the neuron emits a spike:

$$\frac{dU_i^{(l)}}{dt} = -\frac{1}{\tau_{\text{mem}}}\left(\left(U_i^{(l)} - U_{\text{rest}}\right) + RI_i^{(l)}\right) + S_i^{(l)}(t)\left(U_{\text{rest}} - \vartheta\right). \tag{7}$$

3   CNN-SNN Fusion Framework

In the federated framework, a centralized server orchestrates multiple clients, each potentially equipped with either an SNN or a CNN model. The overarching goal is to train a global model without necessitating the transmission of raw data from the clients. It includes three phases, initialization, local training, and aggregation.

– **Initialization:** The federated learning process commences with the initialization phase, during which a global model is instantiated and distributed to all participating clients by the centralized server.
  Each client receives the initial model parameters, serving as the foundational framework for subsequent training iterations.
– **Local training phase:** In the local training phase, individual clients train their respective local datasets to fine-tune the global model parameters. For SNNs, local training entails fine-tuning synaptic weights, thresholds, and other parameters critical for optimizing spike timings and firing rates. Employing the FedAvg algorithm, clients update model parameters and upload their parameters to the server.

– **Aggregation:** After receiving the parameters, the server conducts an aggregation with the average function and outputs the final result, which is the global model.

To fully demonstrate the effectiveness of the CNN-SNN fusion framework, we have devised five distinct modes, refer to Fig. 2, each tailored to specific functionalities and scenarios:

– **Federated CNN Mode (C-C):** In this mode, the algorithm exclusively operates in the domain of CNNs. The training process encompasses all CNN clients, fostering a unified and optimized CNN-based approach across the network.
– **Federated SNN Mode (S-S):** By copntrast, the federated SNN mode focuses solely on SNNs. It orchestrates the training of all SNN clients.
– **Federated CNN for SNN Mode (C-SC):** This mode intertwines the modalities of both CNNs and SNNs. Initially, CNN models undergo training and are then uploaded to a centralized server. Then, all clients, regardless of whether they are using CNN or SNN, get these CNN weights from the server. This hybrid approach optimizes resources by leveraging CNN weights across the network.
– **Federated SNN for CNN Mode (S-SC):** Similarly, the federated SNN for CNN mode combines CNN and SNN capabilities. Here, SNN models undergo training and are uploaded to the server. All clients, regardless of their inherent modality, then fetch these SNN weights from the server. This strategy optimizes network efficiency by capitalizing on SNN weights across diverse client devices.
– **CNN-SNN Fusion Mode (SC-SC):** The CNN-SNN fusion mode amalgamates the modalities of both CNNs and SNNs, refer to Fig. 3. Clients independently train their local models, contributing to a diverse and robust set of weights. The server orchestrates weight aggregation, culminating in a unified, comprehensive model. Subsequently, all clients retrieve these aggregated weights, embodying a fusion of CNN and SNN capabilities across the network.

4   Experimental Results

The experiments assess five distinct frameworks using the MNIST dataset [2]. In each framework, an equal number of CNN and SNN clients undergo 200 global epochs, with each client performing 2 local epochs.

Table 2. Accuracy comparisons of different modes.

N/P:10/2		C-C	S-S	C-SC		S-SC		SC-SC	
		CNN	SNN	CNN	SNN	CNN	SNN	CNN	SNN
IID		98.930	99.160	95.680	89.310	47.780	95.870	**97.470**	95.690
Non-IID	Alpha = 1	98.950	98.610	**97.740**	93.570	54.240	97.560	95.6500	94.2700
	Alpha = 0.5	98.570	97.890	97.900	92.770	45.300	97.360	**97.500**	90.710
	Alpha = 0.125	62.790	74.100	57.620	51.210	38.960	**73.110**	58.920	61.710

4.1 Model Architectures and Data Processing

Table 1 presents the architectures of the CNN and SNN models utilized in the experiments. The inputs to the SNN clients are temporal discrete pulse signals, generated from continuous signals with a temporal length set to 20 time steps and following a Poisson distribution [5]. The activation function in the SNN is based on the Integrate-and-Fire neuron model, corresponding to IFNode in Table 1, which enables the SNN to process spiking signals. Furthermore, a sigmoid surrogate gradient function is employed to facilitate backpropagation training in the SNN.

The data for the CNN and SNN clients are randomly distributed, non-overlapping, and remain constant across epochs from the MNIST dataset. In non-IID scenarios, a Dirichlet distribution is employed to allocate sample proportions among different clients for each class, generating non-IID data [23], with the parameter alpha governing the degree of non-IIDness, where lower values indicate higher degrees of non-IIDness.

4.2 Comparison of Five Frameworks

In this series of experiments, we configured the number of clients to 10 and uploaded one SNN weight and one CNN weight each time. Additionally, the non-IID data set is further divided into three different levels of non-independence, represented by different alpha values. Lower alpha values indicate higher non-independence, which makes the task of generalizing the model more challenging.

From the results in Fig. 4, we observe that the proposed CNN-SNN fusion framework (SC-SC) can converge under both IID and various degrees of non-IID data. Secondly, within the SC-SC framework, there exists a convergence difference between SNN and CNN due to the misalignment of different modal data. Their gradients compete during fusion, with the dominant side suppressing the performance of the weaker side during training. In this experiment, SNN clients are the dominant side.

Additionally, compared to the C-SC and S-SC frameworks, the SC-SC framework exhibits smaller convergence differences between SNN and CNN. This is because the SC-SC framework merges the gradients of two modal models, allowing the server to simultaneously learn knowledge from both SNN and CNN

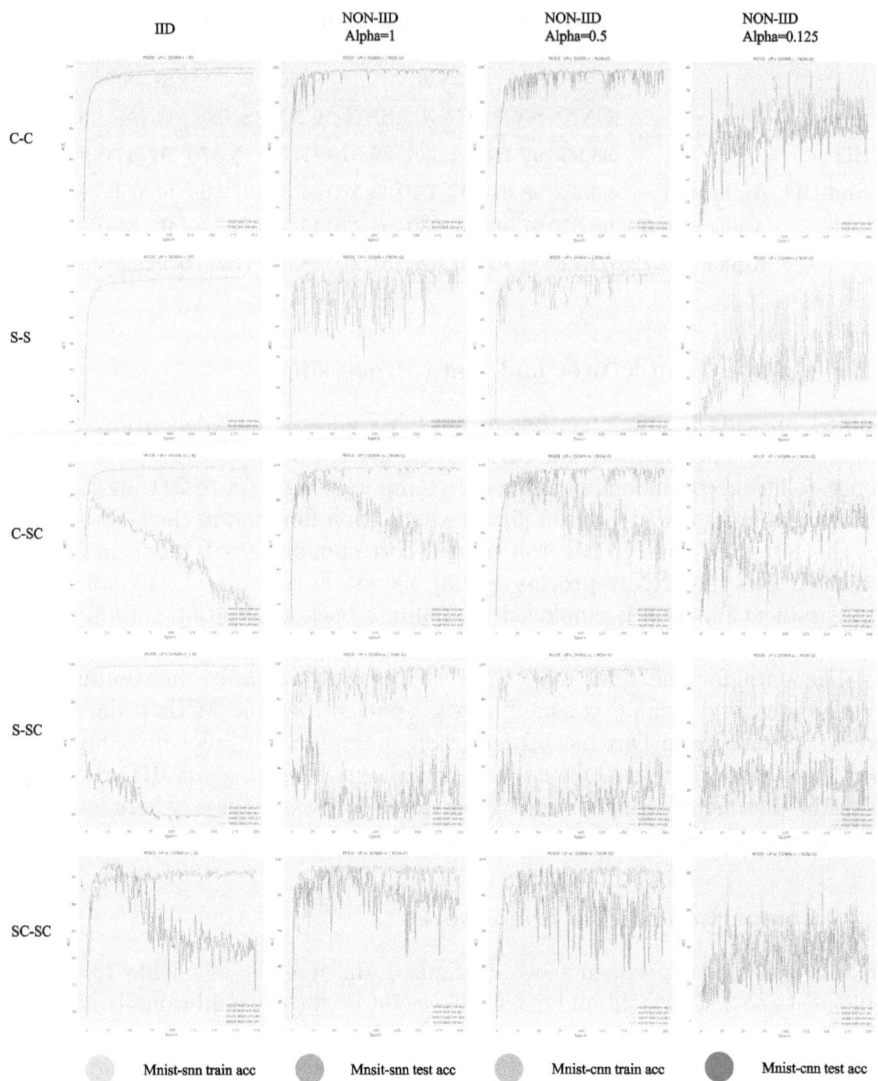

Fig. 4. Accuracy of five frameworks under IID and Non-IID scenarios.

clients, while C-SC and S-SC models can only learn from one type of client. Furthermore, as the degree of Non-IID data increases, the differences between CNN and SNN results gradually decrease in the C-SC, S-SC, and SC-SC frameworks. This indicates that non-IID data helps alleviate competition suppression issues in training different modalities.

Finally, compared to the C-C and S-S frameworks, the performance of the SC-SC framework on each modality is slightly lower than the corresponding single-modality frameworks (S-S and C-C). This is because the current framework does

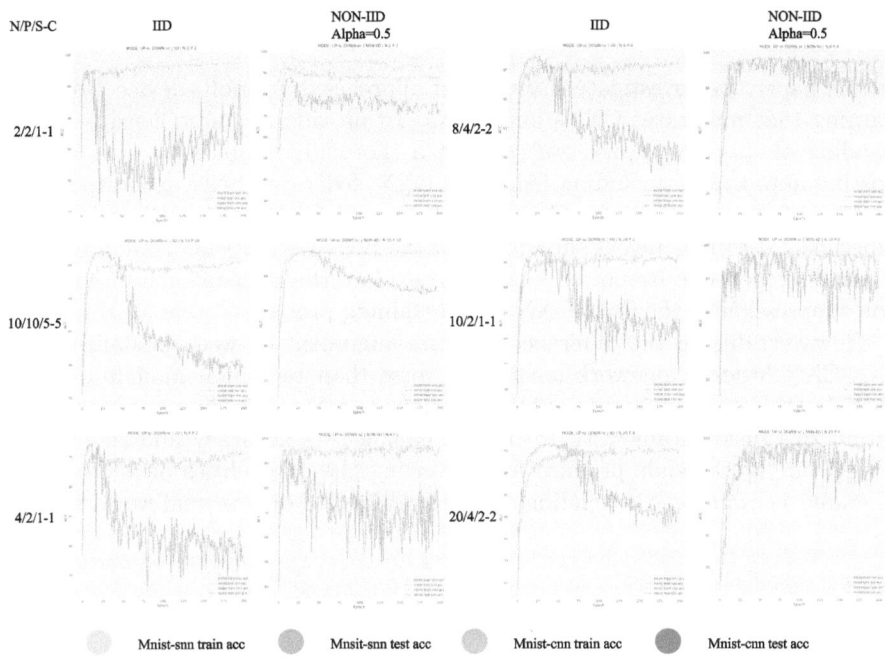

Fig. 5. Accuracy of SC-SC framework for different numbers of clients.

not consider mutual promotion between different modalities. We will explore this direction in future research.

Table 2 shows the optimal results of the five frameworks in Fig. 4 under four different data conditions. For the C-SC, S-SC and SC-SC frameworks, we chose the results corresponding to the optimal mean of the CNN and SNN.

4.3   Competitive Suppression in SC-SC

This set of experiments investigates the SC-SC framework by varying the number of clients (denoted as N) and the number of uploads (denoted as P). This variation aims to further explore the issue of competition suppression within the framework. Each configuration of N/P considers both IID and non-IID (with alpha = 0.5) scenarios.

Observations from Fig. 5 are as follows. As the values of N/P increase, the convergence discrepancy between SNN and CNN decreases gradually. In the IID scenario, role reversal between superior and inferior parties is more likely to occur. Initially, in the IID column, CNN clients (blue curve) tend to be dominant, but later, it transitions to SNN clients (orange curve) becoming more dominant. However, non-IID significantly reduces the competition suppression problem in SC-SC federated training.

5 Conclusion

In this paper, we investigate a variety of approaches to multi-device federated learning that integrates CNNs and SNNs. To provide a comprehensive understanding of this framework, we conduct a thorough comparison with various existing approaches, including federated CNN, federated SNN, federated CNN for SNN, federated SNN for CNN, and federated CNN with SNN fusion. The experimental results reveal superiority of the SNN-CNN fusion compared with other heterogeneous frameworks and also explore the phenomenon of competition suppression in the SNN-CNN fusion training process.

However, due to the differences and misalignment between modalities, the SNN-CNN fusion framework is slightly worse than the single-modality framework. In the future, we aim to explore alignment and transfer learning techniques within this fusion framework to further enhance its accuracy and robustness. This future work holds promise for advancing the capabilities of multi-device federated learning and extending its applicability to diverse real-world scenarios.

References

1. Custers, B., Sears, A.M., Dechesne, F., Georgieva, I., Tani, T., Van der Hof, S.: EU Personal Data Protection in Policy and Practice. Springer, Cham (2019)
2. Deng, L.: The MNIST database of handwritten digit images for machine learning research. IEEE Signal Process. Mag. **29**(6), 141–142 (2012)
3. Ghosh-Dastidar, S., Adeli, H.: Spiking neural networks. Int. J. Neural Syst. **19**(04), 295–308 (2009)
4. Gu, J., et al.: Recent advances in convolutional neural networks. Pattern Recogn. **77**, 354–377 (2018)
5. Heeger, D., et al.: Poisson model of spike generation. Handout, University of Standford **5**(1–13), 76 (2000)
6. Hunsberger, E., Eliasmith, C.: Spiking deep networks with LIF neurons. arXiv preprint arXiv:1510.08829 (2015)
7. Ji, S., et al.: Emerging trends in federated learning: From model fusion to federated x learning. Int. J. Mach. Learn. Cybern. 1–22 (2024)
8. Johnson, R., Zhang, T.: Accelerating stochastic gradient descent using predictive variance reduction. In: Advances in Neural Information Processing Systems, vol. 26 (2013)
9. Koo, M., Srinivasan, G., Shim, Y., Roy, K.: sBSNN: stochastic-bits enabled binary spiking neural network with on-chip learning for energy efficient neuromorphic computing at the edge. IEEE Trans. Circuits Syst. I Regul. Pap. **67**(8), 2546–2555 (2020)
10. Kornijcuk, V., et al.: Leaky integrate-and-fire neuron circuit based on floating-gate integrator. Front. Neurosci. **10**, 212 (2016)
11. Lobo, J.L., Del Ser, J., Bifet, A., Kasabov, N.: Spiking neural networks and online learning: an overview and perspectives. Neural Netw. **121**, 88–100 (2020)
12. Lu, Y., Fan, L.: An efficient and robust aggregation algorithm for learning federated CNN. In: Proceedings of the 2020 3rd International Conference on Signal Processing and Machine Learning, pp. 1–7 (2020)

13. McMahan, B., Moore, E., Ramage, D., Hampson, S., y Arcas, B.A.: Communication-efficient learning of deep networks from decentralized data. In: Artificial Intelligence and Statistics, pp. 1273–1282. PMLR (2017)
14. Merenda, M., Porcaro, C., Iero, D.: Edge machine learning for AI-enabled IoT devices: a review. Sensors **20**(9), 2533 (2020)
15. Rashid, N., Demirel, B.U., Al Faruque, M.A.: AHAR: adaptive CNN for energy-efficient human activity recognition in low-power edge devices. IEEE Internet Things J. **9**(15), 13041–13051 (2022)
16. Skatchkovsky, N., Jang, H., Simeone, O.: Federated neuromorphic learning of spiking neural networks for low-power edge intelligence. In: ICASSP 2020-2020 IEEE International Conference on Acoustics, Speech and Signal Processing (ICASSP), pp. 8524–8528. IEEE (2020)
17. Venkatesha, Y., Kim, Y., Tassiulas, L., Panda, P.: Federated learning with spiking neural networks. IEEE Trans. Signal Process. **69**, 6183–6194 (2021)
18. Wang, H., Yurochkin, M., Sun, Y., Papailiopoulos, D., Khazaeni, Y.: Federated learning with matched averaging. arXiv preprint arXiv:2002.06440 (2020)
19. Wang, Y., Duan, S., Chen, F.: Efficient asynchronous federated neuromorphic learning of spiking neural networks. Neurocomputing **557**, 126686 (2023)
20. Yang, H., et al.: Lead federated neuromorphic learning for wireless edge artificial intelligence. Nat. Commun. **13**(1), 4269 (2022)
21. Yang, Q., Liu, Y., Chen, T., Tong, Y.: Federated machine learning: concept and applications. ACM Trans. Intell. Syst. Technol. (TIST) **10**(2), 1–19 (2019)
22. Zhang, X., Mavromatis, A., Vafeas, A., Nejabati, R., Simeonidou, D.: Federated feature selection for horizontal federated learning in IoT networks. IEEE Internet Things J. **10**(11), 10095–10112 (2023)
23. Zhu, H., Xu, J., Liu, S., Jin, Y.: Federated learning on non-IID data: a survey. Neurocomputing **465**, 371–390 (2021)

Synthetic Data Aided Federated Learning Using Foundation Models

Fatima Z. Abacha[1]([⊠]) [ID], Sin G. Teo[2] [ID], Lucas C. Cordeiro[1] [ID],
and Mustafa A. Mustafa[1,3] [ID]

[1] The University of Manchester, Manchester, UK
{fatima.abacha,lucas.cordeiro,mustafa.mustafa}@manchester.ac.uk
[2] Institute for Infocomm Research, A*STAR, Singapore, Singapore
teosg@i2r.a-star.edu.sg
[3] COSIC, KU Leuven, Leuven, Belgium

Abstract. In scenarios where the data distribution amongst Federated Learning (FL) participants is Non-Independent and Identically distributed (Non-IID), FL suffers from the well-known problem of data heterogeneity. This leads to significantly degraded FL performance, as the global model tends to struggle to converge. To solve this problem, we propose Differentially Private Synthetic Data Aided Federated Learning Using Foundation Models (DPSDA-FL) - a novel data augmentation strategy that aids in homogenizing the local data present on the clients' side. DPSDA-FL improves the training of the local models by leveraging differentially private synthetic data generated from foundation models. We demonstrate the effectiveness of our approach by evaluating it on the benchmark image dataset: CIFAR-10. Our experimental results show that DPSDA-FL can improve the global model's class recall and classification accuracy by up to 26% and 9%, respectively, in FL with Non-IID issues.

Keywords: Federated Learning · Non-IID Data · Foundation Models

1 Introduction

Federated Learning (FL) enables the training of a machine learning model by several parties without sharing their data with each other [16]. The training process is orchestrated by a third party, which is usually a central server. In FL, each client uses its private data to train its model, known as the local model, while the server uses an aggregation algorithm to construct a global model from the local models. The process runs for several iterations until a global model with the desired performance is achieved [22]. This global model is then broadcast to all the clients so they can use it for inference on their test dataset.

FL protects against data leakage as each client's private training data is not disclosed to any other party. It can facilitate collaboration between institutions that deal with sensitive data, such as health and financial data [2]. Regulations

H. Yu et al. (Eds.): FL 2024 Workshops, LNAI 15501, pp. 106–118, 2025.
https://doi.org/10.1007/978-3-031-82240-7_8

such as the General Data Protection Regulation (GDPR) and Health Insurance Portability and Accountability Act (HIPAA) control how sensitive data are stored and shared within and between institutions to protect the privacy of the individuals whose data is captured [27]. FL can aid collaborators in adhering to these regulations, as no data is shared between the clients during the training or inference process.

However, FL comes with its challenges, as studies have shown that the global model struggles to converge when the data distribution amongst the clients is statistically heterogeneous [13,25]. This implies that the data distribution is Non-Independent and Identically distributed (Non-IID). A client may hold data from some classes, but not all classes present in the global dataset or clients could hold data for all classes but in different quantity. This statistical heterogeneity of local data could result in each local model being very different from other local models, leading to a global model that performs at a subpar level [14]. Also, when clients train their local model on data that does not contain certain classes from the global set or only a few samples from specific classes, the models are likely to be biased towards those underrepresented groups [10]. This could have devastating consequences when these models are deployed in safety-critical situations such as healthcare and finance.

The presence of biases could also disincentivize clients from participating in FL collaboration as they would lose trust in the system. For instance, imagine a collaboration between pharmaceutical companies training a model to determine the effectiveness of several drugs on an ailment and having the drug from one company consistently being predicted as the most effective because they provide more data as a result of conducting more experiments than the others [20]. Data heterogeneity, as such, is a challenge that needs to be addressed to obtain trustworthy FL models.

Some existing work [25] have proposed a global data-sharing strategy to tackle the challenge of FL with Non-IID data. The server is posited to have a uniformly distributed dataset in its possession. This global data is then shared amongst the clients to harmonize their data distribution to alleviate the impact of data heterogeneity. Other approaches such as FedProx [13] introduce a regularization term to the local model loss function on the client side, this mitigates the effect of data heterogeneity and enhances the convergence of the global model. The work of [14] employs Generative Adversarial Networks (GANs) to produce synthetic data to solve the problem of Non-IID data in FL. The synthetic data is then augmented with the clients' local data to improve the stability of the FL training process. While these proposed methods have improved the performance of FL with data heterogeneity, they are constrained by certain limitations. The assumption that the server possesses a uniformly distributed global dataset in [25] is impractical in real-world FL scenarios. In contrast, the regularization technique employed by FedProx [13] is not effective in extreme cases of data heterogeneity. On the other hand, solutions such as [14] that utilize GANs may produce low-quality and non-diverse synthetic data, as GANs are known to suffer from instabilities such as mode collapse during training.

Considering the limitations above, we propose a novel data augmentation process, that is more effective than existing solutions in FL by using foundation models to generate differentially private synthetic data. To our knowledge, this is the first work that employs pre-trained foundation models to generate differentially private synthetic data to tackle the problem of Non-IID data in FL. Thus, our contributions are as follows:

- We propose Differentially Private Synthetic Data Aided Federated Learning Using Foundation Models (DPSDA-FL) – a new data augmentation strategy to enhance the performance of FL with Non-IID data – and show the effectiveness of utilizing differentially private synthetic data generated from foundation models in cross-silo horizontal FL.
- We conduct experiments and evaluations on the CIFAR-10 dataset and observe an increase in the recall of the global model by up to 26% and an accuracy enhancement of 9%, demonstrating the efficacy of our approach over the baselines. We also provide an analysis of our results to guide further research.

The remaining part of the paper is organised as follows. Section 2 discusses background and related work. Section 3 introduces our methodology and proposes a new data augmentation strategy. Section 4 presents our evaluation. Finally, Sect. 5 concludes this paper.

2   Background and Related Work

2.1   Data Heterogeneity

Data heterogeneity is the degree of diversity in the datasets held by clients participating in FL. Data heterogeneity in FL arises from the differences in data distribution, data quality, and data quantity among participants. It can manifest in various forms in FL. Quantity Skew results from the differences in the amount of data held by clients, while Label Skew results from the differences in the classes of data held by individual clients [18].

Several techniques have been proposed to address the challenge of data heterogeneity in FL. FedProx [13] addresses heterogeneity in FL by integrating a proximal term into the training process. The proximal term reduces the divergence of the local models from the global model by serving as a penalization term for the loss function of the local models. Karimireddy et al. [11] developed the stochastic controlled averaging algorithm, a modification of the federated averaging, which incorporates variance reduction to stabilize the local model towards the global model. However, these techniques are not effective in extreme cases of data heterogeneity. Another line of work uses GANs to mitigate the effects of data heterogeneity by generating additional training data for local data augmentation [21] of which our method aligns with. However, despite using a similar approach to the GAN-based data augmentation methods, we locally generate differentially private synthetic data using foundation models to mitigate the effects of data heterogeneity, our solution generates more diverse synthetic data that is of higher quality than the GAN-based approaches.

2.2 Generative Adversarial Networks

Generative adversarial networks (GANs) are deep learning models comprising of two networks: the generator and the discriminator. The generator produces synthetic data mimicking real data, challenging the discriminator to distinguish between them [9]. Synthetic data from GANs share the statistical distribution of real datasets and, as such, can be used for dataset augmentation, enhancing model performance [1].

Zhang et al. [24] trained a GAN at the server side using FL and then shared the synthetic data across clients to improve the performance of FL. Li et al. [14] proposed Synthetic Data Aided Federated Learning (SDA-FL), where all clients receive a portion of locally synthetically generated data globally shared by the server. Despite the effectiveness of GAN-based methods in combating data heterogeneity problems in FL and enhancing the performance of the global model, these works have limitations. The instability of training GANs can result in low-quality synthetic samples with low utility [3].

Recent works have addressed the underperformance of GANs in generating high-quality synthetic data by adopting diffusion models. Diffusion models are generative deep learning architectures that generate synthetic data by iteratively adding noise to real data and then removing this noise through a reverse diffusion process [23]. Diffusion models have been shown to produce high-quality data for computer vision applications [3,5]. Diffusion models, however, can be challenging to train due to their high computational requirements, which are often beyond the reach of many. However, the emergence of foundation models has made access to pre-trained diffusion models more accessible.

2.3 Foundation Models

Foundation models are a class of generative AI trained on large-scale data and can be modified to undertake various tasks with high precision [26]. Models like Open AI's Stable Diffusion and DALL.E [19] have become widely accessible. These pre-trained models can be used to generate high-utility synthetic data.

Differentially Private Synthetic Data: Synthetic data has been demonstrated to inadvertently reveal sensitive information about the original dataset generated from [8]. Consequently, integrating privacy-preserving techniques into the synthetic data generation process is imperative. Differential Privacy (DP) is a method that introduces randomness while computing statistics to maintain the privacy of the underlying information [6]. It has emerged as the standard approach for enhancing the privacy of synthetic data due to its ability to offer provable privacy guarantees. Consequently, diffusion models can be trained using DP to safeguard the privacy of the synthetic data they produce.

In [7], by finetuning pre-trained diffusion models with tens of millions of parameters, high utility data with low Fréchet inception distance were generated privately. The synthetic data was employed for a downstream classification task, and state-of-the-art results were attained. A more recent method, PRIV-IMAGE [12], generates differentially private synthetic images using foundation models by strategically selecting pre-training data. While this approach is effective, it incurs significant memory and time overheads. Another notable technique is Private Evolution (PE) [15], an algorithm that fine-tunes pre-trained diffusion models to generate synthetic data from private datasets while maintaining differential privacy. PE has demonstrated state-of-the-art results in image synthesis and requires no pre-training. In this study, we leverage PE to generate synthetic data for data augmentation.

3 DPSDA-FL: Differentially Private Synthetic Data Aided Federated Learning Using Foundation Models

This section proposes our novel technique, DPSDA-FL, that generates differentially private synthetic data for FL using foundation models. Figure 1 gives a high-level overview of our proposal. DPSDA-FL works in two main stages, Stage 1 in which each Cross-Silo FL client uses a foundation model to locally generate differentially private synthetic data from their private data and then share part of the synthetic data with the central server to form a global synthetic data which will be utilized in Stage 2. In the next stage, the server distributes the global synthetic data to clients to enable them to augment their local data with the diverse and high-quality synthetic data. This augmentation leads to a less heterogeneous local data distribution by allowing clients to possess synthetic data from classes they do not possess or classes they possess a very limited sample from. This subsequently leads to a more stable local model training that enhances the performance of the global model both in terms of its recall capability and its accuracy. A more detailed overview of how DPSDA-FL works is presented below:

1. **Unique label count information sharing:** At the start of the training process, clients share their unique label counts with the server to form a globally unique label count. This information will be used to share the synthetic global data with clients to ensure each client receives differentially private synthetic data from their deficient classes.
2. **Local clients' synthetic data generation using foundation models:** To generate our differentially private synthetic data, we utilize the image-guided diffusion model DPSDA [15], as our foundation model. DPSDA is based on improved diffusion [5]. To ensure the privacy of local training data, a local copy of the diffusion model is downloaded and hosted locally on the client's devices. It mitigates privacy risks associated with diffusion models memorizing their training data, as in [4]. The local synthetic data D_{csyn} are then shared with the server to construct the global synthetic data D_{Gsyn}.
3. **Global synthetic data distribution:** The server then shares the differentially private synthetic data from the previous step with the local clients. The local data class information possessed by the server guides effective distribution, so each client only receives data from classes it lacks.

4. **Local data augmentation:** Clients utilize the received synthetic data to augment their local data and homogenize the local data distribution. These synthetic data are of high quality and can enhance local model training.

5. **Federated training:** With more stable local training aided by the augmented local datasets at each client's side, clients proceed to train a federated global model jointly. Note that DPSDA [15] does not necessitate any pre-training to generate the synthetic data, and the clients are assumed to be health institutions that can afford reasonable computational resources.

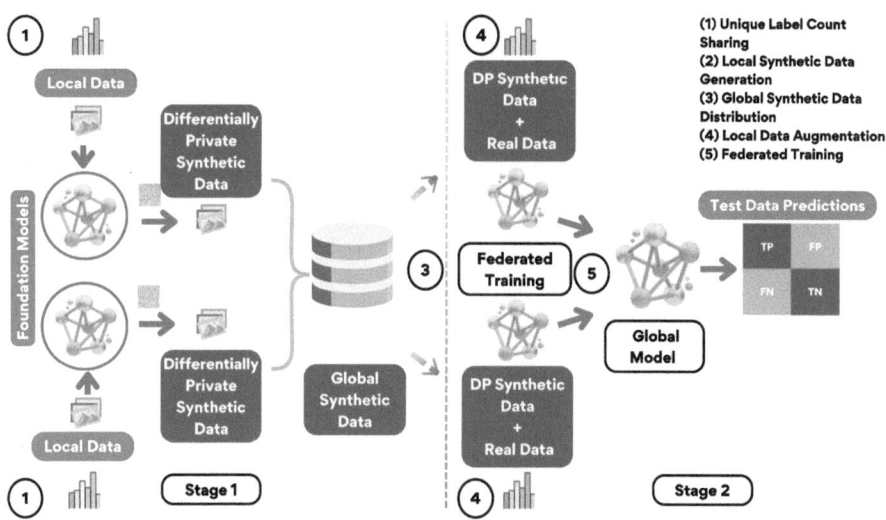

Fig. 1. DPSDA-FL: Differentially Private Synthetic Data Aided Federated Learning Using Foundation Models

Algorithm 1 outlines the pseudocode for DPSDA-FL. We consider a FL setting with a single semi-trusted central server S and N clients denoted by $\{C_1, C_2, ...C_N\}$. A horizontal FL setup is one where the data across the FL clients is partitioned horizontally, and clients share similar feature sets but different sample spaces. Each client possesses a local dataset D_c, which is a subset of the global dataset D_G. D_G follows a normal distribution and consists of k classes of data. However, D_c does not follow a normal distribution as the data distribution amongst the clients is Non-IID. Some clients may possess fewer samples than others, leading to quantity skew or some classes of data but not others resulting in label skew. As we are considering a cross-silo FL setup, all the clients participate in training rounds, and each local model L_n contributes to the global model aggregation. The objective 1 is to produce a single global model G that performs well on the global test data.

Algorithm 1 DPSDA-FL

1: **Input Parameters:**
2: N: Number of clients.
3: T: Total number of rounds.
4: α: Learning rate.
5: w_t: Initial model parameters.
6: w_{t+1}: Updated model parameters.

7: **Initialization**
8: Clients share their unique label counts with the server
9: Clients generate DP synthetic data using Foundation Models
10: **for** $i = 1$ to N **do**
11:     Generate D_{syn}^i from D_c^i
12:     Send D_{syn}^i to server
13: **end for**
14: Server forms global D_{Gsyn} from D_{syn}^i
15: Distribute D_{Gsyn} using unique label count
16: **for** $t = 1$ to T **do**
17:     Send w_t to all clients
18:     **for** $i = 1$ to N **do**
19:         Augment D_c^i with D_{Gsyn}
20:         Train model L_i to update w_{t+1}^i
21:         Server Initializes w_0
22:         Send w_{t+1}^i to server
23:     **end for**
24:     Aggregate $w_{t+1} = \frac{1}{N} \sum_{i=1}^{N} w_{t+1}^i$
25: **end for**
26: Repeat until convergence

$$\min_{w} \mathcal{L}_G(w), \quad \text{where} \quad \mathcal{L}_G(w) = \frac{1}{N} \sum_{n=1}^{N} \mathcal{L}_n(w) \tag{1}$$

Here $\mathcal{L}_G(w)$ is the global loss, $\mathcal{L}_n$ the loss function of each client and w the parameters of the model.

4   Evaluations

4.1   Experimental Settings

Below we describe the experimental settings used in our evaluation. These settings are also summarised in Table 1.

Dataset: We performed our experiments on the CIFAR-10 dataset, which is a benchmark dataset used for image recognition. It consists of 50,000 training samples and 10,000 testing samples. The dataset is mostly utilized to evaluate the classification accuracy of Convolutional Neural Networks (CNN). We used

Table 1. Experimental settings

Name	Value
FL architecture	Cross-Silo Horizontal FL
Dataset	CIFAR-10
NN architecture	CNN
Number of clients	5
Number of local epochs	2
Number of global rounds	20
Learning rate	0.1
Batch size	32
Optimizer	Stochastic gradient descent

the entire 10,000 images to test the accuracy of the global model for our approach and the baselines.

Differentially Private Synthetic Dataset: We deployed five pre-trained diffusion models to generate synthetic local data for each client. To limit privacy risks associated with the honest but curious server, we assumed each client only generated and shared at most 50% of its number of classes. We generated 5000 differentially private synthetic images for each class of the CIFAR-10 dataset and selected a subset to be used for augmentation. The generated images were 64×64; they were resized to 32×32 to match the size of the CIFAR-10 images.

Data Distribution: We evaluated the effectiveness of our approach by simulating real world FL participants with varying data distributions that follow a Non-IID fashion. The local data distribution of each client is not representative of the global dataset. To simulate extreme label skew for our experiments, we followed the work [13]; each client received samples from only two classes.

Neural Network Architecture: We used CNN for all our experiments. The CNN includes two convolutional layers, each followed by a ReLU activation and a max-pooling layer. It also includes two fully connected layers followed by a ReLU activation. The final output layer uses a log-softmax activation to produce class probabilities. We used stochastic gradient descent (SGD) and negative log-likelihood as our local model optimizer and loss function.

Cross-Silo Horizontal FL: In cross-silo horizontal FL (HFL), clients are usually smaller in number compared to cross-device horizontal FL, where there are many devices collaboratively training a model. Also, unlike cross-device HFL, where a fraction of clients are selected to participate in each round, in cross-silo HFL, all the clients usually participate in all communication rounds. Cross-silo setups are also traditionally made up of larger institutions with abundant computational resources serving as clients compared to cross-device, where there are typically resource-constrained smaller devices participating in the training process.

Evaluation Metrics: We used the top-1 accuracy of the global model to evaluate how effectively our data augmentation technique can enhance FL. We also measured and compared the recall of the global model produced by the baselines and our approach. Recall is an essential metric for machine learning models that are deployed in safety-critical sectors such as healthcare, where FL is a good candidate. This is because false positives in such domains entail significant consequences. We reported the mean and standard deviation of the global model accuracy from running each experiment three times. We also reported the mean of the recall.

Baselines: As baselines, we used the two well-established approaches for implementing federated learning systems.

- **Federated Averaging (FedAvg)**: To compare the effectiveness of our approach, we used federated averaging [16], which is the vanilla version of FL where clients share their local model parameters with the central server, which is then aggregated to form an updated global model.
- **Federated Optimization (FedProx)**: We implemented FedProx [13] with the same number of clients as in our work and used the value of 0.001 for mu, which is the proximal term that aids in combating the effect of data heterogeneity in FL with Non-IID Data.

4.2   Results and Discussion

Our experimental results are summarised in Tables 2 and 3, as well as in Fig. 2. We visualized our models' performances using confusion matrices as they provide a clear insight into the model's ability to make correct predictions for both positive and negative cases. The darker shades of colour in each matrix represent these correct predictions.

Table 2. Classification accuracy of the global model in FedAvg and FedProx compared with DPSDA-FL with 5 clients

Approach	Data Augmentation	Synthetic Data Shared (in %)	Number of Classes	Global Model Accuracy
FedAvg	No	0	2	28.30 ± 2.20%
FedProx	No	0	2	31.70 ± 2.26%
DPSDA-FL	Yes	50	2	37.20 ± 0.44%

Table 3. Recall of the global model in FedAvg and FedProx compared with DPSDA-FL with 5 clients

Approach	Recall of the Plane Class	Recall of the Cat Class	Recall of the Ship Class	Recall of the Truck Class
FedAvg	55.9%	15.6%	35.1%	46.5%
FedProx	40.6%	19.3%	53.2%	44.6%
DPSDA-FL	58.86%	42.4%	58.6%	56.46.0%

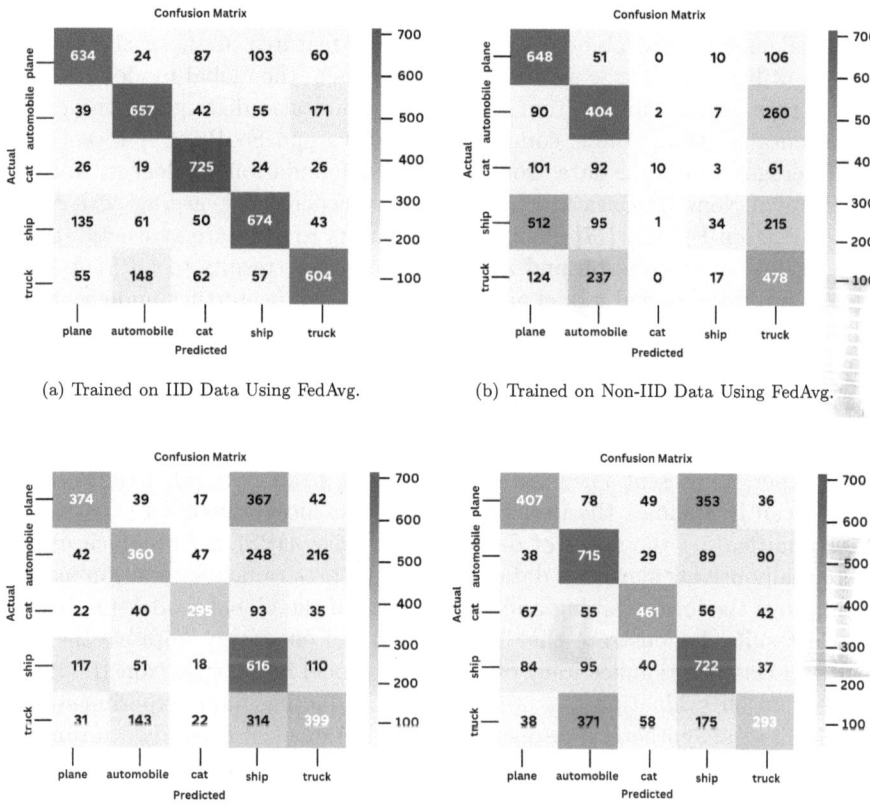

(a) Trained on IID Data Using FedAvg.   (b) Trained on Non-IID Data Using FedAvg.

(c) Trained on Non-IID Data Using FedProx.   (d) Trained on Non-IID Data Using DPSDA FL.

Fig. 2. Confusion matrices highlighting the correct predictions and misclassifications made by the various approaches

Our findings reveal a promising outcome. For the global FL model trained on IID Data using FedAvg, which represents the most ideal case, as depicted in Fig. 2a, the majority of classes were correctly identified, as evidenced by a darkened diagonal. In contrast, the global model trained on Non-IID using FedAvg, where each client possesses data from only 2 classes, struggles to correctly identify positive and negative cases, as shown in Fig. 2b. This struggle highlights the challenge faced by models in such scenarios. The global model trained using FedProx Fig. 2c shows a better performance than FedAvg, due to the proximal term added to the loss function of local clients to prevent significant divergence. However, DPSDA-FL demonstrated an even more accurate and enhanced global model, as shown in Table 2 and Fig. 2d. This can be attributed to the more stable local training for clients aided by the differentially private synthetic data.

The recall of the classes for which the differentially private synthetic data generated by the foundation models is shared with other clients tends to improve as well, as shown in Table 3. This suggests that the local models that make up the global model were able to effectively learn features of those classes from the high utility and diverse synthetic data. As such, the global model is able to identify more data samples from those classes and also distinguish the classes more accurately than others, compared to FedAvg and FedProx. A recent work that leverages synthetic data from pretrained foundation models to mitigate the effects of Non-IID Data in FL, "Generative Federated Learning with Stable Diffusion" (Gen-FedSD) [17] utilizes text prompts to generate synthetic images for local data augmentation and achieves comparable results to DPSDA-FL in terms of improved global model accuracy. These findings further underscore the viability and potential of synthetic data from pretained foundation models in enhancing the performance of FL with Non-IID Data.

5   Conclusion

In this paper, we present a new data augmentation strategy that has the potential to significantly enhance the performance of cross-silo horizontal FL with Non-IID. By mitigating the effect of data heterogeneity, DPSDA-FL, which utilizes differentially private synthetic data generated by pre-trained foundation models, can improve the local training and convergence of the global model. Our experimental results demonstrate that DPSDA-FL can effectively improve the class recall and classification accuracy of the global model in FL with Non-IID issues.

We plan on evaluating our approach by conducting more experiments and generating local synthetic data using a limited number of private data samples. We also leave experimenting with other datasets that do not overlap with the training datasets of the foundation models for future work.

Acknowledgements. This work was supported by The University of Manchester and EPSRC through the EnnCore project [EP/T026995/1].

References

1. Antoniou, A., Storkey, A., Edwards, H.: Data augmentation generative adversarial networks (2018). http://arxiv.org/abs/1711.04340 [cs, stat]
2. Aouedi, O., Sacco, A., Piamrat, K., Marchetto, G.: Handling privacy-sensitive medical data with federated learning: challenges and future directions. IEEE J. Biomed. Health Inform. 1–14 (2022). https://doi.org/10.1109/JBHI.2022.3185673. conference Name: IEEE Journal of Biomedical and Health Informatics

3. Azizi, S., Kornblith, S., Saharia, C., Norouzi, M., Fleet, D.J.: Synthetic data from diffusion models improves imagenet classification (2023). http://arxiv.org/abs/2304.08466 [cs]

4. Carlini, N., et al.: Extracting training data from diffusion models (2023). http://arxiv.org/abs/2301.13188 [cs]

5. Dhariwal, P., Nichol, A.: Diffusion models beat GANs on image synthesis. In: Advances in Neural Information Processing Systems, vol. 34, pp. 8780–8794. Curran Associates, Inc. (2021). https://proceedings.neurips.cc/paper_files/paper/2021/hash/49ad23d1ec9fa4bd8d77d02681df5cfa-Abstract.html

6. Dwork, C., Roth, A.: The algorithmic foundations of differential privacy. foundations and trends® in theoretical computer science **9**(3-4), 211–407 (2013). https://doi.org/10.1561/0400000042, http://www.nowpublishers.com/articles/foundations-and-trends-in-theoretical-computer-science/TCS-042

7. Ghalebikesabi, S., et al.: Differentially private diffusion models generate useful synthetic images (2023). http://arxiv.org/abs/2302.13861. [cs, stat]

8. Giomi, M., Boenisch, F., Wehmeyer, C., Tasnádi, B.: A unified framework for quantifying privacy risk in synthetic data (2022). http://arxiv.org/abs/2211.10459. [cs]

9. Goodfellow, I.J., et al.: Generative adversarial networks (2014). http://arxiv.org/abs/1406.2661 [cs, stat]

10. Hao, W., et al.: Towards fair federated learning with zero-shot data augmentation. In: 2021 IEEE/CVF Conference on Computer Vision and Pattern Recognition Workshops (CVPRW), pp. 3305–3314. IEEE, Nashville, TN, USA (2021). https://doi.org/10.1109/CVPRW53098.2021.00369, https://ieeexplore.ieee.org/document/9522726/

11. Karimireddy, S.P., Kale, S., Mohri, M., Reddi, S.J., Stich, S.U., Suresh, A.T.: SCAFFOLD: stochastic controlled averaging for federated learning (2021). http://arxiv.org/abs/1910.06378. [cs, math, stat]

12. Li, K., Gong, C., Li, Z., Zhao, Y., Hou, X., Wang, T.: PrivImage: differentially private synthetic image generation using diffusion models with semantic-aware pretraining (2024). http://arxiv.org/abs/2311.12850. [cs]

13. Li, T., Sahu, A.K., Zaheer, M., Sanjabi, M., Talwalkar, A., Smith, V.: Federated optimization in heterogeneous networks (2020). http://arxiv.org/abs/1812.06127 [cs, stat]

14. Li, Z., Shao, J., Mao, Y., Wang, J.H., Zhang, J.: Federated learning with GAN-based data synthesis for Non-IID clients (2022). http://arxiv.org/abs/2206.05507. [cs]

15. Lin, Z., Gopi, S., Kulkarni, J., Nori, H., Yekhanin, S.: Differentially private synthetic data via foundation model APIs 1: images (2024). http://arxiv.org/abs/2305.15560. [cs]

16. McMahan, H.B., Moore, E., Ramage, D., Hampson, S.: Communication-efficient learning of deep networks from decentralized data. In: Proceedings of the 20th International Conference on Artificial Intelligence and Statistics (AISTATS) (2017). http://proceedings.mlr.press/v54/mcmahan17a/mcmahan17a.pdf

17. Morafah, M., Reisser, M., Lin, B., Louizos, C.: Stable diffusion-based data augmentation for federated learning with Non-IID data (2024). http://arxiv.org/abs/2405.07925 [cs]

18. Qu, L., Balachandar, N., Rubin, D.L.: An experimental study of data heterogeneity in federated learning methods for medical imaging (2021). http://arxiv.org/abs/2107.08371. [cs]

19. Ramesh, A., Dhariwal, P., Nichol, A., Chu, C., Chen, M.: Hierarchical text-conditional image generation with CLIP latents (2022). http://arxiv.org/abs/2204.06125. [cs]

20. Rance, J., Svoboda, F.: Attacks of fairness in federated learning (2023). http://arxiv.org/abs/2311.12715. [cs]

21. Razavi-Far, R., Ruiz-Garcia, A., Palade, V., Schmidhuber, J.: Generative Adversarial Learning: Architectures and Applications, Intelligent Systems Reference Library, vol. 217. Springer, Cham (2022). https://doi.org/10.1007/978-3-030-91390-8

22. Shahid, O., Pouriyeh, S., Parizi, R.M., Sheng, Q.Z., Srivastava, G., Zhao, L.: Communication efficiency in federated learning: achievements and challenges (2021). http://arxiv.org/abs/2107.10996. [cs]

23. Yang, L., et al.: Diffusion models: a comprehensive survey of methods and applications. ACM Comput. Surv. **56**(4), 1–39 (2024)

24. Zhang, L., Shen, B., Barnawi, A., Xi, S., Kumar, N., Wu, Y.: FedDPGAN: federated differentially private generative adversarial networks framework for the detection of COVID-19 pneumonia (2021). http://arxiv.org/abs/2104.12581. [cs, eess]

25. Zhao, Y., Li, M., Lai, L., Suda, N., Civin, D., Chandra, V.: Federated learning with non-IID data (2018). https://doi.org/10.48550/arXiv.1806.00582. [cs, stat]

26. Zhou, C., et al.: A comprehensive survey on pretrained foundation models: a history from BERT to ChatGPT (2023). http://arxiv.org/abs/2302.09419. [cs]

27. Zhou, C., Fu, A., Yu, S., Yang, W., Wang, H., Zhang, Y.: Privacy-preserving federated learning in fog computing. IEEE Internet Things J. **7**(11), 10782–10793 (2020)

Leveraging Unstructured Text Data for Federated Instruction Tuning of Large Language Models

Rui Ye[1], Rui Ge[1], Fengting Yuchi[1], Jingyi Chai[1], Yanfeng Wang[1,2], and Siheng Chen[1,2(✉)]

[1] Shanghai Jiao Tong University, Shanghai, China
sihengc@sjtu.edu.cn
[2] Shanghai AI Lab, Shanghai, China

Abstract. Federated instruction tuning enables multiple clients to collaboratively fine-tune a shared large language model (LLM) that can follow humans' instructions without directly sharing raw data. However, existing literature impractically requires that all the clients readily hold instruction-tuning data (i.e., structured instruction-response pairs), which necessitates massive human annotations since clients' data is usually unstructured text instead. Addressing this, we propose a novel and flexible framework FedIT-U2S, which can automatically transform unstructured corpus into structured data for federated instruction tuning. FedIT-U2S consists two key steps: (1) few-shot instruction-tuning data generation, where each unstructured data piece together with several examples is combined to prompt an LLM in generating an instruction-response pair. To further enhance the flexibility, a retrieval-based example selection technique is proposed, where the examples are automatically selected based on the relatedness between the client's data piece and example pool, bypassing the need of determining examples in advance. (2) A typical federated instruction tuning process based on the generated data. Overall, FedIT-U2S can be applied to diverse scenarios as long as the client holds valuable text corpus, broadening the application scope of federated instruction tuning. We conduct a series of experiments on three domains (medicine, knowledge, and math), showing that our proposed FedIT-U2S can consistently and significantly brings improvement over the base LLM.

Keywords: Federated Learning · Large Language Models · Instruction Tuning

1 Introduction

Instruction tuning has become one of the most imperative components in training contemporary instruction-followed large language models (LLMs) [1–4], where typically, the training samples are collected from diverse sources by a central

---

R. Ye and R. Ge—Equal contribution.

H. Yu et al. (Eds.): FL 2024 Workshops, LNAI 15501, pp. 119–131, 2025.
https://doi.org/10.1007/978-3-031-82240-7_9

party [5–7]. However, these data could contain sensitive (e.g., private or proprietary) information that cannot be directly shared, making such centralized learning paradigm inapplicable especially for domains such as medicine [8] and finance [9].

Addressing this, federated learning [10,11] has emerged as a well-suited technique to achieve instruction tuning of LLMs without direct data sharing. In federated instruction tuning (FedIT), each party (i.e., client) keeps its private data locally and shares the instruction-tuned LLM with the central server, while the server aggregates LLMs from multiple parties and distributes the aggregated LLM back to participating parties. Such paradigm has attracted massive attention and interests from both academia [12–14] and industry [15–17].

Despite extensive efforts dedicated to FedIT, existing methods impractically rely on the assumption that each party possesses structured instruction-tuning data (i.e., instruction-response pairs), which significantly constrains the real-world applicability of FedIT. In practice, while clients may possess valuable data locally, this data often exists in an unstructured format (just strings of text) rather than naturally aligns with the structured format required for IT [18]. Consequently, current FedIT systems face challenges in scalability, as they necessitate manual annotation of data by each client.

To fill this gap, we propose a novel and flexible framework FedIT-U2S, which can automatically transform unstructured corpus into structured instruction-tuning data for FedIT, bypassing the massive human efforts required for data annotation. Specifically, FedIT-U2S consists of two key steps: few-shot instruction-tuning data generation and FedIT on the generated data. (1) The server first distributes an open-sourced general LLM and a few examples (could be as few as only one) to participating clients. During data generation, each client queries the LLM to generate multiple instruction pairs, where each pair is generated by feeding the LLM with a prompt that is composed of few examples as the context and a sampled piece of its unstructured data. To further enhance the generality and scalability of FedIT-U2S, we propose a retrieval-based example selection approach, where for each sampled piece of unstructured data, similarity scores are computed by comparing it with all the examples sent from the server, after which the top-k examples are selected as the few-shot examples in the context for data generation. (2) Subsequently, typical federated instruction tuning is launched based on the general LLM and the generated datasets in the previous step. Considering communication and computation efficiency, LoRA [19] is applied and therefore only a small set of parameters are learned and communicated. Overall, our FedIT-U2S framework makes FedIT system as practical as Google's GBoard application (next word prediction) [20], where the supervision data directly comes from user's data without any manual effort.

To verify the effectiveness of our proposed framework, we conduct a series of experiments covering three domains (i.e., medicine, knowledge, and math). We show that across these domains, our FedIT-U2S consistently improves the performance of the general LLM on the corresponding downstream task. Besides, we show the effectiveness of several designs, including retrieval-based example selection and filtering during data generation, providing potential directions for further improving the performance of FedIT-U2S.

Our contributions are as follows:

1. We propose the first end-to-end framework (FedIT-U2S) for directly leveraging unstructured data for federated instruction tuning of large language models.
2. We propose a retrieval-based example selection technique and a few-shot data generation mechanism, which automatically selects examples for higher relatedness and generates structured data in an expected manner.
3. We verify the effectiveness of FedIT-U2S through a series of experiments on multiple domains.

2   Related Work

Federated Learning of Large Language Models. Federated learning is a privacy-preserving machine learning paradigm that enables multiple clients to collaboratively train machine learning models without sharing their raw data [10, 11]. With the rise of large language models (LLMs), researchers have recently begun to consider federated training of LLMs to safeguard client data privacy or to address the scarcity of publicly available data [12,21], which has attracted massive attention and interests from both academia [12–14] and industry [15–17].

Specifically, OpenFedLLM [12] offers an integrated framework and provides a comprehensive empirical study to show the potential of federated instruction tuning of LLMs (FedIT). Similarly, FederatedScope-LLM [17] and FedML-LLM [15] provide frameworks that implement FedIT; while FedLLM-Bench [13] offers real-world datasets and benchmarks. Besides frameworks and benchmarks [22], a series of methods are proposed to target various perspectives including safety alignment [23], privacy [24], heterogeneous computation [25].

However, existing literature assumes that client data is structured in the form of instruction-response pairs, overlooking the reality that client data often exists in an unstructured format. In such cases, clients are required to annotate data before participating in FedIT, which is labor-intensive and limits its broader adoption. In this paper, we address this issue for the first time by proposing FedIT-U2S, a method that automates the transformation of unstructured client data into structured data prior to FedIT. This reduces the need for manual annotation and broadens the applicability of FedIT.

Data Generation in Large Language Models. The quality and quantity of data play a critical role in the training of large language models. However, manually generating and annotating data is labor-intensive and hard to scale up. Addressing this, the community turns to using LLMs to generate high-quality data [26–29]. For example, Self-Instruct [30] leverages 8 in-context examples to prompt LLMs for generating new instruction samples. WizardLM [26] instructs ChatGPT to generate diverse instructions via evolving prompt. MATRIX [31] instructs the LLMs to generate data for value alignment via social simulation. Genie [18] employs few-shot methods [32] to transform unstructured data

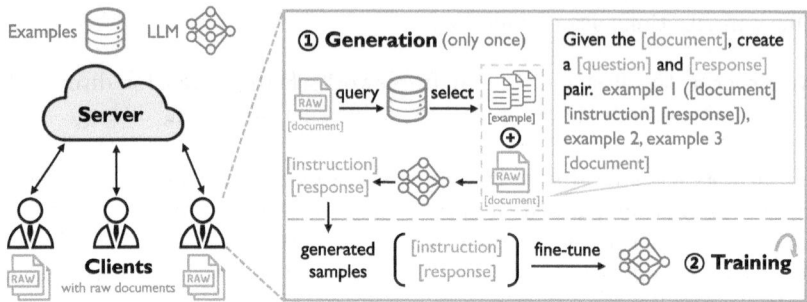

Fig. 1. Overview of our proposed FedIT-U2S. It consists of two key steps: data generation and FedIT. Data generation is required only once before FedIT. (1) For each raw unstructured data piece, clients select a few examples by retrieving from an example database to construct a few-shot template, prompting the LLM to generate an instruction-response pair. (2) Typical federated instruction tuning starts based on the generated structured instruction-tuning data.

into three kinds of structured data. Instruction Pre-training [27] generates instruction-tuning data to augment pre-training.

In this paper, we for the first time consider utilizing clients' unstructured data for FedIT of LLMs by leveraging the LLMs for data generation. We apply few-shot generation technique for its simplicity and effectiveness; while we believe that there could be other techniques applied to our scenario.

3   Methodology

In this section, we first introduce the overall framework of our proposed FedIT-U2S (Fig. 1), which consists of two key steps: few-shot instruction-tuning data generation (which transforms unstructured data into structured instruction-tuning data pairs) and federated instruction tuning on the generated data. Then, we detail our design of retrieval-based example selection for few-shot data generation.

3.1   Pipeline of FedIT-U2S

At the beginning of FedIT-U2S, the server first distributes an open-sourced general LLM (denoted by θ^*) and a set of examples (unstructured and structured text pairs, denoted by $\mathcal{O}$) to participating clients.

Step 1: Few-Shot Instruction-Tuning Data Generation. Suppose there are M clients in the system and each client m holds an unstructured dataset $\mathcal{D}_m^u = \{d_i\}_{i=1}^{N_m}$, where d_i is a data piece and N_m denotes the number of data pieces. Since such unstructured data cannot be directly used for instruction tuning, it conventionally requires each client's efforts to manually create instruction-response pairs for tuning, which is costly and faces the challenges of scaling up.

To address this, we design to automatically transform the unstructured data into a structured instruction-response format via a few-shot data generation process, which leverages LLM's in-context learning capability [32].

Specifically, upon receiving example set $\mathcal{O} = \{(d_i, x_i, y_i)\}_{i=1}^{O}$, where O is the example number, d_i is an unstructured data document, x_i and y_i is the document-grounded instruction and response respectively, each client selects several (denoted by k) examples as few-shot examples prompt the LLM θ^*. Denote the instruction for generation as I and the selected examples as $\mathcal{S} = \{(\hat{d}_i, \hat{x}_i, \hat{y}_i)\}_{i=1}^{k}$, given a user's data piece d, the prompt P is constructed as: $P = Concat(I, \mathcal{S}, d)$, where $Concat$ denotes the concatenation operation (see full prompt in Appendix A). Note that these examples can be either randomly selected for diversity or selected according to relatedness between user data and examples for better diversity-relatedness trade-off, which will be detailed in Sect. 3.2. Based on the prompt, the LLM θ^* will generate an instruction-response pair: $(x, y) = f(P; \theta^*)$. Therefore, by iterating on client's unstructured dataset $\mathcal{D}_m^u = \{d_i\}_{i=1}^{N_m}$, we obtain a structured dataset for instruction tuning: $\mathcal{D}_m^s = \{x_i, y_i\}_{i=1}^{N_m}$.

Since the responses of LLMs are in an open-ended form and there are randomness during generation, some generated data might fall short in terms of data quality. Therefore, additional data filtering is necessary for enhancing the data quality. Here, we consider two filtering mechanisms: rule-based filtering to remove data with undesired format and reward-based filtering to ensure the quality of selected data. Specifically, we first filter out data that does not follow the format of instruction-response pair. Secondly, we use an publicly available reward model to score the generated data samples and select the top two-thirds samples. This enables us to select data that is more aligned with human preference since reward model is trained to model human preference.

Step 2: Federated Instruction Tuning on the Generated Data. With the generated data, a typical process of federated instruction tuning is started. Considering computation and communication efficiency, we apply LoRA [19] as the parameter-efficient fine-tuning technique. Suppose there are T rounds of federated learning rounds in total. At each round t, the server sends the model parameters θ^t to each available client. Then, each client m initializes its local trainable parameters with θ^t, keeps the base model parameters θ^* fixed, and starts supervised fine-tuning on its generated dataset $\mathcal{D}_m^s = \{x_i, y_i\}_{i=1}^{N_m}$, where the model learns to predict the response y_i given the instruction x_i. By fine-tuning for several steps, each client m obtains a fine-tuned model parameters θ_m^t and sends it to the server. Finally, the server aggregates model parameters of clients to obtain the global model parameters for the next round: $\theta^{t+1} = \sum_m p_m \theta_m^t$, where $p_m = \frac{N_m}{\sum_i N_i}$ is the relative dataset size of client m.

3.2 Retrieval-Based Example Selection for Few-Shot Generation

The chosen examples (i.e., the context) in the prompt could significantly affect the behaviour of LLMs [33,34], resulting in different quality of the generated data. Therefore, to generate high-quality structured data, selecting appropriate few-shot examples is essential. Generally, examples that closely match the target text in terms of content and structure tend to produce more effective results. However, in practical applications, manually identifying suitable examples can be a time-consuming process, making it inflexible in adapting to diverse scenarios. To mitigate this challenge, we propose a retrieval-based example selection method for few-shot generation which automatically selects few-shot examples from a mixed example pool according to similarity between user data and examples.

Given the set of examples sent from the server $\mathcal{O} = \{(d_i, x_i, y_i)\}_{i=1}^{O}$, each client aims to select k examples for each of its sampled unstructured data piece. Specifically, for each data piece d, we compute the similarity $Sim(d, d_i)$ for each d_i in the example pool $\mathcal{O}$ using BERT Score as the metric, which gives a similarity score that reflects the relatedness between the target data piece and the example's content. Subsequently, we rank the similarity scores and select top-k examples $\mathcal{S} = \{(\hat{d}_i, \hat{x}_i, \hat{y}_i)\}_{i=1}^{k}$, which are mostly likely to guide the LLM to generate high-quality and highly-related data. The other procedures remain unchanged as in Sect. 3.1.

4   Experiments

4.1   Experimental Details

Training Dataset. We consider three datasets for our experiments [27], which cover domains including medicine, knowledge, and math. Specifically, Pub-MedQA [35] is a medical dataset for biomedical research question answering with corresponding abstracts as the context. HotpotQA [36] is a dataset of Wikipedia-based questions with supporting facts as the context. AQUA_RAT [37] is a math dataset for algebraic word problems answering. The problems, together with solutions, form the context. We select 10,000 samples from each dataset for the experiments [27], with each sample comprising a piece of original unstructured text, along with a human annotated instruction and response, both derived from the text. Only the unstructured text is used in our method FedIT-U2S, while the human annotated instruction-response pairs are used to implement FedAvg as a reference to verify the effectiveness of our method.

Implementation Details. Our implementation is based on the open-sourced codebase OpenFedLLM[1] [12]. We use Vicuna-7B [38] as the base model and set the learning rate as $2e^{-5}$ with a batch size of 16. The communication round is set to 200 and 2 clients are sampled out of 5 each round to participate federated instruction tuning. We use *reward-model-deberta-v3-large-v2* as the reward model following [18]. We select $k = 3$ examples for few-shot generation.

Evaluation Metrics. (1) BERT Score: BERT Score [39] is an evaluation metric for natural language generation that measures the similarity between a

---

[1] https://github.com/rui-ye/OpenFedLLM.

candidate sentence and reference sentences by leveraging contextual embeddings from pre-trained language models like BERT. **(2) ROUGE-L:** ROUGE-L [40] is an evaluation metric used for summarization and text generation tasks, focusing on the longest common subsequence (LCS) between a candidate sentence and a reference sentence. ROUGE-L evaluates the extent to which the candidate sentence preserves the order and content of the reference, providing a more holistic assessment of the generated text's quality. We select 50 samples from each dataset to serve as the test set. We compare the model-generated responses to the gold standard answers (i.e., human-annotated answers in the test set) by calculating BERT Score and ROUGE-L to assess performance.

Table 1. Experiments on three datasets: PubMedQA (medical), HotpotQA (knowledge), and AQUA_RAT (math). BERT stands for BERT Score. Our proposed FedIT-U2S consistently brings performance improvement compared to base model. FedIT-U2S (Filtered) hugely fills the gap between base model and FedAvg on human-annotated data, indicating the effectiveness of our proposed method in bypassing massive human efforts in annotation.

	PubMedQA		HotpotQA		AQUA_RAT	
	BERT	ROUGE-L	BERT	ROUGE-L	BERT	ROUGE-L
Base Model	0.1483	0.1496	0.0566	0.2380	-0.0171	0.1529
FedIT-U2S	0.1876	0.1727	0.1774	0.2942	0.0885	0.2383
FedIT-U2S (Filtered)	0.2043	0.1859	0.2439	0.3226	0.1131	0.2452
FedAvg on Human Data	0.2306	0.2017	0.2701	0.3531	0.1381	0.2890

Compared LLMs. (1) The base LLM, i.e., the Vicuna model without additional tuning; (2) the base LLM tuned via FedAvg on human-annotated data, which serves as a performance reference; (3) the base LLM tuned by our FedIT-U2S without filtering technique; and (4) the base LLM tuned by our FedIT-U2S with filtering technique.

4.2   Experimental Results

Comparisons with Baselines. In Table 1, we compare models trained via our methods on generated data with base model and model trained via FedAvg [10] on human-annotated data (as a reference). Experiments are conducted on three datasets and evaluated by two metrics. From the table, we see that (1) our methods consistently and significantly improves the performance of the base model across datasets and evaluation metrics, indicating the effectiveness of our proposed methods. Specifically, in HotpotQA, our method can achieve 0.1873 higher BERT Score (0.2439 v.s. 0.0566). (2) Our methods hugely fill the gap between base model and that tuned via FedAvg on human data, further verifying FedIT-U2S's effectiveness. However, there is still a room for improvement, calling for more future works to further enhance the performance. With the increasing generation capability of LLMs [28,29], we even believe that there is potential for surpassing this baseline (FedAvg on human data). (3) Although the data filtered using the reward model is smaller in quantity, it brings a more significant improvement to the model's performance, indicating the importance of data quality in this scenario.

Analysis of Example Selection for Few-Shot Generation. The effectiveness of few-shot generation may heavily rely on the chosen examples in the context. Therefore, here, we deeply analyze the example selection by conducting a series of experiments on HotpotQA dataset since we observe a large improvement in previous experiments. In this experiment, the example pool has 50 samples in total, covering five domains: medicine, math, knowledge, common sense, and daily life. We consider the following setups of few-shot generation in our proposed FedIT-U2S: ① Random 0 + 3: 3 out-domain examples are randomly selected (e.g., for medical task, examples from other domains are randomly selected); ② Random 1 + 2: 1 in-domain and two out-domain examples are randomly selected; ③ Fixed 3 + 0: 3 fixed in-domain examples are selected for all generation; ④ Random 3 + 0: 3 in-domain examples are randomly selected; ⑤ Retrieval-based Selection: 3 examples are automatically selected from a mixed example pool by our retrieval-based example selection technique.

Table 2. Experiments on HotpotQA dataset for analysis of example selection during few-shot data generation. The results show that our proposed automated retrieval-based selection technique can achieves comparable performance compared to selecting in-domain examples (which requires prior knowledge).

Experimental Setup	Bert Score	ROUGE-L
Base Model	0.0566	0.2380
① Random 0 + 3 (3 out-domain examples)	0.0868	0.2211
② Random 1 + 2 (1 in-domain and 2 out-domain examples)	0.1143	0.2426
③ Fixed 3 + 0 (3 fixed in-domain examples)	0.1774	0.2942
④ Random 3 + 0 (3 randomly selected in-domain examples)	0.2128	0.3054
⑤ **Retrieval-based Selection from A Mixed Pool**	0.2035	0.2994

The experimental results are shown in Table 2. (1) Compared to the base model, ①, which introduces out-domain examples for few-shot generation, does not bring evident improvement while ②-⑤ all bring consistent improvement. This indicates the importance of selecting appropriate examples for few-shot data generation. (2) Comparing ①, ②, and ④, we can see that increasing the number of in-domain examples consistently brings more performance improvement, indicating the value of introducing in-domain examples to facilitate generation. (3) Comparing ③ and ④, we see that randomly selecting in-domain examples performs better than selecting fixed examples, indicating the value of example diversity in generation. (4) Comparing ④ and ⑤, we see that our proposed retrieval-based selection from a mixed pool performs comparably to selecting examples from a in-domain pool (which requires prior knowledge), indicating the effectiveness of our retrieval-based selection technique. This result suggests that equipped with this technique, our proposed FedIT-U2S framework can be automatically deployed in various domains without much prior knowledge.

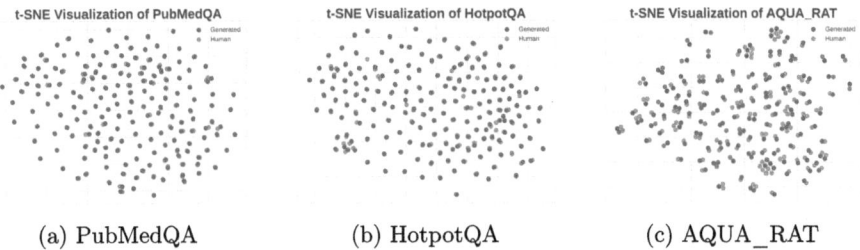

| (a) PubMedQA | (b) HotpotQA | (c) AQUA_RAT |

Fig. 2. The t-SNE visualization of embeddings of instruction-response pairs in Pub-MedQA, HotpotQA and AQUA_RAT. Blue dots represent generated data, while red dots represent human-annotated data. The close proximity of each pair of red and blue dots indicates that the generated data closely aligns with the human-annotated data. (Color figure online)

Comparisons of Generated and Human-Annotated Data. To better understand our method, we further analyze the characteristics of our generated data by comparing it with human-annotated data from two perspectives: embedding visualization and case studies.

(1) Embedding visualization: Here, we use t-SNE [41] to visualize the data points of generated and human-annotated data. For each dataset, 200 generated and human-annotated sample pairs, sharing the same context, are selected. The embeddings of the concatenated instruction and response texts are extracted via *sentence-transformers*[2] and mapped to a two-dimensional space via t-SNE. The final 2D embeddings are plotted as shown in Fig. 2, where blue and red dots represent generated and human-annotated data respectively. From the figure, we observe close proximity between the generated and human data points, indicating a high degree of alignment between the generated and human data across the datasets.

(2) Case Study: In Fig. 3, we show a specific example of generated data sample from PubMedQA. The human-annotated data sample with the same context is also given for comparison. Instructions of both samples ask about the effectiveness of HA injections in treating knee OA. The generated response conveys a meaning similar to human-annotated response based on the context.

These two aspects of comparison demonstrate that our generated data is highly similar to the manually annotated data in both content and structure, reflecting the high quality of the generated data.

---

[2] https://huggingface.co/sentence-transformers/all-MiniLM-L6-v2.

Context

Methods: Fourty-eight patients with knee OA were included in this study. The patients were randomized into two groups: one group received HA injections (average molecular weight [MW] 1.5 million Da), and the other group received placebo containing 0.9% saline. Three injections of HA or placebo were given at weeks 1, 2 and 3. The evaluation instruments were: Visual Analog Scale (VAS); Likert Scale; Lequesne<ndex; the Western Ontario and McMaster Universities (WOMAC) Index for Osteoarthritis pain, stiffness, and function, and WOMAC pain subgroups (pain on walking, climbing stairs, at night, on sitting and lying down, on standing); the number of analgesics taken; changes in knee flexion angle; and patient satisfaction. Assessment was performed at weeks 1, 3, 5, and 14 after the first injection.

Results: Significant improvement for almost all parameters was noted in both groups (P<0.05). There was no statistically significant difference between change in outcome after HA or placebo treatment (P>0.05), except for WOMAC pain subscore on walking at final assessment (week 14) which showed greater improvement in the HA-treated group (35.2% versus 9.1%; P=0.01).

Human-labeled Instruction & Response

Instruction: Is hyaluronate sodium effective in the management of knee osteoarthritis?

Response: HA treatment was effective in the management of knee OA and improved knee pain and functional outcome, but there was no statistically significant difference in functional and symptom improvement with respect to saline (placebo) injection.

Generated Instruction & Response

Instruction: Is HA injection effective for knee OA?

Response: The results suggest that HA may be an effective treatment for knee OA, with no significant difference between HA and placebo treatments.

Fig. 3. Example illustration.

5   Conclusions

This paper proposes FedIT-U2S, which directly leverages clients' unstructured text data to achieve federated instruction tuning of large language models. FedIT-U2S consists of two key steps: few-shot instruction-tuning data generation and federated instruction tuning on the generated data. During data generation, for each unstructured data piece, a client firstly selects related examples via a retrieval-based example selection mechanism and then uses these examples for guiding the LLM to generate instruction-response pair based on the data piece. A typical process of federated instruction tuning is then conducted based on the generated data. Experiments on three domains (medicine, knowledge, and math) verify the effectiveness of our proposed FedIT-U2S. Our method for the first time enables clients with unstructured data to be involved in the process of federated instruction tuning, which occupy a large proportion in practice and are underutilized previously. We believe that this work can contribute to broadening the application scope of federated instruction tuning.

A   Appendix

Listing 1.1. Few-shot prompt template

```
Given the next [document], create a [question] and [answer]
pair that are grounded in the main point of the document,
don't add any additional information that is not in the
document. The [question] is by an information-seeking user
and the [answer] is provided by a helping AI Agent.

[document]: {The content of document 1}
```

```
### Response:
[question]: {The content of question 1}
[answer]: {The content of answer 1}

[document]: {The content of document 2}

### Response:
[question]: {The content of question 2}
[answer]: {The content of answer 2}

[document]: {The content document 3}

### Response:
[question]: {The content of question 3}
[answer]: {The content of answer 3}

[document]: {The content of the target text}

### Response:
```

References

1. OpenAI. GPT-4 technical report. arXiv preprint arXiv:2303.08774 (2023)
2. Touvron, H., et al.: Llama 2: open foundation and fine-tuned chat models. arXiv preprint arXiv:2307.09288 (2023)
3. Jiang, A.Q., et al.: Mistral 7B. arXiv preprint arXiv:2310.06825 (2023)
4. Yang, A., et al.: Qwen2 technical report. arXiv preprint arXiv:2407.10671 (2024)
5. Ouyang, L., et al.: Training language models to follow instructions with human feedback. NIPS **35**, 27730–27744 (2022)
6. Wei, J., et al.: Finetuned language models are zero-shot learners. In: ICLR (2021)
7. Zhou, C., et al.: Lima: less is more for alignment. arXiv preprint arXiv:2305.11206 (2023)
8. Singhal, K., et al.: Towards expert-level medical question answering with large language models. arXiv preprint arXiv:2305.09617 (2023)
9. Wu, S., et al.: Bloomberggpt: a large language model for finance. arXiv preprint arXiv:2303.17564 (2023)
10. McMahan, B., Moore, E., Ramage, D., Hampson, S., y Arcas, B.A.: Communication-efficient learning of deep networks from decentralized data. In: Artificial Intelligence and Statistics, pp. 1273–1282. PMLR (2017)
11. Kairouz, P., et al.: Advances and open problems in federated learning. Found. Trends® Mach. Learn. **14**(1–2), 1–210 (2021)
12. Ye, R., et al.: Openfedllm: training large language models on decentralized private data via federated learning. In: Proceedings of the 30th ACM SIGKDD Conference on Knowledge Discovery and Data Mining, pp. 6137–6147 (2024)
13. Ye, R., et al.: Fedllm-bench: realistic benchmarks for federated learning of large language models. arXiv preprint arXiv:2406.04845 (2024)
14. Zhang, J., et al.: Towards building the federated GPT: federated instruction tuning. arXiv preprint arXiv:2305.05644 (2023)

15. FedML Inc. Federated learning on large language models (LLMS) (2023). https://doc.fedml.ai/federate/fedllm. Accessed 31 Mar 2024
16. Fan, T., et al.: Fate-LLM: a industrial grade federated learning framework for large language models. arXiv preprint arXiv:2310.10049 (2023)
17. Kuang, W., et al.: Federatedscope-LLM: a comprehensive package for fine-tuning large language models in federated learning. arXiv preprint arXiv:2309.00363 (2023)
18. Yehudai, A., et al.: Genie: achieving human parity in content-grounded datasets generation (2024)
19. Hu, E.J., et al.: Lora: low-rank adaptation of large language models. In: ICLR (2021)
20. Hard, A., et al.: Federated learning for mobile keyboard prediction. arXiv preprint arXiv:1811.03604 (2018)
21. Villalobos, P., Sevilla, J., Heim, L., Besiroglu, T., Hobbhahn, M., Ho, A.: Will we run out of data? An analysis of the limits of scaling datasets in machine learning. arXiv preprint arXiv:2211.04325 (2022)
22. Collins, L., Wu, S., Oh, S., Sim, K.C.: Profit: benchmarking personalization and robustness trade-off in federated prompt tuning. In: International Workshop on Federated Learning in the Age of Foundation Models in Conjunction with NeurIPS 2023 (2023)
23. Ye, R., Chai, J., Liu, X., Yang, Y., Wang, Y., Chen, S.: Emerging safety attack and defense in federated instruction tuning of large language models. arXiv preprint arXiv:2406.10630 (2024)
24. Sun, Y., Li, Z., Li, Y., Ding, B.: Improving loRA in privacy-preserving federated learning. In: The Twelfth International Conference on Learning Representations (2024)
25. Cho, Y.J., Liu, L., Xu, Z., Fahrezi, A., Joshi, G.: Heterogeneous lora for federated fine-tuning of on-device foundation models. In: International Workshop on Federated Learning in the Age of Foundation Models in Conjunction with NeurIPS 2023 (2023)
26. Xu, C., et al:. Wizardlm: empowering large language models to follow complex instructions. arXiv preprint arXiv:2304.12244 (2023)
27. Cheng, D., Yuxian, G., Huang, S., Bi, J., Huang, M., Wei, F.: Instruction pre-training: language models are supervised multitask learners (2024)
28. Adler, B., et al.: Nemotron-4 340b technical report. arXiv preprint arXiv:2406.11704 (2024)
29. Dubey, A., et al.: The llama 3 herd of models. arXiv preprint arXiv:2407.21783 (2024)
30. Wang, Y., et al:. Self-instruct: aligning language model with self generated instructions. arXiv preprint arXiv:2212.10560 (2022)
31. Pang, X., et al.: Self-alignment of large language models via monopolylogue-based social scene simulation. In: Forty-First International Conference on Machine Learning (2024)
32. Brown, T.B., et al.: Language models are few-shot learners (2020)
33. Brown, T.B., et al.: Language models are few-shot learners. In: Proceedings of the 34th International Conference on Neural Information Processing Systems, pp. 1877–1901 (2020)
34. Dong, Q., et al.: A survey for in-context learning. arXiv preprint arXiv:2301.00234 (2022)
35. Jin, Q., Dhingra, B., Liu, Z., Cohen, W.W., Lu, X.: Pubmedqa: a dataset for biomedical research question answering (2019)

36. Yang, Z., et al.: Hotpotqa: a dataset for diverse, explainable multi-hop question answering (2018)
37. Ling, W., Yogatama, D., Dyer, C., Blunsom, P.: Program induction by rationale generation: learning to solve and explain algebraic word problems (2017)
38. Chiang, W.-L., et al.: Vicuna: an open-source chatbot impressing GPT-4 with 90%* chatgpt quality (2023). https://vicunalmsys.org. Accessed 14 Apr 2023
39. Zhang, T., Kishore, V., Felix, W., Weinberger, K.Q., Artzi, Y.: Bertscore: evaluating text generation with bert (2020)
40. Lin, C.-Y.: ROUGE: a package for automatic evaluation of summaries. In: Text Summarization Branches Out, Barcelona, Spain, pp. 74–81. Association for Computational Linguistics (2004)
41. Van der Maaten, L., Hinton, G.: Visualizing data using t-SNE. J. Mach. Learn. Res. **9**(11) (2008)

FEDLEGAL: A Real-World Federated Learning Benchmark for Legal Natural Language Processing

Zhuo Zhang[1,2(✉)], Xiangjing Hu[1], Jingyuan Zhang[5], Yating Zhang[5], Hui Wang[2], Lizhen Qu[4], and Zenglin Xu[2,3]

[1] Harbin Institute of Technology, Shenzhen, China
iezhuo17@gmail.com
[2] Peng Cheng Lab, Shenzhen, China
wangh06@pcl.ac.cn
[3] Fudan University, Shanghai, China
xuzenglin@fudan.edu.cn
[4] Monash University, Melbourne, Australia
Qu@monash.edu.cn
[5] Hangzhou, China

Abstract. The sensitive nature of legal data demands that legal AI focuses on privacy-preserving and decentralized learning approaches. Federated Learning (FL) has emerged as a promising method for enabling multiple participants to collaboratively train a shared model while safeguarding their sensitive information. Despite its potential, no prior work has explored the use of FL in legal NLP. To address this gap, we introduce FEDLEGAL, the new real-world FL benchmark for legal NLP, encompassing five legal NLP tasks and one privacy task derived from Chinese court data. Our comprehensive experiments highlight the unique challenges posed by real-world non-IID data in FL. This benchmark aims to drive further research on privacy protection in FL using real-world datasets, and model deployment in resource-limited environments. The code and datasets of FEDLEGAL are available here.

Keywords: Federated Learning · Legal NLP · Data Resource

1 Introduction

The exponential growth of legal data has far exceeded the capacity of human legal practitioners to effectively learn, understand, and utilize it [13]. With most of this data being text-based, this "information overload" has driven the need for advanced legal Natural Language Processing (NLP) techniques, which aim to deliver accessible legal services to both professionals and the general public [34]. Many of these techniques rely on machine learning, which typically requires centralized datasets for training. However, this approach raises significant privacy

J. Zhang and Y. Zhang—Independent Researcher.

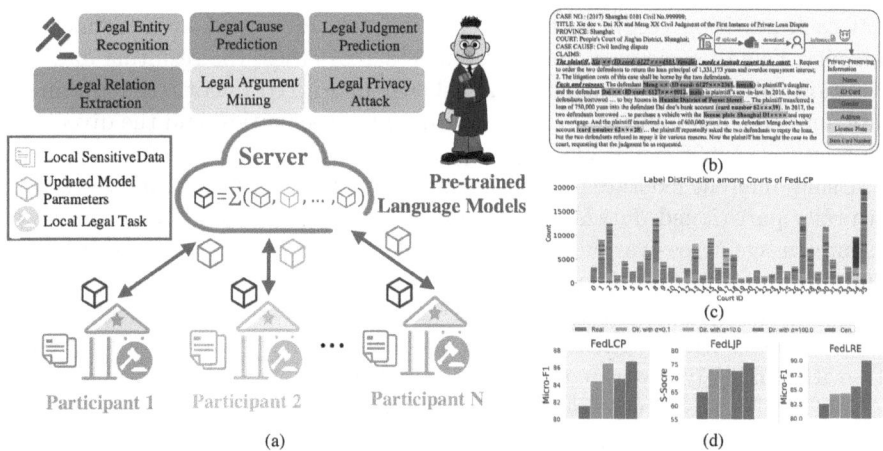

Fig. 1. The overview of FEDLEGAL (a) and Characteristics of FEDLEGAL: (b) demonstrating the rich sensitive information in a legal document; (c) depicting the data size (unbalanced) and label distributions (non-IID) among real-world courts; (d) showing heuristic sampling methods may bury the realistic difficulty of non-IID in real-world applications.

concerns and increases the risk of violating data protection laws such as the General Data Protection Regulation (GDPR).

To mitigate these issues, federated learning (FL) has emerged as a promising solution, offering a balance between data utility and privacy by training models without sharing sensitive data [29]. As illustrated in Fig. 1(a), FL allows participants' local machines to collaborate with one or more servers to train a model in a decentralized manner while ensuring data privacy. However, despite its potential, FL still faces unresolved challenges related to data heterogeneity [12], privacy vulnerabilities [14], and system inefficiencies [25].

In particular, differences between local data distributions of participants impose a special challenge when they are not Independently and Identically Distributed (non-IID) [39]. Although non-IID data is common in practice, most studies rely on artificially created non-IID datasets using heuristic sampling methods [17,30], due to the scarcity of real-world non-IID datasets. However, these artificially partitioned datasets tend to be less challenging for FL algorithms than naturally occurring non-IID data. As demonstrated in Fig. 1(d), FL algorithms applied to heuristically sampled datasets achieve substantially higher F1 scores than when applied to natural non-IID data.

To advance FL research in the legal domain, we introduce the new FL benchmark for legal NLP, named FEDLEGAL. This benchmark includes five key legal NLP tasks based on real-world legal texts from Chinese courts: Legal Cause Prediction (FEDLCP), Legal Argumentation Mining (FEDLAM), Legal Entity Recognition (FEDLER), Legal Relation Extraction (FEDLRE), and Legal Judgment Prediction (FEDLJP). Additionally, we introduce a privacy attack task, FEDLPA, to assess the risk of privacy leakage. To maintain the natural distribution of the data, we partition the datasets by cities or case categories, ensuring that each partition contains data from a different city court or a distinct case category. Due to socio-economic differences across cities, the resulting data distributions are distinctly non-IID. As shown in Fig. 1(c), both the volume of data and label distributions vary significantly between cities, and the divergence between case categories is even more pronounced.

Using different federated algorithms, we conduct the first empirical study on naturally partitioned datasets to assess model performance, privacy risks, and resource usage across various legal NLP tasks. To prevent privacy leakage while retaining the key features of sensitive data (as shown in Fig. 1(b)), we replace personally identifiable information (PII) and sensitive attributes, such as names and addresses, with synthetic data in the same format (e.g., substituting real IDs with randomly generated fake IDs). Furthermore, we provide a fully modular and easily extensible codebase to advance FL research in the legal domain. Our extensive experiments on legal NLP tasks reveal several important findings previously unreported in FL studies: (1) On the natural non-IID data of most of the legal NLP tasks, there is still a large performance gap between FL algorithms and supervised algorithms on centralized data. (2) For FL algorithms, it is more challenging to achieve high performance on the *natural* non-IID local distributions of almost all legal NLP tasks than that on the distributions sampled by heuristic sampling algorithms. Heuristically split data exhibit different research problems than naturally partitioned data. (3) The natural non-IID data partitions pose more challenges to small and shallow language model models [26] than their large and deep counterparts.

2   Preliminaries

This section starts with reviewing the concepts, problem formulations, and challenges of federated learning, followed by providing an overview of the lifecycle of the lawsuit in the Chinese court system.

2.1   Federated Learning

FL is a distributed learning technology that collaboratively learns a shared global model from multiple isolated participants (or silos), while preserving privacy [22, 23,29]. In a typical FL cross-silo setup, there is a server that coordinates the FL process and aggregates model information (e.g., model gradients) collected from scattered participants.

FedAvg [29] is the first and one of the most widely used FL algorithms, whose details are outlined in Algorithm 1. At the beginning of each communication round, the server sends model parameters W to each participating silo. Then, the silo trains on local private data $\mathcal{D}_k$ (*SiloLocalTraining*) and subsequently uploads the updated model parameters. The server monitors and collects the updated model parameters from the silo. After collecting the model parameters from all the silos, the server aggregates all model updates according to Eq. (1). The above process is repeated until the global model converges.

Algorithm 1: Training process of FedAvg

Parameters: Silo set $\mathcal{S}$; Communication round $\mathcal{T}$; Local epoch number $\mathcal{E}$; The shared global model parameters $\mathcal{W}^0$ on server; The local learning rate η; The local dataset $\mathcal{D}_k$ of the k-th silo ;

ServerGlobalUpdating:
for each communication round $t = 1$ to $\mathcal{T}$ **do**

> **for** each silo $k \in |\mathcal{S}|$ **in parallel do**
> > | SiloLocalTraining$(k, \mathcal{W}^{t-1})$
> **end**
>
> **Receive** participant-uploaded parameters $\mathcal{W}_k^t$
> Perform global aggregation by:
>
> $$\mathcal{W}^t = \sum_{k=1}^{|\mathcal{S}|} \frac{|\mathcal{D}_k|}{\sum_{k=1}^{|\mathcal{S}|} |\mathcal{D}_k|} \mathcal{W}_k^t \quad (1)$$

end

SiloLocalTraining $(k, \mathcal{W}^t)$:

> **for** epoch $e = 1$ to $\mathcal{E}$ **do**
> > | $\mathcal{W}_k^t \leftarrow \mathcal{W}_k^t - \eta \frac{\partial \mathcal{L}_k}{\partial \mathcal{W}_k^t}$
> **end**
> **Send** $\mathcal{W}_k^{t+1}$ to the server

As elaborated in Algorithm 1, we identify three main challenges in FL as follows. (1) Training models with FL algorithms on the non-IID local data $\mathcal{D}_k$ between silos often leads to inferior performance than that with centralized training, as demonstrated in previous work [29,37]. (2) Although FL aims to protect the participants' private data, prior studies [3,35,40] show that the local training data can be partially reconstructed from the gradients uploaded by participants, resulting in privacy leakage . (3) Resource-constrained FL requires high frequency communication between the server and participants to accelerate model convergence. However, these participants[1] often have limited computing resources and communication bandwidth [31], which prevent them from training large-scale pre-trained models.

2.2   The Lifecycle of Lawsuit

The procedure for legal cases can be broadly divided into three phases in chronological order: (1) At **Pre-trial** stage, plaintiffs submit the claims and evidence to the court, and judges conduct a desk review of the case and read through the files to get a rough picture; During this stage, Legal AI techniques can be applied to assist both plaintiffs and judges with process work or paperwork. (2) In **Trial**

---

[1] FL participants are typically privacy-sensitive institutions (e.g., courts) or edge devices (e.g., personal mobile phones).

Table 1. Task descriptions and statistics of FEDLEGAL. Cls., IE., Reg., Pri. represent the text classification, information extraction, regression, and privacy attack tasks, respectively. The cells in # Instances represent the total number of samples for each task. The cells in # Loc. represent the mean of data volume from local train/dev/test on all silos. The cells in # Glo. represent the volume of global dev/test data. Considering the trade-off between the time consumed by the attack and the batch size of local training, the volume of data for FEDLPA is generally tiny.

Task Type	Dataset	Metrics	Case Source	# Instances	# Silos	# Loc.	# Glo.	Pre-Trial	Trial	After-Trial
Cls.	FEDLCP	Micro/Macro-F1	Civil	199,284	36	3,542/443/443	19,928/19,929	✔		
	FEDLAM	Micro-F1	Civil	4,866	15	207/26/26	487/487	✔	✔	
IE.	FEDLER	Pre./Rec./Micro-F1	Criminal	2,282	10	146/18/19	228/229	✔		✔
	FEDLRE	Macro-F1	Criminal	5,923	10	379/47/48	592/593	✔		✔
Reg.	FEDLJP	S-Score/Acc@0.2	Criminal	59,431	24	1,584/198/199	5,943/5,944			✔
Pri.	FEDLPA	Pre./Rec./F1	Civil	80	1	-	-	-	-	-

stage, two or more parties get chances to cross-examine in the court; During this stage, the judge needs to summarize the dispute focusing on the views of different parties and inquire about their concerns. This part of the work can be assisted with Legal AI system by providing some suggestions through the analysis over past cases. (3) In many cases, the judge may not directly pronounce sentence in court at the end of trial, instead several weeks/months should be spent at **After-trial** stage to let the judge further review the information obtained during trial and then make the final decision. In addition, the prosecutor's office and the court are responsible for supervising the quality of judgments or even analyzing criminal clues or patterns with some structural data.

3 FEDLEGAL

To facilitate the research on the incorporation of FL and LegalAI, we present the legal FL benchmark FEDLEGAL with natural non-IID partitions and practical private information. FEDLEGAL consists of six critical legal tasks which covers a broad range of task types, federated participant numbers, and natural non-IID data as shown in Table 1.

3.1 Tasks

FEDLCP The task of **L**egal **C**ause **P**rediction aims to automatically predict causes, namely case categories (e.g., private lending disputes), of civil cases. A system tackling this task is commonly used to assist plaintiffs with limited legal knowledge to choose the correct category of a case in the filing process at the pre-trial stage.

FEDLJP **L**egal **J**udgment **P**rediction is a regression task that automatically predicts the duration of a sentence given the facts identified by a judge. Noteworthy, the goal of this task is to provide predicted judgements as references to users. Based on estimated judgements, lawyers can tailor their arguments, assess legal risks and provide appropriate advice to litigants. Similarly, judges may double check their judgements if there are discrepancies.

FedLER The task of **Legal Entity Recognition** aims to extract crime-related entities (e.g. instruments of crime, stolen amount and alcohol level in blood) from case documents. In practice, the extracted entities contribute to sorting out the gist of a case and characterization of a crime.

FedLRE Based on the outputs of FedLER, this task detects relations among entities and classifies entity pairs into specific types, such as a certain drug and its weight. These relations are then utilized to organize massive entities and avoid misplaced relations for subsequent analysis.

FedLAM **Legal Argument Mining** seeks to identify arguments and dispute focuses between a plaintiff and a defendant from court transcripts and estimate their argument types. To well understand a case, judges are required to summarize those arguments and investigate them during a trial. Before analyzing arguments and dispute focuses, cases are divided into different categories and are assigned to the corresponding courts. Law firms are usually specialized in only one or a handful of case categories. As cases are organized by case categories before analyzing arguments, we partition data by case categories in this benchmark.

FedLPA **Legal Privacy Attack** aims to evaluate privacy leaks in federated learning. Concretely, FedLegal provides a well-designed privacy attack dataset FedLPA containing 80 privacy-sensitive examples extracted from FedLJP. As shown in Fig. 3, such attack data includes privacy-sensitive attributes (e.g., age and gender) with various types, such as numbers and characters. Note that this is the *first* real-world privacy attack dataset for FL. We hope that FedLPA can facilitate studies of FL in terms of privacy protection.

3.2   Dataset

The source data for all tasks are collected from the public legal judgements that are anonymized and released by the Supreme Court of China[2]. The FedLCP dataset is collected from the results of a rigorous charge determination process, and the FedLJP dataset directly uses the official court decisions. Regarding the datasets for FedLAM, FedLER and FedLRE tasks, we establish a data schema and the corresponding annotation guidelines, and recruit a team of five law school students for annotation. A legal professional oversees the process, answering questions about annotation standards and performing quality checks. On average, annotating a sample takes about three minutes per person. The Kappa scores [28] among five annotators are 92%, 96%, 96% for each respective task. The sentences provided for FedLPA are manually created by the annotators to simulate real-world cases.

---

[2] https://wenshu.court.gov.cn/.

Practitioners and researchers aim to improve FL algorithms that customize models to perform well on each distinct local dataset and build a global model to perform well on all partitions without customization. The above two goals in FL are often difficult to achieve altogether, especially on significantly heterogeneous data partitions [18]. Unfortunately, the existing FL benchmarks only focus on one of the two goals but rarely take both into consideration [8]. Thus, accurately evaluating the pros and cons of different FL algorithms for both goals is difficult with existing FL benchmarks. For example, an optimal model personalized for a single data partition does not necessarily perform well on all partitions.

In light of above analysis, we build a local and a global evaluation set for each task in FEDLEGAL. For the local one, we divide each local partition into the local train/valid/test sets by 8:1:1. For the global evaluation set, we collect the training data of all partitions and divide the union into the global train/valid/test sets with the ratios of 8:1:1. During the global FL training, the global train set is partitioned for each participant w.r.t. either courts or case categories for respective tasks. Table 1 shows the basic statistics of each dataset in FEDLEGAL.

3.3   Framework Design

To facilitate research on FL in the legal domain, we build a general FL framework for legal tasks. Our framework is based on FedLab [38], a lightweight open-source framework for FL simulation. However, FedLab contains only basic FL framework components (e.g., communication configurations and FL algorithms), which lack APIs for downstream tasks. Therefore, on top of FedLab, we further establish the training pipelines for various legal tasks. Meanwhile, our framework integrates HuggingFace[3], which is widely recognized for its rich pre-trained models for NLP applications. Thus this framework is suitable for practitioners to study Legal NLP problems in FL settings using the *state-of-the-art* pre-trained language models.

4   Experiment

In this section, we first show the performance of different FL algorithms on FEDLEGAL (see Sect. 4.2). To obtain a clear understanding of the practical challenges of FL in real-world applications, we conduct an in-depth investigation on FEDLEGAL, covering privacy leakage analysis (see Sect. 4.3) and resource-constrained FL scenario (see Sect. 4.4).

4.1   Experiment Setup

Baseline Algorithms. Our experiment adopts the four typical FL algorithms for each legal task. The first two are classic and global FL algorithms: **FedAvg** [29] is the oft-cited FL algorithm that collaboratively trains a global FL model across participants, and **FedProx** [23] addresses statistical heterogeneity in FL by introducing L_2 proximal term during the local training process.

---

[3] https://huggingface.co/.

The last is the personalized FL method **FedOPT** [32] is an extended version of FedAvg, which respectively uses two gradient-based optimizers in participants and servers. **Ditto** [22], which excels at tackling the competing constraints of accuracy, fairness, and robustness in FL. Besides the FL family, we also include the local training algorithm: **Standalone** refers to the training model only using local data on each participant without collaborations between participants, and **Centralized** refers to the ideal centralized training setting where the server could collect all participants' data. Since pre-trained language models (PLMs) have been *de facto* base model architecture in NLP research nowadays, we adopt RoBERTa-WWM [9] released by HggingFace[4] for all tasks.

Evaluation Strategies. As described in Sect. 3.2, for a comprehensive evaluation, our experiments test all algorithms using two evaluation strategies: 1) Global test performance (GLOBAL) is evaluated on the global test set and used to determine whether the model has learned global knowledge. The better results of GLOBAL indicate that the model is closer to the centralized training. 2) Local test performance (LOCAL) is evaluated on each local test set and averaged by all participants. The LOCAL is more practical in real-world applications than GLOBAL because it shows performance improvement without centralizing all local data.

Table 2. The GLOBAL performances of different FL methods on FEDLEGAL.

	FEDLCP		FEDLJP		FEDLER			FEDLRE	FEDLAM
	Micro-F1	Macro-F1	S-Score	Acc@0.2	Pre.	Rec.	Micro-F1	Macro-F1	Micro-F1
Standalone	61.54	8.33	52.65	17.84	65.74	69.69	67.56	62.84	16.21
FedAvg	**81.56**	19.29	65.01	27.81	**82.84**	87.25	84.99	82.62	35.51
FedProx	81.09	18.46	65.76	28.30	82.81	87.25	**84.97**	82.51	34.11
FedOPT	81.03	**19.30**	65.77	30.33	81.29	**88.09**	84.55	80.74	**35.73**
Ditto	81.32	19.28	**65.93**	**30.53**	78.06	86.82	82.20	**88.21**	28.63
Centralized	86.74	39.90	75.72	36.46	85.74	87.37	86.54	90.04	79.62

Table 3. The LOCAL performances of different FL methods on FEDLEGAL. Underlined numbers denote either superior or acceptable performance for Standalone.

	FEDLCP		FEDLJP		FEDLER			FEDLRE	FEDLAM
	Micro-F1	Macro-F1	S-Score	Acc@0.2	Pre.	Rec.	Micro-F1	Macro-F1	Micro-F1
Standalone	<u>88.01</u>	<u>51.28</u>	53.77	9.58	73.42	82.57	77.66	82.02	<u>60.43</u>
FedAvg	87.47	48.22	63.52	26.10	78.15	82.08	79.95	89.76	45.94
FedProx	**87.59**	48.35	63.75	27.77	78.44	82.29	80.21	**89.94**	44.77
FedOPT	87.31	48.88	**64.59**	**28.32**	**79.49**	86.22	82.67	87.02	47.75
Ditto	87.44	**49.73**	60.65	23.99	73.37	82.45	77.56	84.19	**66.18**
Centralized	86.42	48.21	75.53	36.33	82.12	85.06	83.47	92.35	78.14

---

[4] https://huggingface.co/hfl/chinese-roberta-wwm-ext.

Table 4. The LOCAL performance of Standalone and FedAvg with different data ratios on FEDLCP.

Data Ratios	0.1	0.5	1.0
Standalone	44.38	56.92	88.01
FedAvg		72.38	79.51	87.47

Table 5. The GLOBAL performance comparisons between artificially sampled local partitions (Dir.) and their natural non-IID counterparts on FEDLEGAL. Underlined numbers indicate the lowest performance and also imply the more challenging non-IID. FEDLCP and FEDLAM adopt Label-level Dir. Partition, FEDLJP and FEDLRE adopt Quantity-level Dir. Partition, FEDLER adopts Clustering-level Dir. Partition.

	FEDLCP		FEDLJP		FEDLER			FEDLRE	FEDLAM
	Micro-F1	Macro-F1	S-Score	Acc@0.2	Pre.	Rec.	Micro-F1	Macro-F1	Micro-F1
Centralized	86.74	39.90	75.72	36.46	85.74	87.37	86.54	90.04	79.62
Dir. 0.1	84.43	38.28	73.31	34.22	81.10	88.85	84.80	84.33	42.44
Dir. 1.0	86.52	37.48	73.39	34.59	82.39	88.51	85.34	84.41	40.95
Dir. 10.0	84.76	33.58	72.74	35.18	81.25	88.24	84.58	85.61	42.99
Natural non-IID	81.56	19.29	65.01	27.81	82.84	87.25	84.99	82.62	35.51

Training Details. The number of silos involved in federated training for each task are listed in Table 1. Our experiments mainly focus on the cross-silo FL scenario, where all silos participate in training at each communication round. In silo local training, we adopt AdamW optimizer for RoBERTa-WWM. Considering the trade-off between computation and communication, we set the local training epoch to 1 and the communication rounds to 20 throughout experiments except for FEDLAM. Since FEDLAM is a highly non-IID task, we set the communication round to 50 on this task to ensure that the federated model can be fully trained.

4.2 Utility Experiment

We first conduct experiments to investigate different baseline algorithms' utility on FEDLEGAL. The experimental results demonstrate that *federated learning is crucial and efficient for privacy-sensitive downstream tasks (compared with Standalone), while there is still significant room for performance improvement using the real-world data partitions (compared with Centralized).*

The GLOBAL and LOCAL performances are shown in Table 2 and 3 respectively. FL algorithms outperform Standalone training on GLOBAL and LOCAL in the majority of FEDLEGAL tasks. This can be attributed to FL's privacy-preserving training manner which enables the model to harness knowledge from all participants, leading to a significant performance boost. We also observe

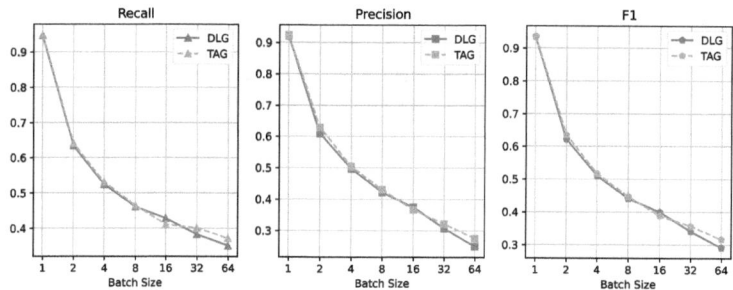

Fig. 2. Privacy attack results of DLG and TAG on FEDLPA under different local training batch sizes. The higher metric means more serious privacy breaches.

that Standalone exhibits either superior or acceptable LOCAL performance in FEDLCP and FEDLAM. Compared with other tasks, each participant in FEDLCP has enough local data, which allows the local model to be fully trained and achieves better performance in local tests. As shown in Table 4, when there is only a small amount of data locally, Standalone's LOCAL performance drops precipitously while the FL algorithm still performs well. This emphasizes the advantages of FL for collaborative model training in situations where local data is limited and centralized collection of data is prohibited. As for FEDLAM, we presume that its strong non-IID features lead to the LOCAL performance better than federated algorithms.

Upon comparing various FL algorithms, we find that they possess unique pros and cons, specific to different tasks. While FedAvg may not attain the best performance in all tasks, its margin of difference from the best-performing algorithm is minimal. FedProx can achieve similar performances as FedAvg, consistent with the finding of [24]. FedOPT, an advanced federation algorithm, attains superior performance in most tasks, which aligns with prior research [24]. As a personalized FL algorithm, Ditto can achieve better performance results on LOCAL but struggles on GLOBAL. FEDLEGAL exhibits the clear trade-off between global and personalized models, providing a more comprehensive evaluation of different FL algorithms. Comparing the FL algorithm with centralized training, we found a sharp performance gap between the FL algorithm on GLOBAL and LOCAL due to the complex real-world data heterogeneity in FEDLEGAL. In this sense, we believe FEDLEGAL can facilitate the FL community to develop more robust FL algorithms.

We further scrutinize the contrast between natural partitioning and commonly employed artificially split methods in non-IID settings. For this analysis, we utilize oft-cited FedAvg and the applicable artificially split methods in each task. As shown in Table 5, compared with artificially split datasets, we find that *the natural non-IID is notably more arduous to address in federated scenarios across all tasks.* Moreover, we uncover that artificially split methods may fail to accurately reflect the attendant non-IID complexities, such as those exhibited in FEDLJP with α values[5] of 1.0 and 10.0 and FEDLAM with α values

---

[5] A lower value of α generates a high distribution shift.

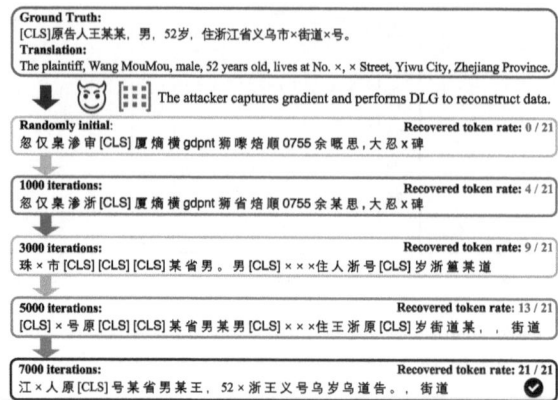

Fig. 3. Recover progress of gradient attack on an example of FEDLPA.

of 0.1 and 1.0. These experimental findings provide further justification for our motivation to develop our FEDLEGAL.

4.3 Privacy Experiment

In FL systems, the server updates the global model by aggregating participant-uploaded model gradients, maintaining privacy by not directly accessing local data. However, prior work [40] has demonstrated the potential privacy breaches in which participants' training data can be partially reconstructed from gradients. To analyze the privacy leakage of FL, we adopt two gradient-based privacy attack methods: DLG (Deep Leakage from Gradients) [40] and TAG (Gradient Attack on Transformer-based Models) [10] in our privacy attack dataset FEDLPA. Both attack methods can effectively recover the original data from the participant-uploaded gradients. For the evaluation metrics, we follow [33] and use *precision* (the average percentage of recovered words in the target texts), *recall* (the average percentage of words in the target texts are predicted), and *F1 score* (the harmonic mean between precision and recall).

Figure 2 shows privacy attack results of DLG and TAG on FEDLPA under different local training batch sizes, we find that attackers can still efficiently reconstruct the data from the participant-uploaded gradients even in privacy-preserving FL. Figure 2 also shows that data is more likely to leak when the local batch size is small. To attain a clearer understanding of gradient attacks, we show the recovery progress of gradient attacks on an example of FEDLPA in Fig. 3. Although the existing gradient attack can effectively recover every token in the sentence, *it is hard for the attacker to recover the order of tokens.* This outcome also reveals the potential privacy risks arising from the unordered bag of words even though it may be challenging for an attacker to obtain the exact original training data from the gradient. Overall, FEDLPA provides an available privacy attack dataset, which researchers can use to simulate privacy attacks and study privacy defenses in the FL setting.

4.4   Resource Cost

This section analyzes resource-intensive situations in real-world federated systems, including communication overhead in federated training and computational resources of local participants.

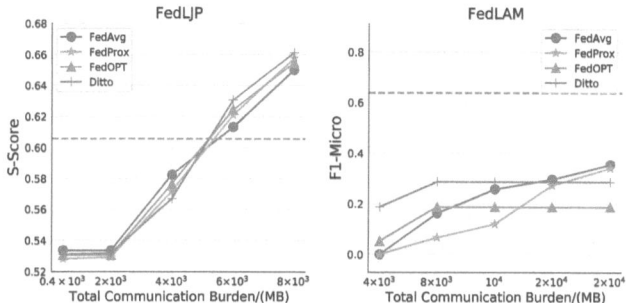

Fig. 4. Performance versus Communication Budgets on FEDLJP and FEDLAM. The horizontal dashed line indicates the acceptable performance, which is 80% of centralized training's performance.

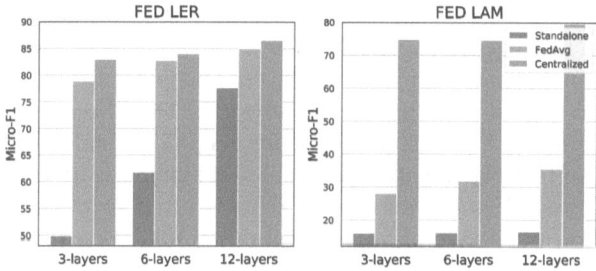

Fig. 5. Performance with different model sizes on FEDLER and FEDLAM in federated and local training settings. The *x-layers* denotes the number of RoBERTa's encoder layers.

The Effect of Communication. We investigate the performance versus communication budgets on FEDLJP and FEDLAM, which is illustrated in Fig. 4. *Although FL can make the model attain the desired performance by multiple communications (e.g., more than 80% performance of centralized training), it also requires an extremely heavy communication cost.* For example, the local model has to upload about 6 GB communication overhead cumulatively when FL algorithms achieve the desired performance on FEDLJP. Such cumbersome communication overhead is unacceptable in a real-world federation system, especially when the local client has limited transmission bandwidth. With the increasing scale of PLMs, communication overhead becomes a significant bottleneck for landing PLMs in real-world FL scenarios. In this sense, developing communication-friendly and PLMs-empowered FL algorithms is necessary. Besides, we find that vanilla FedAvg and FedProx algorithms show better performance and robustness in GLOBAL performance under extremely non-IID task FEDLAM.

The Resource-Constrained Computation. Participants in the FL system typically have limited computation resources, thereby it is practical to consider small federated models to reduce the computation costs. Figure 5 shows the performances of different sizes of models in federated and local training settings for FEDLER and FEDLAM tasks. We find that *smaller models suffer drastic performance degradation in FL,* despite reducing the training cost of local clients. Note that, the performance of FL is still weaker than the results of Centralized setting. This result is contrary to that in [24], where they experimentally demonstrate that a small-scale model can still achieve competitive performance. We speculate that this result may be due to the real-world data heterogeneity in FEDLEGAL, and [24] uses a heuristic partitioning method. Based on this, FEDLEGAL could be better to reflect the trade-off between local computational resources and performance.

5   Related Work

Legal Artificial Intelligence (LegalAI) provides intelligent support for legal professionals, enhancing the efficiency of lawyers and judges while offering affordable services to the public. Significant advances have been made in LegalAI applications, including legal judgment prediction [6,27], legal information extraction [2,5,5], legal text classification [7], legal text summarization [1,11], and legal question answering [19]. However, legal data is often scattered across various regions or courts, and due to privacy concerns, consolidating this data-especially non-public records—is impractical. This limits the potential of data-driven algorithms in the legal field.

Federated learning (FL) [29] has become a leading approach for decentralized machine learning in privacy-sensitive settings. Several FL benchmarks, such as LEAF [4], FedScale [20], pFL-Bench [8], FedCV [15], and FedNLP [24], have facilitated progress in standardized FL evaluation. These benchmarks typically simulate non-IID data through heuristic sampling [17,21,30], but this may overlook the complexity of real-world data heterogeneity [36]. In contrast, FEDLEGAL uses real-world datasets, preserving natural non-IID partitioning. Recent FL benchmarks, such as FLamby [36] for healthcare and the first real-world FL image classification dataset [16], focus on image tasks but lack task diversity. FEDLEGAL addresses this by covering a wider range of NLP tasks and introducing the first practical privacy attack dataset, FEDLPA, to advance FL research on privacy vulnerabilities.

6   Conclusion

This chapter proposes the *first* real-world federated learning benchmark for legal NLP (FEDLEGAL), which contains five NLP tasks and one privacy task. The benchmark features a large number of FL participants and natural non-IID data partitions. On this dataset, we conduct the extensive empirical study, including performance comparisons, privacy leakage, and resource-constrained analysis. The experimental results reveal that FL algorithms are effective for real-world applications but our benchmark poses new challenges on natural non-IID partitions. In addition, we build a lightweight and easy-to-extend codebase to facilitate FL research in the legal domain. We hope that FEDLEGAL would facilitate the development of novel and practical FL algorithms for real-world legal applications.

References

1. Aletras, N., Tsarapatsanis, D., Preotiuc-Pietro, D., Lampos, V.: Predicting judicial decisions of the European court of human rights: a natural language processing perspective. PeerJ Comput. Sci. **2**, e93 (2016)
2. Angelidis, I., Chalkidis, I., Koubarakis, M.: Named entity recognition, linking and generation for Greek legislation. In: JURIX. Frontiers in Artificial Intelligence and Applications, vol. 313, pp. 1–10. IOS Press (2018)
3. Boenisch, F., Dziedzic, A., Schuster, R., Shamsabadi, A.S., Shumailov, I., Papernot, N.: When the curious abandon honesty: federated learning is not private. arXiv preprint arXiv:2112.02918 (2021)
4. Caldas, S., et al.: LEAF: a benchmark for federated settings. CoRR abs/1812.01097 (2018)
5. Cardellino, C., Teruel, M., Alemany, L.A., Villata, S.: Legal NERC with ontologies, Wikipedia and curriculum learning. In: EACL (2), pp. 254–259. Association for Computational Linguistics (2017)
6. Chalkidis, I., Androutsopoulos, I., Aletras, N.: Neural legal judgment prediction in english. In: ACL (1), pp. 4317–4323. Association for Computational Linguistics (2019)
7. Chalkidis, I., Fergadiotis, M., Malakasiotis, P., Androutsopoulos, I.: Large-scale multi-label text classification on EU legislation. In: ACL (1), pp. 6314–6322. Association for Computational Linguistics (2019)
8. Chen, D., Gao, D., Kuang, W., Li, Y., Ding, B.: pFL-bench: a comprehensive benchmark for personalized federated learning. In: Thirty-Sixth Conference on Neural Information Processing Systems Datasets and Benchmarks Track (2022). https://openreview.net/forum?id=2ptbv_JjYKA
9. Cui, Y., et al.: Pre-training with whole word masking for Chinese bert. arXiv preprint arXiv:1906.08101 (2019)
10. Deng, J., et al.: Tag: gradient attack on transformer-based language models. arXiv preprint arXiv:2103.06819 (2021)
11. Duan, X., et al.: Legal summarization for multi-role debate dialogue via controversy focus mining and multi-task learning. In: CIKM, pp. 1361–1370. ACM (2019)
12. Ge, S., Wu, F., Wu, C., Qi, T., Huang, Y., Xie, X.: Fedner: medical named entity recognition with federated learning. arXiv preprint arXiv:2003.09288 (2020)

13. Gomes, M., Oliveira, B., Sousa, C.: Enriching legal knowledge through intelligent information retrieval techniques: a review. In: EPIA Conference on Artificial Intelligence, pp. 119–130. Springer (2022)
14. Gupta, S., Huang, Y., Zhong, Z., Gao, T., Li, K., Chen, D.: Recovering private text in federated learning of language models. arXiv preprint arXiv:2205.08514 (2022)
15. He, C., et al.: Fedcv: a federated learning framework for diverse computer vision tasks. CoRR abs/2111.11066 (2021)
16. Jain, S., Jerripothula, K.R.: Federated learning for commercial image sources. In: Proceedings of the IEEE/CVF Winter Conference on Applications of Computer Vision, pp. 6534–6543 (2023)
17. Ji, S., Jiang, W., Walid, A., Li, X.: Dynamic sampling and selective masking for communication-efficient federated learning. arXiv preprint arXiv:2003.09603 (2020)
18. Kairouz, P., et al.: Advances and open problems in federated learning. Found. Trends® Mach. Learn. **14**(1–2), 1–210 (2021)
19. Khazaeli, S., et al.: A free format legal question answering system. In: Proceedings of the Natural Legal Language Processing Workshop 2021, pp. 107–113. Association for Computational Linguistics, Punta Cana, Dominican Republic (2021). https://doi.org/10.18653/v1/2021.nllp-1.11. https://aclanthology.org/2021.nllp-1.11
20. Lai, F., et al.: Fedscale: benchmarking model and system performance of federated learning at scale. In: ICML. Proceedings of Machine Learning Research, vol. 162, pp. 11814–11827. PMLR (2022)
21. Li, Q., Diao, Y., Chen, Q., He, B.: Federated learning on non-IID data silos: an experimental study. arXiv preprint arXiv:2102.02079 (2021)
22. Li, T., Hu, S., Beirami, A., Smith, V.: Ditto: fair and robust federated learning through personalization. In: International Conference on Machine Learning, pp. 6357–6368. PMLR (2021)
23. Li, T., Sahu, A.K., Zaheer, M., Sanjabi, M., Talwalkar, A., Smith, V.: Federated optimization in heterogeneous networks. Proc. Mach. Learn. Syst. **2**, 429–450 (2020)
24. Lin, B.Y., et al.: FedNLP: benchmarking federated learning methods for natural language processing tasks. In: Findings of the Association for Computational Linguistics: NAACL 2022, pp. 157–175. Association for Computational Linguistics, Seattle, United States (2022). https://doi.org/10.18653/v1/2022.findings-naacl.13. https://aclanthology.org/2022.findings-naacl.13
25. Liu, R., et al.: No one left behind: inclusive federated learning over heterogeneous devices. arXiv preprint arXiv:2202.08036 (2022)
26. Liu, Y., et al.: Roberta: a robustly optimized bert pretraining approach. arXiv preprint arXiv:1907.11692 (2019)
27. Ma, L., et al.: Legal judgment prediction with multi-stage case representation learning in the real court setting. In: SIGIR, pp. 993–1002. ACM (2021)
28. McHugh, M.L.: Interrater reliability: the kappa statistic. Biochemia Medica **22**(3), 276–282 (2012)
29. McMahan, B., Moore, E., Ramage, D., Hampson, S., y Arcas, B.A.: Communication-efficient learning of deep networks from decentralized data. In: Artificial Intelligence and Statistics, pp. 1273–1282. PMLR (2017)
30. Morafah, M., Vahidian, S., Chen, C., Shah, M., Lin, B.: Rethinking data heterogeneity in federated learning: Introducing a new notion and standard benchmarks. arXiv preprint arXiv:2209.15595 (2022)

31. Pfeiffer, K.Y., Rapp, M., Khalili, R., Henkel, J.: Federated learning for computationally-constrained heterogeneous devices: a survey. ACM Comput. Surv. (2023)
32. Reddi, S.J., et al.: Adaptive federated optimization. In: International Conference on Learning Representations (2021). https://openreview.net/forum?id=LkFG3lB13U5
33. Song, C., Raghunathan, A.: Information leakage in embedding models. In: Proceedings of the 2020 ACM SIGSAC Conference on Computer and Communications Security, pp. 377–390 (2020)
34. Sun, C., Zhang, Y., Liu, X., Wu, F.: Legal intelligence: algorithmic, data, and social challenges. In: Proceedings of the 43rd International ACM SIGIR Conference on Research and Development in Information Retrieval, pp. 2464–2467 (2020)
35. Sun, J., Li, A., Wang, B., Yang, H., Li, H., Chen, Y.: Provable defense against privacy leakage in federated learning from representation perspective. arXiv preprint arXiv:2012.06043 (2020)
36. du Terrail, J.O., et al.: FLamby: datasets and benchmarks for cross-silo federated learning in realistic healthcare settings. In: Thirty-Sixth Conference on Neural Information Processing Systems Datasets and Benchmarks Track (2022). https://openreview.net/forum?id=GgM5DiAb6A2
37. Weller, O., Marone, M., Braverman, V., Lawrie, D., Van Durme, B.: Pretrained models for multilingual federated learning. In: Proceedings of the 2022 Conference of the North American Chapter of the Association for Computational Linguistics: Human Language Technologies, pp. 1413–1421. Association for Computational Linguistics, Seattle, United States (2022). https://doi.org/10.18653/v1/2022.naacl-main.101. https://aclanthology.org/2022.naacl-main.101
38. Zeng, D., Liang, S., Hu, X., Wang, H., Xu, Z.: Fedlab: a flexible federated learning framework. J. Mach. Learn. Res. **24**(100), 1–7 (2023). http://jmlr.org/papers/v24/22-0440.html ´
39. Zhao, Y., Li, M., Lai, L., Suda, N., Civin, D., Chandra, V.: Federated learning with non-IID data. arXiv preprint arXiv:1806.00582 (2018)
40. Zhu, L., Liu, Z., Han, S.: Deep leakage from gradients. In: Advances in Neural Information Processing Systems, vol. 32 (2019)

Lightweight Unsupervised Federated Learning with Pretrained Vision Language Model

Hao Yan[1] and Yuhong Guo[1,2(✉)]

[1] Carleton University, Ottawa, Canada
haoyan6@cmai.carleton.ca, yuhong.guo@carleton.ca
[2] Canada CIFAR AI Chair, Amii, Canada

Abstract. Federated learning aims to tackle the "isolated data island" problem, where it trains a collective model from physically isolated clients while safeguarding the privacy of users' data. However, supervised federated learning necessitates that each client labels their data for training, which can be both time-consuming and resource-intensive. Moreover, the training and transmission of deep models present challenges to the computation and communication capabilities of the clients. To address these two inherent challenges in supervised federated learning, we propose a novel lightweight unsupervised federated learning approach that leverages unlabeled data on each client to perform lightweight model training and communication by harnessing pretrained vision-language models, such as CLIP. By capitalizing on the zero-shot prediction capability and the well-trained image encoder of the pre-trained CLIP model, we have carefully crafted an efficient and resilient self-training approach. Additionally, to address data heterogeneity within each client, we propose a class-balanced text feature sampling strategy for generating synthetic instances in the feature space to support local training. The experimental results demonstrate that our proposed method greatly enhances model performance in comparison to CLIP's zero-shot predictions and even outperforms supervised federated learning benchmark methods given limited computational and communication overhead.

Keywords: Lightweight Unsupervised Federated Learning · Pretrained Vision-Language Models · Data Heterogeneity

1 Introduction

Deep learning has achieved state-of-the-art performance across various benchmarks, primarily driven by the emergence of ultra-deep neural networks and the availability of centralized training data. While potential information hides in huge amount of personal or corporate data, learning from these isolated data islands poses a fundamental challenge in preserving privacy of user data. To address this challenge, federated learning [27] was introduced as an interactive approach involving communication between a central server and individual clients. In this process, clients download initial model parameters from the server, update these parameters locally, and then upload the updated parameters back to the server. The server aggregates these updates and sends the aggregated parameters back to the clients. While FedAvg [27] achieves rapid convergence when the data distribution among clients is homogeneous, heterogeneity in data distribution leads to biased local models and reduces the efficiency of federated learning [26]. Subsequent research efforts have sought to enhance the training efficiency of heterogeneous federated learning, both at the client side [15,16,18,20,21,32,34] and on the server side [7,11,26,29].

However, standard supervised federated learning faces two significant challenges. Firstly, it requires data annotation on every client, which is both time and resource-intensive. Secondly, updating deep models within the client and frequently transferring these models between the server and clients induce substantial computational and communication resources, particularly on edge devices such as mobile phones. Addressing these challenges has been the focus of only a few recent works. Some have explored semi-supervised federated learning, assuming that a portion of the data in each client is labeled [5,13]. Lu et al. [23] proposed federated learning from unlabeled data while under the strong assumption of known precise label frequencies on each client. Lin et al. [22] proposed federated learning with positive and unlabeled data and assumed that each client labels only a portion of data from certain classes.

In this paper, we propose a novel lightweight unsupervised federated learning approach to simultaneously address the aforementioned annotation and resource demanding challenges. Our approach focuses on a setting where data annotation on each client is unnecessary, while restricting to lightweight model training on each client to accommodate computation and communication limitations. The contemplation of this learning approach is prompted by recent advancements in pretrained vision-language models, such as CLIP [28], which train both image and text encoders on large datasets of image-caption pairs and facilitate zero-shot predictions on downstream tasks by generating pairs of visual and textual features. While pretrained vision-language models can offer initial annotations through zero-shot prediction, achieving satisfactory or optimal model performance in the demanding context of lightweight and unsupervised federated learning still necessitates the development of novel methodologies.

To this end, we develop a novel method, Federated Self-Training with Class-Balanced Data Generation (FST-CBDG), to perform lightweight unsupervised federated learning by utilizing the text and image encoders of pretrained vision-language models. First, in the preparation stage, we generate the textual embeddings of all relevant classes using the pretrained text encoder on the server side and distribute them to participating clients along with the pretrained image encoder. Subsequently, in the federated learning stage, we form the prediction model by putting a lightweight linear classification layer on top of the pretrained image encoder, and conduct standard federated average learning solely on the linear layer. This learning scheme imposes minimal computational and communication overhead on each client. Additionally, the weight parameters of the linear classification layer can be conveniently initialized using the textual features of the corresponding class categories, which facilitates efficient federated learning by leveraging the zero-shot prediction capabilities of the pretrained vision-language model. Nevertheless, the crux of the matter is the efficient enhancement of initial models on each client within the constrained parameter space. Hence, we have carefully designed a self-training strategy aimed at improving the quality of predicted pseudo-labels and enhancing overall model performance. Moreover, to address the challenges and mitigate the negative impact of heterogeneous data distribution on local clients, we introduce a class-balanced data generation module to produce augmenting data from a Gaussian sampling model that leverages class-relevant text features. To evaluate our proposed approach, we conducted experiments on standard federated learning benchmarks under the "lightweight unsupervised federated learning" setting. The experimental results demonstrate that the proposed method achieves substantial improvements over CLIP's zero-shot prediction and even outperforms supervised federated learning benchmark methods given limited computational and communication overhead.

2   Related Works

Federated Learning. Federated learning was introduced to address the challenge of training models based on isolated data islands. Majority studies focus on fully supervised federated learning settings, requiring every client has fully labeled data. The foundational FedAvg [27] is a simple approach of averaging local model parameter updates on the server and sending them back to clients for further local updates. It demonstrates rapid convergence and approximation of centralized learning when client data adhered to an independently and identically distributed (i.i.d.) pattern. However, heterogeneity in data distribution among clients, which is common in real-world scenarios, introduces non-i.i.d. challenges, resulting in biased local models and slower model convergence. Subsequent research endeavors aimed to enhance heterogeneous federated learning. These approaches target both client and server-side improvements. FedProx [21] enforces local parameter updates to stay close to the global model. FedNova [34] tackles the issue of objective inconsistency by employing a normalized averaging method. SCAFFOLD [15] employs control variates to reduce variance in local updates. MOON [20] corrects local updates by maximizing the agreement between local and global representations through contrastive learning. FedNTD [18] generates outputs from global and local models, discarding logits belonging to the ground-truth class while minimizing the KL divergence between the modified predictions. FedBR [10] reduces learning biases on local features and classifiers through mix-max optimization. FedDisco [36] aggregates local model parameters based on the discrepancy between local and global category distributions on the server. FedSMOO [31] adopts a dynamic regularizer to align local and global objectives and employs a global sharpness-aware minimization optimizer to find consistent flat minima. FedCLIP [24] utilizes the pretrained CLIP model for federated learning while under the traditional supervised setting.

Semi-supervised Federated Learning. Recent works have relaxed the full supervision requirement and explored semi-supervised scenarios. FedMatch [13] integrates federated learning and semi-supervised learning with an inter-client consistency loss. FedRGD [37] employs consistency regularization loss and group normalization for local updates on the client side, along with a grouping-based model averaging method for aggregation on the server side. SemiFL [5] employs semi-supervised learning approaches for local updates and assumes extra labeled data on the server for aggregated model fine-tuning. Other works go even further to relax data annotation requirements. FedPU [22] assumes that each client labels only a portion of data from specific classes and uses positive and unlabeled learning methods for local updates. FedUL [23] introduces federated learning with only unlabeled data, but requires knowledge of precise label frequencies for each client.

Pretrained Vision-Language Models. Pretrained Vision-Language Models have gained popularity for their ability to learn image and text encoders from large image-text datasets. These models exhibit promising zero-shot prediction capabilities. CLIP [28] trains paired image and text encoders mainly used for image classification and retrieval. ALIGN [14] trains visual and language representations using noisy image and alt-text data. Subsequent models emphasize diverse tasks or expand the CLIP model. BLIP [19] focuses on language-image pretraining for both vision-language understanding and generation with filtered captions. FLAVA [30] learns representations from paired and unpaired images and text, featuring multimodal and unimodal encoders. SimVLM [35] simplifies training complexity with large-scale weak supervision and a prefix language modeling objective. AltCLIP [1] extends CLIP's text encoder to a multilingual text encoder for multilingual understanding. FashionCLIP [2] and PLIP [12] finetune the CLIP model on special types of data. Recent research has harnessed such pretrained vision-language models, primarily CLIP, for various downstream applications. LADS [6] employed CLIP to generate augmented domain-specific visual embedding for domain adaptation. CLIPSeg [25] extended CLIP by incorporating a transformer-based decoder for semantic segmentation tasks. ViLD [8] conducted knowledge distillation from a pretrained open-vocabulary image classification model into a two-stage detector for object detection. pFedPrompt [9] adapted CLIP with prompt learning techniques for personalized supervised federated learning.

3   Proposed Method

In this section, we present the proposed method, Federated Self-Training with Class-Balanced Data Generation (FST-CBDG), for achieving lightweight unsupervised federated learning, where only unlabeled data, and limited computation and communication resources are available on each local client. The method centers on constructing a lightweight unsupervised federated learning framework by harnessing pretrained vision-language models, particularly CLIP, devising an

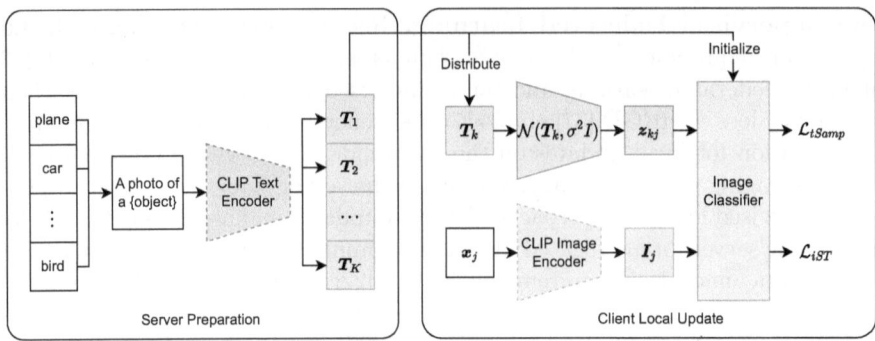

Fig. 1. Framework of the proposed FST-CBDG method for lightweight unsupervised federated learning. In the server preparation stage, the CLIP image encoder and the categorical text features extracted using the CLIP text encoder are distributed to each client. During local training, extracted image features from the fixed CLIP image encoder are used for self-training of the linear classifier. Synthetic instances are generated in the feature space via class-balanced Gaussian sampling to address the data heterogeneity problem.

effective self-training mechanism to improve noisy pseudo-labels and hence model performance through moving average soft label updates, and tackling the data imbalance and heterogeneity problem on local clients via class-balanced data generation. The framework of the proposed FST-CBDG method is presented in Fig. 1. We elaborate this approach in subsequent subsections.

3.1   Lightweight Unsupervised Federated Learning Framework

Deep classification models typically consist of a deep feature encoder that maps high-dimensional raw image data to high-level feature representations and a shallow classifier to make predictions based on these high-level representations. However, training deep models on clients requires substantial labeled data and computational resources, and transmitting these models between clients and the server demands expensive communication bandwidth. To bypass such demanding training and communication requirements and realize lightweight unsupervised federated learning, we propose to initialize a federated learning framework by utilizing the recent pretrained vision-language models, particularly CLIP, for their impressive zero-shot transfer capabilities on downstream tasks.

CLIP trains image and text encoders using extensive datasets of image-caption pairs, offering well trained encoders that can extract visual and textual features in aligned feature spaces. With such aligned encoders, zero-shot image classification can be easily achieved by mapping extracted test image features based on cosine similarity to the text features extracted from sentences constructed from candidate category names. For unsupervised federated learning, we leverage CLIP's zero-shot prediction capability to prepare the federated learning model at the server side. Specifically, we first deploy CLIP's text encoder to extract textual features for the set of predefined class categories. For example, to obtain the textual feature vector for the class "plane", a sentence such like "a photo of a plane" can be input to CLIP's text encoder, resulting in the desired textual feature vector. Next, we form a prediction model by adding a linear classification layer on top of the pretrained and fixed CLIP image encoder, which produces a multi-class probabilistic classifier

$$f(\mathbf{z}; W, \mathbf{b}) = \mathrm{softmax}(W\mathbf{z} + \mathbf{b}) \tag{1}$$

in the aligned feature space $\mathcal{Z}$. A linear classifier is chosen for two compelling reasons:

- Linear classifiers have significantly fewer parameters compared to full-fledged deep models, offering a lightweight training and transmitting mechanism for federated learning when fixing the pretrained CLIP image encoder.
- The weight parameters W of the linear classifier can be initialized with textual features extracted from the CLIP text encoder for the predefined class categories, while setting $\mathbf{b} = 0$. Based on the zero-shot prediction capability of the CLIP model, this initialization not only provides the ability of predicting initial pseudo-labels for unlabeled data, but also can substantially enhance the convergence rate of the subsequent federated learning.

The textual features of the class categories and the initialized prediction model can be subsequently distributed to all the clients to produce the initial pseudo-labels on the unlabeled data and start the lightweight federated learning process: In each round, each client makes local updates on the linear classifier, which is then uploaded to the server for model aggregation; we adopt the simple average aggregation procedure of FedAvg. Therefore, we obtain a feasible initial framework for lightweight unsupervised federated learning.

3.2   Resilient Self-training with Evolving Pseudo-labels

Employing the pseudo-labels generated from CLIP model's zero-shot predictions as targets for federated learning, however, can often yield suboptimal results due to the low quality of these initial labels. An observation worth noting is that on benchmark datasets these initial predicted probabilities for each class are typically close to each other, and the CLIP zero-shot model tends to make low-confidence predictions on the unlabeled data. To empirically demonstrate the characteristics of the predicted probability vectors from the zero-shot CLIP model, we conducted an entropy analysis using a dataset of 1000 randomly sampled images from CIFAR-10 [17]. To elaborate, let's denote an image as $\boldsymbol{x}_j$ and its extracted image features as $\boldsymbol{I}_j$. We also denote the text features for each class k as $\boldsymbol{T}_k$, where $1 \leq k \leq K$, with K being the total number of classes. The probability vector resulting from the CLIP zero-shot prediction for image $\boldsymbol{x}_j$ can be calculated as

$$\boldsymbol{p}_j = [p_{j1}, \cdots, p_{jK}] = \mathrm{softmax}([\boldsymbol{I}_j \cdot \boldsymbol{T}_1, \cdots, \boldsymbol{I}_j \cdot \boldsymbol{T}_K]). \tag{2}$$

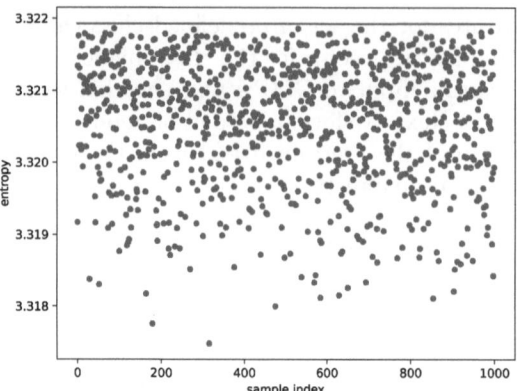

Fig. 2. Entropy distribution of predicted probability vectors. Green dots represents the entropy for each sample and red line denotes the upper bound of the entropy ($\log_2 10 \approx 3.322$). (Color figure online)

The confidence level of the prediction can then be measured using the entropy value of the vector $\boldsymbol{p}_j$: $H(\boldsymbol{p}_j) = -\sum_{k=1}^{K} p_{jk} \log p_{jk}$. The upper bound for this entropy is $\log K$, which can only be reached when the predicted probability vector is a uniform vector. The results of this analysis are visualized in Fig. 2 which shows the entropy values corresponding to the 1000 image samples as well as the upper bound for the entropy of a probability vector with $K = 10$ classes. From the figure, it is evident that the entropy values for all the sampled images are very close to the upper bound value of $\log_2 10$. This observation demonstrates that the zero-shot CLIP model often produces probability vectors that are close to a uniform distribution across classes, resulting in low-confidence predictions.

To address the challenge posed by low-confidence initial pseudo-labels, we have devised a carefully crafted self-training method to progressively update and improve the pseudo-labels. It is evident that generating one-hot pseudo-labels from the low-confidence predictions during linear classifier training can often result in large errors and degrade the training process. Therefore, we opt for using soft pseudo-labels for self-training and update these labels using a moving average approach. In the t-th iteration, we use the following cross-entropy loss on *images* as the *Self-Training* objective for the linear classifier $f(\cdot)$ on each client:

$$\mathcal{L}_{iST} = -\mathbb{E}_{\boldsymbol{I}_j}[\boldsymbol{q}_j^t \cdot \log f(\boldsymbol{I}_j; W, \mathbf{b})] \tag{3}$$

As stated in the previous subsection, the weight matrix W is initialized with the text features $\boldsymbol{T} = [\boldsymbol{T}_1, \cdots, \boldsymbol{T}_K]^\top$ and the bias vector $\mathbf{b}$ is initialized as $\mathbf{0}$ vector. The soft pseudo-labels, denoted as $\boldsymbol{q}_j$ are initially set to the CLIP zero-shot predicted probability vector, i.e. $\boldsymbol{q}_j^0 = \boldsymbol{p}_j$ and then updated with the model's prediction outputs. To obtain smooth and progressive updates of pseudo-labels and mitigate the risk of oscillations, we adopt the following weighted moving average update:

$$\boldsymbol{q}_j^t = \beta \boldsymbol{q}_j^{t-1} + (1 - \beta) f(\boldsymbol{I}_j; W, \mathbf{b}) \tag{4}$$

where β is the hyper-parameter that controls the updating rate. This progressive update strategy can promptly incorporate the progress of the classifier training to improve the quality of pseudo-labels, while maintaining stability by accumulating the previous predictions.

3.3   Class-Balanced Data Generation

A significant challenge in federated learning arises from the non-i.i.d. data distribution across clients, which often results in class imbalances and introduces bias during local model training, thereby diminishing the convergence rate of the global model. Regrettably, unsupervised federated learning exacerbates this situation since errors accumulated in the pseudo-labels further impede the convergence of the local models. Fortunately, there is a silver lining in the form of text features extracted from the CLIP text encoder for the relevant classes. As the CLIP model is trained using paired image-text data, the text features and image features pertaining to the same category exhibit a high degree of similarity, and the text feature vectors $\{T_1, \cdots, T_K\}$ can be regarded as class prototypes for the corresponding categories in the aligned image-text feature space $\mathcal{Z}$.

Using the K text feature vectors—class prototype vectors—as additional labeled instances from their corresponding classes for training the local model however provides limited supervision and may lead to overfitting. Feature-level Gaussian augmentation has demonstrated effectiveness in recent works [4,38]. Motivated the clustering assumption that data belonging to the same class are usually close to each other in the high level feature space, we propose to model each class as a Gaussian distribution $\mathcal{N}(T_k, \sigma^2 I)$ around the class prototype vector T_k in the feature space $\mathcal{Z}$, where I denotes the identity matrix and $\sigma^2 I$ represents a diagonal covariance matrix. Then we can generate a set of synthetic instances for each k-th class in the feature space by randomly sampling feature vectors from the Gaussian distribution $\mathcal{N}(T_k, \sigma^2 I)$, aiming to augment the pseudo-labeled training data and mitigate data heterogeneity and class imbalance. Specifically, we generate n_k instances for each class k as follows:

$$\{z_{kj} \sim \mathcal{N}(T_k, \sigma^2 I) | 1 \leq k \leq K, 1 \leq j \leq n_k\} \tag{5}$$

They can be used as labeled instances to help train the classifier by minimizing following cross-entropy loss:

$$\mathcal{L}_{tSamp} = -\sum_{k=1}^{K} \sum_{j=1}^{n_k} \mathbf{1}_k \cdot \log f(z_{kj}; W, b) \tag{6}$$

where $\mathbf{1}_k$ denotes the one-hot vector with a single 1 at the k-th entry.

To tackle the class imbalance problem at local clients, we further propose a class-balanced sampling strategy that generates more synthetic instances for the minority classes compared to the majority classes. To illustrate this, let's denote the number of images categorized into the k-th class based on the pseudo-labels ($k = \arg\max_{k'} q_{jk'}^t$) on the considered client as m_k. The class-balanced sampling

---

Algorithm 1: FST-CBDG

    Input   : Number of classes K, total number of communication rounds R, learning rate η.

1 **for** *each class* $k \leftarrow 1$ **to** K **do**
2 | Obtain class name {object} and construct: a photo of a {object}.
3 | Extract text feature $\boldsymbol{T}_k$ using the CLIP text encoder from the sentence.
4 **end**
5 Initialize the parameters of the linear classifier $\boldsymbol{W} = [\boldsymbol{T}_1, \cdots, \boldsymbol{T}_K]^\top$ and $\boldsymbol{b} = \boldsymbol{0}$.
6 Distribute the text features $\{\boldsymbol{T}_k\}_{k=1}^K$ and CLIP image encoder to each client.
7 **for** *each round* $r \leftarrow 1$ **to** R **do**
8 | Server samples participated clients for training in this round.
9 | **for** *each client* c **do**
10 | Download model parameters $\boldsymbol{W}_c^r$ and $\boldsymbol{b}_c^r$ to local machine.
11 | **for** *each iteration* **do**
12 | Update soft pseudo labels for each $\boldsymbol{x}_j$ via Equation (4).
13 | Calculate self-training loss $\mathcal{L}_{iST}$ via Equation (3).
14 | Sample synthetic instances via Equation (5) and (7).
15 | Calculate synthetic loss $\mathcal{L}_{tSamp}$ via Equation (6).
16 | Update model parameters $\boldsymbol{W}_c^r \leftarrow \boldsymbol{W}_c^r - \eta \nabla_{\boldsymbol{W}_c^r}(\mathcal{L}_{iST} + \lambda \mathcal{L}_{tSamp})$ and $\boldsymbol{b}_c^r \leftarrow \boldsymbol{b}_c^r - \eta \nabla_{\boldsymbol{b}_c^r}(\mathcal{L}_{iST} + \lambda \mathcal{L}_{tSamp})$
17 | **end**
18 | Upload updated model parameters $\boldsymbol{W}_c^r$ and $\boldsymbol{b}_c^r$ to the server.
19 | **end**
20 | $\boldsymbol{W}^{r+1} \leftarrow \mathbb{E}_c[\boldsymbol{W}_c^r]$ and $\boldsymbol{b}^{r+1} \leftarrow \mathbb{E}_c[\boldsymbol{b}_c^r]$
21 **end**

---

strategy determines the number of synthetic instances, n_k, based on the following balancing equation:

$$m_k + n_k = (1 + \gamma)m_{k^*}, \quad 1 \le k \le K \tag{7}$$

where k^* denotes the class index with the largest number of predicted images on the considered client, such that $k^* = \arg\max_{k' \in \{1, \cdots, K\}} m_{k'}$; and $\gamma > 0$ controls the number of synthetic instances to be sampled for class k^*, specifically as $n_{k^*} = \gamma m_{k^*}$.

By utilizing all the pseudo-labeled real instances and generated synthetic instances, the linear classifier on each client is updated to minimize the following overall objective:

$$\min_{\boldsymbol{W}, \boldsymbol{b}} \quad \mathcal{L}_{iST} + \lambda \mathcal{L}_{tSamp} \tag{8}$$

where λ is the trade-off parameter. The overall training algorithm for the proposed lightweight unsupervised federated learning method, FST-CBDG, is presented in Algorithm 1.

4   Experiments

4.1   Experimental Settings

Datasets Partition. Following the experimental settings in [18], we have conducted experiments on three datasets: CIFAR-10 [17], CIFAR-100 [17], and CINIC-10 [3]. To emulate the federated learning scenario, we divide the data among $N = 100$ clients, ensuring no overlap. In each communication round, a random 10% of the clients participate in the federated training process. We have considered both homogeneous (i.i.d.) and heterogeneous (non-i.i.d.) data distribution settings. In the homogeneous setting, the data is evenly split and distributed to each client. In contrast, the heterogeneous setting involves the use of two widely recognized partition methods: *Sharding* and *Latent Dirichlet Allocation (LDA)*. *Sharding* involves sorting the data based on the labels and then dividing them into Ns shards where s represents the number of shards per client. Each client subsequently randomly selects s shards without replacement to constitute its local data. The parameter s controls the data heterogeneity, with smaller values of s leading to higher levels of data heterogeneity. We conducted experiments on all three datasets using various values: CIFAR-10 (s values of 2, 3, 5, and 10), CIFAR-100 (s value of 10) and CINIC-10 (s value of 2). On the other hand, the *LDA* method partitions each class of data to each client according to a Dirichlet distribution with a parameter α. For any given class k, each client i randomly samples a proportion p_{ki} of the data belonging to class k, where $p_{ki} \sim Dir(\alpha)$ and $\sum_{i=1}^{N} p_{ki} = 1$. The parameter α controls the data heterogeneity within each client, with smaller values of α indicating more severe data heterogeneity. In our experiments, we used various α values for the three datasets, CIFAR-10 (α values of 0.05, 0.1, 0.3, 0.5), CIFAR-100 (α value of 0.1) and CINIC-10 (α value of 0.1). It's important to note that in the context of unsupervised federated learning, all data within each client are unlabeled.

Implementation Details. CLIP offers various pretrained image encoders with different model architectures. Specifically, we chose a simple variant, 'RN50', in which the global average pooling layer of the original ResNet-50 model is replaced with an attention pooling mechanism [28]. The pretrained text encoder is based on a modified Transformer model [33]. The linear classifier has a input size of 1024, which matches the output size of the CLIP image encoder. We optimized the linear classifier using mini-batch Stochastic Gradient Descent (SGD) with a learning rate of 0.01, a momentum of 0.9 and a weight decay of 10^{-5}. For the proposed method, we set the moving average parameter of the pseudo-label updating β, to 0.9, and the class-balanced sampling parameter γ to 0. The trade-off parameter between the self-training and text sampling losses λ was set to 1. Given the lightweight setting, we limited the number of communication rounds to 10, and each client performed 1 local update epoch for each round. These settings were chosen to align with the computational and communication capacities of the local clients.

Table 1. Testing accuracy (%) under homogeneous data distribution. All methods utilize a pretrained and fixed CLIP image encoder (RN50). Supervised means training with labeled data while unsupervised means training with unlabeled data.

Methods	Supervised	CIFAR-10	CIFAR-100	CINIC-10
CLIP-ZS	-	68.7	39.0	63.2
CLIP-FC-Centralized	✓	77.5	42.9	70.4
FedAvg	✓	73.3	37.8	66.0
FedNTD	✓	72.8	39.8	66.2
FST-CBDG (ours)	✗	74.0	43.2	66.3

Table 2. Testing accuracy (%) under heterogeneous data distribution. All methods utilize a pretrained and fixed CLIP image encoder (RN50). Supervised means training with labeled data while unsupervised means training with unlabeled data.

		NIID Partition Strategy: Sharding					
Methods	Supervised	CIFAR-10				CIFAR-100	CINIC-10
		$s=2$	$s=3$	$s=5$	$s=10$	$s=10$	$s=2$
CLIP-ZS	-	68.7				39.0	63.2
CLIP-FC-Centralized	✓	77.5				42.9	70.4
FedAvg	✓	32.3	42.0	43.5	47.7	34.1	30.9
FedNTD	✓	42.0	64.1	47.6	55.6	26.6	35.8
FST-CBDG (ours)	✗	72.0	72.8	73.6	73.2	43.3	65.9

		NIID Partition Strategy: LDA.					
Method	Supervised	CIFAR-10				CIFAR-100	CINIC-10
		$\alpha=0.05$	$\alpha=0.1$	$\alpha=0.3$	$\alpha=0.5$	$\alpha=0.1$	$\alpha=0.1$
FedAvg	✓	20.1	32.4	41.9	45.1	16.4	29.1
FedNTD	✓	26.6	28.2	37.1	52.9	15.9	26.6
FST-CBDG (ours)	✗	71.5	71.9	72.2	72.4	43.1	65.0

Baselines. In our experiments, we compared our proposed method, FST-CBDG, with two baseline approaches and two representative supervised federated learning methods. CLIP-ZS represents using the pretrained CLIP model to make zero-shot prediction on the testing data. CLIP-FC-Centralized denotes that we train a linear classifier based on the fixed CLIP image encoder with SGD optimizer in a centralized manner. The classifier was trained on all the training data with labels and evaluated on the testing data. As comparison, FedAvg [27] and FedNTD [18] are adapted to train a linear classifier based on the fixed CLIP image encoder (RN50 variant) with labeled training data in each client. Our proposed method, FST-CBDG, differs from the above methods as it trains a linear classifier in a federated manner, but all the data in each client are unlabeled. This introduces a more challenging setting compared to the supervised federated learning methods.

4.2   Experimental Results

Performance on Homogeneous Data. In our evaluation under the homogeneous data distribution setting, we compared the performance of the proposed FST-CBDG method with several baselines, including CLIP-ZS, CLIP-FC-Centralized, FedAvg, and FedNTD, on three datasets: CIFAR-10, CIFAR-100, and CINIC-10. Here are the key findings from the results in Table 1. CLIP-ZS achieves decent performance on all three datasets. It serves as a strong baseline, leveraging the pretrained CLIP model's transfer capabilities. CLIP-FC-Centralized, which trains a linear classifier using the fixed CLIP image encoder and labeled training data in a centralized manner, significantly improves performance compared to CLIP-ZS. FedAvg and FedNTD, these supervised federated learning methods, which also train linear classifiers based on the fixed CLIP image encoder but with labeled data, outperform CLIP-ZS predictions. Our proposed method, FST-CBDG, which operates in a federated manner with unlabeled data, outperforms CLIP-ZS by a significant margin on all three datasets. It even surpasses the performance of the supervised federated learning methods, FedAvg and FedNTD. Notably, FST-CBDG achieves performance that is close to the centralized and supervised baseline, CLIP-FC-Centralized.

Performance on Heterogeneous Data. In our evaluation under the more challenging setting of heterogeneous data distribution, we considered two different data construction strategies: *Sharding* and *LDA*. Here are the key findings from the results in Table 2. Compared with the CLIP-ZS baseline, our method FST-CBDG consistently enhances model performance across all three datasets in the challenging heterogeneous setting. FST-CBDG also outperforms the supervised federated learning methods across different datasets and heterogeneous data partition strategies even though our method trains the model without labels. It's interesting to notice that the supervised federated learning methods fail under the lightweight heterogeneous federated learning setting even though labeled data are given. With limited communication rounds and local update epochs, FedAvg and FedNTD cannot preserve the initial performance of the CLIP zero-shot predictions. On the one hand, the strong supervision from the labeled data introduce negatives transferring effect to the linear model. On the other hand, data heterogeneity in the local client leads to biased local models thus biased aggregated global model while FedAvg and FedNTD failed to address this under the lightweight setting. However, our method FST-CBDG not only consistently improve the performance starting from the CLIP zero-shot prediction through the proposed resilient self-training method, but also reduce the influence of data heterogeneity by sampling synthetic instances.

Computation and Communication Efficiency. The proposed lightweight federated learning from unlabeled data framework significantly reduces the computation and communication requirements for the local clients. Since the training and communication overload only involves a linear classifier, the overall computation and communication efficiency are primarily impacted by the convergence

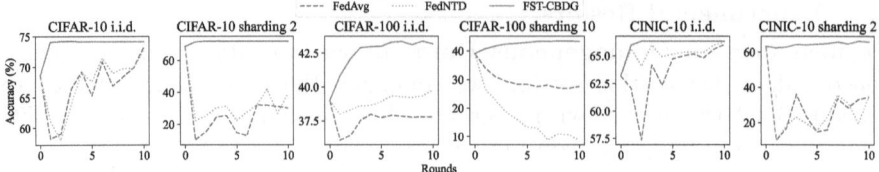

Fig. 3. Curves of the testing accuracy (%) w.r.t. communication rounds for the proposed method FST-CBDG and the two comparison methods, FedAvg and FedNTD under homogeneous (i.i.d.) and heterogeneous (Sharding) data distribution.

Table 3. Ablation study to evaluate each component. Test accuracy (%) on each dataset under i.i.d. and non-i.i.d. (Sharding) data distribution.

Method	CIFAR-10		CIFAR-100	
	$s=2$	i.i.d.	$s=10$	i.i.d.
CLIP-ZS	68.7		39.0	
$\mathcal{L}_{iST}$	68.9	68.2	37.5	37.5
$\mathcal{L}_{tSamp}$	68.9	65.7	37.3	35.5
$\mathcal{L}_{tSamp}$ (Centralized)	69.4	69.4	39.1	39.1
$\mathcal{L}_{iST} + \mathcal{L}_{tSamp}$	72.0	74.0	43.3	43.2

speed. Figure 3 displays the testing accuracy curves concerning the communication rounds for all three datasets. FST-CBDG exhibits rapid convergence in both homogeneous and heterogeneous data distribution settings. While the two comparison methods, FedAvg and FedNTD, fail to maintain this initial accuracy, FST-CBDG consistently improves accuracy and achieves near-optimal performance within a few communication rounds: CIFAR-10 (1 round), CIFAR-100 (6 rounds), and CINIC-10 (1 round). This indicates that the proposed method significantly improves the computation and communication efficiency for the federated learning system.

4.3 Ablation Study

Components. In our ablation study, we examined the effects of the self-training loss and synthetic instance sampling loss in our proposed method. The results are presented in Table 3. Denoted as $\mathcal{L}_{iST}$, training the local linear classifier with the self-training loss alone does not lead to performance gain over the CLIP-ZS baseline under both homogeneous and heterogeneous settings. Fitting the linear classifier with local client data only disrupts the original fine-grained textual features from the CLIP textual encoder with image features from local data, introducing negative transfer effects and decreasing the original CLIP zero-shot performance. On the other hand, denoted as $\mathcal{L}_{tSamp}$, fine-tuning the linear classifier with synthetic textual instances only also decreases the CLIP model zero-shot performance. As revealed in Fig. 2, the CLIP zero-shot model tends to make

Table 4. Ablation study to evaluate sampling strategy. Test accuracy (%) on each dataset under i.i.d. and non-i.i.d. (Sharding) data distribution.

Sampling strategy	CIFAR-10		CIFAR-100	
	s=10	i.i.d.	s=10	i.i.d.
Equal sampling	68.6	68.6	37.4	37.4
Balanced sampling	73.2	74.0	43.3	43.2

predictions with high entropy, indicating large similarities among the textual features. Fine-tuning the linear classifier initialized with these textual features based on the hard-labeled synthetic instances leads to overfitting, decreasing the CLIP model zero-shot performance on the downstream task. Centralized training with these synthetic instances, denoted as $\mathcal{L}_{tSamp}$(Centralized), also confirms this. To this end, our method combines both losses $(\mathcal{L}_{iST}+\mathcal{L}_{tSamp})$ to fine-tune the linear classifier, balancing the local and synthetic data fitting. The results demonstrate significant improvements over the baseline, underscoring the necessity of both components for our approach.

Sampling Strategy. We conducted experiments to assess the effectiveness of our proposed class-balanced sampling strategy, as outlined in Eq. 7, by comparing it to another sampling strategy, equal sampling. The equal sampling strategy involves sampling the same number of synthetic instances for each class, irrespective of the number of images per class in the local client. The results are presented in Table 4. In the non-i.i.d. setting, balanced sampling eliminates the effect of data heterogeneity by sampling synthetic instances to balance the local training data in each category. In the i.i.d. setting, as the lack of data annotation, pseudo labels still introduce possible class imbalance and further introduce bias to the local model. As the number of samples for each category is calculated with pseudo-labels, balanced sampling still supplements data for categories with fewer pseudo labeled data. However, equal sampling fails to address both cases. This highlights the effectiveness of our carefully designed sampling strategy in improving model performance.

5   Conclusion

In this paper, we proposed a novel lightweight unsupervised federated learning approach, FST-CBDG, to alleviate the computational and communication costs, as well as the high data annotation requirements typically associated with standard federated learning for deep models. By capitalizing on the petrained visual-language model CLIP, the proposed method devises an efficient and resilient self-training approach to progressively refine the initial pseudo-labels produced by CLIP and learn a linear classifier on top of the fixed CLIP image encoder. Additionally, we propose a class-balanced synthetic instance generation method based on the class prototypes produced by the CLIP text encoder to address data heterogeneity within each client. The experimental results on multiple datasets demonstrate that the proposed method greatly improves model performance in comparison to CLIP's zero-shot predictions and outperforms supervised federated learning benchmark methods given limited computational and communication overhead.

References

1. Chen, Z., Liu, G., Zhang, B.W., Yang, Q., Wu, L.: AltCLIP: altering the language encoder in CLIP for extended language capabilities. In: Findings of the Association for Computational Linguistics: ACL 2023 (2023)
2. Chia, P.J., et al.: Contrastive language and vision learning of general fashion concepts. Sci. Rep. (2022)
3. Darlow, L.N., Crowley, E.J., Antoniou, A., Storkey, A.J.: Cinic-10 is not imagenet or cifar-10. arXiv preprint arXiv:1810.03505 (2018)
4. DeVries, T., Taylor, G.W.: Dataset augmentation in feature space. arXiv preprint arXiv:1702.05538 (2017)
5. Diao, E., Ding, J., Tarokh, V.: Semifl: semi-supervised federated learning for unlabeled clients with alternate training. In: NeurIPS (2022)
6. Dunlap, L., et al.: Using language to extend to unseen domains. In: ICLR (2023)
7. Elgabli, A., Issaid, C.B., Bedi, A.S., Rajawat, K., Bennis, M., Aggarwal, V.: Fednew: a communication-efficient and privacy-preserving newton-type method for federated learning. In: ICML (2022)
8. Gu, X., Lin, T.Y., Kuo, W., Cui, Y.: Open-vocabulary object detection via vision and language knowledge distillation. In: ICLR (2022)
9. Guo, T., Guo, S., Wang, J.: pFedPrompt: learning personalized prompt for vision-language models in federated learning. In: Proceedings of the ACM Web Conference 2023 (2023)
10. Guo, Y., Tang, X., Lin, T.: Fedbr: improving federated learning on heterogeneous data via local learning bias reduction. In: ICML (2023)
11. Hsu, T.M.H., Qi, H., Brown, M.: Measuring the effects of non-identical data distribution for federated visual classification. arXiv preprint arXiv:1909.06335 (2019)
12. Huang, Z., Bianchi, F., Yuksekgonul, M., Montine, T.J., Zou, J.: A visual–language foundation model for pathology image analysis using medical twitter. Nat. Med. (2023)
13. Jeong, W., Yoon, J., Yang, E., Hwang, S.J.: Federated semi-supervised learning with inter-client consistency & disjoint learning. In: ICLR (2021)
14. Jia, C., et al.: Scaling up visual and vision-language representation learning with noisy text supervision. In: ICML (2021)
15. Karimireddy, S.P., Kale, S., Mohri, M., Reddi, S., Stich, S., Suresh, A.T.: Scaffold: stochastic controlled averaging for federated learning. In: ICML (2020)
16. Kim, J., Kim, G., Han, B.: Multi-level branched regularization for federated learning. In: ICML (2022)
17. Krizhevsky, A., Hinton, G., et al.: Learning multiple layers of features from tiny images (2009)
18. Lee, G., Jeong, M., Shin, Y., Bae, S., Yun, S.Y.: Preservation of the global knowledge by not-true distillation in federated learning. In: NeurIPS (2022)

19. Li, J., Li, D., Xiong, C., Hoi, S.: Blip: bootstrapping language-image pre-training for unified vision-language understanding and generation. In: ICML (2022)
20. Li, Q., He, B., Song, D.: Model-contrastive federated learning. In: CVPR (2021)
21. Li, T., Sahu, A.K., Zaheer, M., Sanjabi, M., Talwalkar, A., Smith, V.: Federated optimization in heterogeneous networks. In: MLSys (2020)
22. Lin, X., et al.: Federated learning with positive and unlabeled data. In: ICML (2022)
23. Lu, N., Wang, Z., Li, X., Niu, G., Dou, Q., Sugiyama, M.: Federated learning from only unlabeled data with class-conditional-sharing clients. In: ICLR (2022)
24. Lu, W., Hu, X., Wang, J., Xie, X.: Fedclip: fast generalization and personalization for clip in federated learning. arXiv preprint arXiv:2302.13485 (2023)
25. Lüddecke, T., Ecker, A.: Image segmentation using text and image prompts. In: CVPR (2022)
26. Luo, M., Chen, F., Hu, D., Zhang, Y., Liang, J., Feng, J.: No fear of heterogeneity: classifier calibration for federated learning with non-IID data. In: NeurIPS (2021)
27. McMahan, B., Moore, E., Ramage, D., Hampson, S., y Arcas, B.A.: Communication-efficient learning of deep networks from decentralized data. In: AISTATS (2017)
28. Radford, A., et al.: Learning transferable visual models from natural language supervision. In: ICML (2021)
29. Reddi, S., et al.: Adaptive federated optimization. In: ICLR (2021)
30. Singh, A., et al.: Flava: a foundational language and vision alignment model. In: CVPR (2022)
31. Sun, Y., Shen, L., Chen, S., Ding, L., Tao, D.: Dynamic regularized sharpness aware minimization in federated learning: approaching global consistency and smooth landscape. In: ICML (2023)
32. Tan, Y., Long, G., Ma, J., Liu, L., Zhou, T., Jiang, J.: Federated learning from pre-trained models: a contrastive learning approach. In: NeurIPS (2022)
33. Vaswani, A., et al.: Attention is all you need. In: NeurIPS (2017)
34. Wang, J., Liu, Q., Liang, H., Joshi, G., Poor, H.V.: Tackling the objective inconsistency problem in heterogeneous federated optimization. In: NeurIPS (2020)
35. Wang, Z., Yu, J., Yu, A.W., Dai, Z., Tsvetkov, Y., Cao, Y.: Simvlm: simple visual language model pretraining with weak supervision. In: ICLR (2022)
36. Ye, R., Xu, M., Wang, J., Xu, C., Chen, S., Wang, Y.: Feddisco: federated learning with discrepancy-aware collaboration. In: ICML (2023)
37. Zhang, Z., et al.: Improving semi-supervised federated learning by reducing the gradient diversity of models. In: 2021 IEEE International Conference on Big Data (Big Data) (2021)
38. Zhu, F., Zhang, X.Y., Wang, C., Yin, F., Liu, C.L.: Prototype augmentation and self-supervision for incremental learning. In: CVPR (2021)

Enhancing Causal Discovery in Federated Settings with Limited Local Samples

Xianjie Guo[1] , Liping Yi[2] , Xiaohu Wu[3] , Kui Yu[1]([⊠]) ,
and Gang Wang[2]

[1] School of Computer Science and Information Engineering,
Hefei University of Technology, Hefei, China
xianjieguo@mail.hfut.edu.cn, yukui@hfut.edu.cn
[2] College of Computer Science, Nankai University, Tianjin, China
{yiliping,wgzwp}@nbjl.nankai.edu.cn
[3] National Engineering Research Center of Mobile Network Technologies,
Beijing University of Posts and Telecommunications, Beijing, China
xiaohu.wu@bupt.edu.cn

Abstract. Causal discovery from observational data is crucial for understanding complex systems, but traditional methods often require centralized data, conflicting with growing privacy concerns. Although federated causal discovery (FCD) has emerged as a solution, existing methods struggle when individual clients possess limited local samples. This paper introduces FedECD, a novel approach addressing causal discovery in federated settings with limited local samples. FedECD comprises two phases: 1) Federated Causal Skeleton Optimization and 2) Federated Causal Structure Refinement, both leveraging Bootstrapping techniques to enhance robustness and accuracy across distributed clients. Both phases employ a two-layer aggregation strategy: client-layer aggregates results from Bootstrapped sub-datasets within each client, while server-layer aggregates across all clients. The first phase uses weighted aggregation to iteratively remove false causal edges based on conditional independence tests. In contrast, the second phase utilizes majority voting to determine edge directions, ensuring robust estimation of the true causal structure. Extensive experiments on eight benchmark Bayesian network datasets demonstrate the superiority of FedECD over existing FCD methods, particularly with limited sample sizes. FedECD achieves an average improvement of 7.53% in the Ar_F1 score compared to the best baseline, addressing a critical challenge in FCD.

Keywords: Federated learning · Causal discovery · Bootstrapping · Bayesian network · Limited local samples

1 Introduction

Background. Causal discovery (CD) aims to uncover causal relationships between variables or events, often represented as causal structures, from observational data [4,8,9,11,23]. It is a promising approach to address the limitations

H. Yu et al. (Eds.): FL 2024 Workshops, LNAI 15501, pp. 164–179, 2025.
https://doi.org/10.1007/978-3-031-82240-7_12

of current machine learning techniques, particularly deep learning, which often lack robustness and interpretability [22, 25, 38]. Developing effective CD methods is crucial for realizing the "high-value" transformation of big data [33]. Numerous studies have sought to discover causal relationships in various fields, including medicine [29], computer science [21], and bioinformatics [18], to enable inference and analysis of events.

Traditionally, CD methods require large-scale datasets aggregated from multiple decentralized data centers to achieve satisfactory performance. However, with the development of big data and an increasing international emphasis on data privacy protection, data collection has become increasingly costly and often prohibited by privacy protection laws and regulations [17, 20]. To address these challenges, federated causal discovery (FCD) has emerged as a novel direction [7, 10, 14, 19, 27]. FCD leverages the privacy-preserving capabilities of the federated learning (FL) paradigm [36] to achieve satisfactory CD performance while protecting data privacy, allowing each client (institution or organization) to keep their data local. For example, in healthcare, multiple hospitals may wish to collaboratively discover causal relationships among various symptoms and diseases without sharing sensitive patient data. FCD enables these institutions to jointly learn a causal model while keeping their individual datasets confidential.

Motivation. Although existing FCD algorithms have achieved satisfactory performance in various scenarios (e.g., data heterogeneity [19], nonlinear causal relationships [27], high-dimensional data [10]), they have primarily focused on data privacy issues while overlooking another critical challenge in federated learning scenarios: the limited sample size problem [16]. This problem arises when each FL client holds a very limited number of samples, which can severely degrade the performance of existing FCD methods. To visually illustrate this challenge, we conducted extensive experiments using a state-of-the-art FCD method, FedPC [14], on three benchmark Bayesian network (BN) datasets: Child, Insurance, and Alarm[1]. We generated multiple batches of datasets with varying sample sizes from these BNs. Setting the total number of clients to 10, we allocated an average sample size per client ranging from 150 to 1,000. We then ran the FedPC algorithm under different dataset scenarios and compared the learned causal structures with the ground truth using two common metrics: Ar_F1 and SHD [14]. The experimental results are shown in Fig. 1, and we can observe that when the average sample size per client falls below 350 (in the range [150, 350]), the performance of FedPC drops dramatically. This indicates that the limited sample sizes per client in federated scenarios significantly impact the performance of existing FCD algorithms.

Inspired by existing studies [2, 6] that have demonstrated the efficacy of Bootstrapping [13] in scenarios with limited sample sizes, we pose a critical question: can we leverage Bootstrapping techniques to resample local client data, thereby

---

[1] These benchmark Bayesian networks are publicly available at http://www.bnlearn.com/bnrepository/.

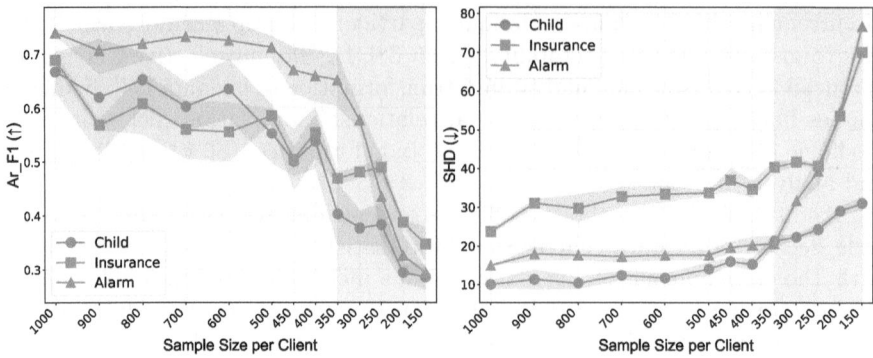

Fig. 1. Performance of the FedPC algorithm under varying sample sizes per client.

addressing the challenges posed by limited sample sizes and ultimately enhancing the performance of FCD in these demanding settings?

Contributions. In this paper, we focus on enhancing FCD performance in scenarios where each FL client holds very limited samples. We propose the FedECD algorithm, which consists of two phases:

- Phase 1: *Federated Causal Skeleton Optimization Using Bootstrapping.*
  FedECD employs a two-layer causal skeleton aggregation strategy. In the first layer, clients internally aggregate causal skeletons learned from resampled sub-datasets generated via Bootstrapping. In the second layer, the server aggregates the causal skeletons returned by each FL client. This strategy helps prevent the loss of true causal edges that might occur due to the small sample sizes of individual clients.
- Phase 2: *Federated Causal Structure Refinement Leveraging Bootstrapping.*
  FedECD utilizes a two-layer causal structure aggregation strategy. In the first layer, clients internally aggregate causal structures learned from resampled datasets generated via Bootstrapping. In the second layer, the server aggregates the causal structures returned by each client. This strategy helps mitigate issues of incorrect edge orientations in causal structures that might arise due to the small sample sizes of individual clients.

To the best of our knowledge, FedECD is the first algorithm to tackle the challenge of limited local samples in FCD scenarios. Extensive experiments on eight benchmark Bayesian network datasets demonstrate the superiority of FedECD over seven state-of-the-art baselines, with an average improvement of 7.53% in the Ar_F1 score compared to the best baseline.

2   Related Work

Federated causal discovery (FCD) has emerged as a critical research direction, addressing the need to uncover causal relationships between variables from decentralized data while preserving privacy. In this section, we provide a comprehensive overview of existing approaches in FCD.

2.1 Continuous Optimization-Based Methods

Early FCD algorithms derived primarily from continuous optimization-based CD methods. These methods became pioneers in FCD largely due to their foundation in gradient descent techniques, which allowed them to directly leverage the various optimization strategies already well-developed in the field of federated learning (FL). This natural compatibility made the extension of CD methods to federated learning settings relatively straightforward and effective.

Specifically, NOTEARS-ADMM [27] adapted the NOTEARS algorithm [40] to a federated setting using the ADMM [3] optimization method. Importantly, the authors proposed two versions: NOTEARS-ADMM for linear causal relationships, and NOTEARS-MLP-ADMM for nonlinear causal relationships. The latter employs multilayer perceptrons (MLPs) to model complex, nonlinear interactions between variables, significantly extending the applicability of the method to more realistic scenarios. Building on this foundation, FedDAG [7] introduced a two-level structure in local models, separating graph structure learning from causal mechanism approximation. This design allowed each client to adapt to its local data characteristics while contributing to the learning of a global causal structure through gradient-based optimization. FedCausal [35] proposed a global optimization formula to aggregate causal graphs from client data while constraining the acyclicity of the global graph. Its flexible optimization objective enables adaptive handling of both homogeneous and heterogeneous data, further advancing FCD's capability in dealing with complex data environments.

2.2 Constraint-Based Methods

Constraint-based methods in FCD focus on learning causal structures through conditional independence tests performed across distributed datasets. FedPC [14] adapted the PC algorithm [30] to a federated setting, introducing a layer-wise aggregation strategy for skeleton learning and a consistent separation sets identifying strategy for skeleton orientation. This approach showed promise in handling larger-scale problems but faced data heterogeneity challenges. Very similar to FedPC, FedC^{2}SL [34] developed a federated conditional independence test protocol to minimize privacy leakages and address client heterogeneity. To further address the challenge of data heterogeneity in FCD, FedCDH [19] introduced a surrogate variable to account for distribution differences across clients. It proposed a federated conditional independence test (FCIT) for skeleton discovery and a federated independent change principle (FICP) for causal direction determination, making no assumptions about specific functional forms.

2.3 Hybrid and Novel Optimization Methods

Some approaches have combined elements from multiple categories or introduced novel optimization techniques. Specifically, DARLS [37] proposed a method simulating an annealing process to search over the space of topological sorts. It used distributed optimization to find the optimal graphical structure, providing theoretical guarantees of convergence to an Oracle solution. FedCSL [10] introduced a federated local-to-global learning strategy to improve scalability for high-dimensional data. It also proposed a novel weighted aggregation strategy to handle uneven sample allocation across clients without compromising privacy. PERI [24] introduced an approach based on distributed min-max regret optimization. By sharing only regret information, PERI achieves federated causal discovery while minimizing the amount of information exchanged between clients and the central server. FED-CD [1] introduced a framework for inferring causal structures from both observational and interventional data in a privacy-preserving manner. It proposed a knowledge aggregation method based on proximity to interventions within the global causal structure.

Although existing FCD approaches have addressed various challenges, including data heterogeneity, scalability, and privacy concerns, a critical issue remains largely unexplored: the performance degradation in scenarios with limited local samples. This challenge is particularly acute in real-world federated learning applications, where individual clients often possess small sample sizes. In this paper, we propose FedECD to tackle this overlooked problem by introducing a novel Bootstrapping-based approach, enhancing causal discovery in federated settings with limited local samples.

3   Preliminaries

3.1   Notations and Assumptions

Let $\mathcal{X} = \{X_1, X_2, ..., X_d\}$ be a set of d variables, and $\mathcal{C} = \{c_1, c_2, ..., c_m\}$ be a set of m clients. We consider a horizontal FL setting, where clients have large overlaps in the variable space but little overlap in the sample space. For each client c_k ($k \in \{1, 2, ..., m\}$), $\mathcal{D}^{c_k} \in \mathbb{R}^{n_{c_k} \times d}$ represents its local dataset, where n_{c_k} is the number of samples. Each sample in $\mathcal{D}^{c_k}$ is independently drawn from the probability distribution $\mathbb{P}^{c_k}(\mathcal{X})$. We define $\mathcal{D}^{\mathcal{C}} = \{\mathcal{D}^{c_1}, \mathcal{D}^{c_2}, ..., \mathcal{D}^{c_m}\}$ as the decentralized dataset and $\mathbb{P}^{\mathcal{C}}(\mathcal{X}) = \{\mathbb{P}^{c_1}(\mathcal{X}), \mathbb{P}^{c_2}(\mathcal{X}), ..., \mathbb{P}^{c_m}(\mathcal{X})\}$ as the decentralized probability distribution set. Causal relationships over $\mathcal{X}$ are often represented by a causal directed acyclic graph (DAG). In a causal DAG, if there is a direct edge $X_{i_1} \rightarrow X_{i_2}$ ($i_1, i_2 \in \{1, 2, ..., d\}$), X_{i_1} is a direct cause of X_{i_2}, and X_{i_2} is a direct effect of X_{i_1} [28].

A causal DAG serves as the fundamental graphical structure for Bayesian networks (BNs), where a BN extends the DAG by associating each node with a conditional probability distribution that quantifies the relationship between a node and its parents, thereby transforming a purely structural representation into a complete probabilistic model capable of encoding both qualitative relationships through its graph structure and quantitative dependencies through its probability distributions.

Definition 1 (Bayesian Network [30]). *Given a causal DAG $\mathcal{G}$ and a joint probability distribution $\mathbb{P}$ over a set of random variables $\mathcal{X}$, the triplet $<$*

$\mathcal{X}, \mathcal{G}, \mathbb{P} >$ *is called a Bayesian network if it satisfies the Markov condition: each variable in $\mathcal{G}$ is conditionally independent of any subset of its non-descendants given its parent variables.*

Definition 2 (D-Separation [30]). *In a causal DAG $\mathcal{G}$, a path γ is d-separated (or blocked) by a variable set $\boldsymbol{S} \subset \mathcal{X}$ if and only if: 1) γ contains a chain $X_{i_1} \to X_{i_3} \to X_{i_2}$ or a fork $X_{i_1} \leftarrow X_{i_3} \to X_{i_2}$ with the middle variable $X_{i_3} \in \boldsymbol{S}$, or 2) γ contains an inverted fork (or collider) $X_{i_1} \to X_{i_3} \leftarrow X_{i_2}$ with $X_{i_3} \notin \boldsymbol{S}$ and X_{i_3}'s descendants $\notin \boldsymbol{S}$.*

Two variables X_{i_1} and X_{i_2} are d-separated by a variable set $\boldsymbol{S}$ if and only if $\boldsymbol{S}$ blocks every path from X_{i_1} to X_{i_2}. We call such a set $\boldsymbol{S}$ a separation set of X_{i_1} from X_{i_2}.

Definition 3 (Faithfulness [30]). *Given a BN $< \mathcal{X}, \mathcal{G}, \mathbb{P} >$, the probability distribution $\mathbb{P}$ is faithful to the DAG $\mathcal{G}$ if and only if for any variables $X_i, X_j \in \mathcal{X}$ and any subset $\boldsymbol{S} \subseteq \mathcal{X} \setminus \{X_i, X_j\}$, the following equivalence holds: $X_i \perp\!\!\!\perp X_j | \boldsymbol{S}$ in $\mathbb{P} \iff X_i$ and X_j are d-separated by $\boldsymbol{S}$ in $\mathcal{G}$.*

The Faithfulness assumption establishes a relation between a probability distribution $\mathbb{P}$ and its underlying DAG $\mathcal{G}$. In a BN, this assumption implies that two variables $X_{i_1}, X_{i_2} \in \mathcal{X}$ that are conditionally independent given a subset $\boldsymbol{S} \subseteq \mathcal{X} \setminus \{X_{i_1}, X_{i_2}\}$ in $\mathbb{P}$ are d-separated by $\boldsymbol{S}$ in $\mathcal{G}$.

Definition 4 (Causal Sufficiency [28,30]). *A set of variables $\mathcal{X}$ satisfies causal sufficiency if and only if for any variables $X_{i_1}, X_{i_2} \in \mathcal{X}$, every common cause of X_{i_1} and X_{i_2} is also in $\mathcal{X}$.*

Under the assumptions of Faithfulness and Causal Sufficiency, we can use conditional independence (CI) tests to find all dependencies or independencies entailed in a BN.

Definition 5 (Conditional Independence). *For $\forall i_1, i_2 \in \{1, 2, ..., d\}$, two variables X_{i_1} and X_{i_2} are conditionally independent given a variable set $\boldsymbol{S} \subseteq \mathcal{X} \setminus \{X_{i_1}, X_{i_2}\}$ if $P(X_{i_1}, X_{i_2}|\boldsymbol{S}) = P(X_{i_1}|\boldsymbol{S})P(X_{i_2}|\boldsymbol{S})$; otherwise, they are conditionally dependent given $\boldsymbol{S}$.*

We denote conditional independence between variables X_{i_1} and X_{i_2} given a set of variables $\boldsymbol{S}$ as $X_{i_1} \perp\!\!\!\perp X_{i_2}|\boldsymbol{S}$. To evaluate these conditional independence relationships in our experiments, we employ the G^2 test [30], a likelihood-ratio alternative to the conventional χ^2 test. The G^2 statistic is defined as:

$$G^2 = 2 \sum_{a,b,v} H_{i_1,i_2,\boldsymbol{S}}^{a,b,v} \ln(\frac{H_{i_1,i_2,\boldsymbol{S}}^{a,b,v} H_{\boldsymbol{S}}^{v}}{H_{i_1,\boldsymbol{S}}^{a,v} H_{i_2,\boldsymbol{S}}^{b,v}}), \tag{1}$$

where $H_{i_1,i_2,\boldsymbol{S}}^{a,b,v}$ denotes the number of counts satisfying $X_{i_1} = a$, $X_{i_2} = b$ and $\boldsymbol{S} = v$, and $H_{\boldsymbol{S}}^{v}$, $H_{i_1,\boldsymbol{S}}^{a,v}$ and $H_{i_2,\boldsymbol{S}}^{b,v}$ are defined similarly. The G^2 statistic is asymptotically distributed as χ^2 with degrees of freedom (df) calculated as:

$$df = (r_{i_1} - 1)(r_{i_2} - 1) \prod_{X_{i_3} \in \boldsymbol{S}} r_{i_3}, \tag{2}$$

where r_{i_1}, r_{i_2} and r_{i_3} are the domains (number of distinct values) of X_{i_1}, X_{i_2} and X_{i_3}, respectively. Given a significance level α and the p-value ρ returned by the G^2 test, under the null hypothesis $H_0 : X_{i_1} \perp\!\!\!\perp X_{i_2}|\boldsymbol{S}$, we conclude that $X_{i_1} \perp\!\!\!\perp X_{i_2}|\boldsymbol{S}$ holds if and only if $\rho > \alpha$.

Federated causal discovery (FCD) aims to identify a causal DAG $\mathcal{G}$ from all local datasets $\mathcal{D}^{c_k}{}_{k\in\{1,2,...,m\}}$ in a privacy-preserving manner. We make the following assumption:

Assumption 1 (Invariant Causal DAG [7]). *All local datasets are uniformly sampled from the same causal DAG $\mathcal{G}$, although the probability distribution of samples for the same variable space can differ across different clients.*

By performing CI tests and identifying d-separation relationships among random variables, we can infer the entire graph structure in a federated setting while preserving data privacy.

3.2   Bootstrapping Technique

This paper proposes a novel Bootstrapping-based approach to enhance causal discovery in federated settings with limited local samples. To understand the rationale behind this choice, it's important first to discuss the concept of ensemble learning and its connection to Bootstrapping.

Ensemble learning is a widely adopted machine learning approach that combines multiple models to solve a problem, often achieving superior generalization performance compared to single models [15]. Bootstrapping [13], a resampling technique, plays a crucial role in creating diverse datasets for ensemble methods. Given an original dataset D_{orig}, the process of resampling through Bootstrapping for generating a sub-dataset D_1 is as follows:

– Randomly selecting an instance from D_{orig} and adding it to D_1. The selected instance is then returned to D_{orig}, allowing for potential resampling.
– Repeating this procedure n times to create D_1 containing n instances.

A key property of Bootstrapping, which makes it particularly useful for our purposes, is captured in the following proposition:

Proposition 1 ([13]). *When generating a sub-dataset D_1 from an original dataset D_{orig} using Bootstrapping, as $n \to \infty$, approximately 36.8% of the samples in D_{orig} will not appear in D_1.*

Proof. For each sample in D_{orig} (with n samples), the probability that it will never be picked up in n times sampling is $(1 - \frac{1}{n})^n$. Since $\lim_{n\to\infty} (1 - \frac{1}{n})^n = \frac{1}{e} \approx 0.368$, when the sample size tends to infinity, approximately 36.8% of the samples in D_{orig} will not be added to D_1 (with n samples).

This property ensures diversity in the resampled datasets, which is crucial for the effectiveness of ensemble learning approaches. In the context of federated causal discovery with limited local samples, Bootstrapping offers a powerful tool to artificially increase the diversity of data available to each client, potentially improving the robustness and statistical reliability of the causal discovery process by generating multiple resampled datasets from the original data distribution.

To address the inherent challenges of limited local sample sizes in federated settings, our proposed method incorporates Bootstrapping to generate multiple statistical replicates of the local datasets. This statistical augmentation enables more reliable causal discovery even when individual clients possess datasets that may be insufficient for traditional causal discovery methods.

4 The Proposed FedECD Method

The FedECD method is designed to address the challenge of causal discovery in federated settings with limited local samples. Our approach leverages Bootstrapping techniques [13] to enhance the robustness and accuracy of causal discovery across distributed clients. The FedECD method consists of two main phases (Fig. 2): 1) *Federated Causal Skeleton Optimization Using Bootstrapping*; and 2) *Federated Causal Structure Refinement Leveraging Bootstrapping*. In both phases, we employ a two-layer (*client-layer* and *server-layer*) aggregation strategy: the *client-layer* aggregates results from Bootstrapped sub-datasets within each client, while the *server-layer* aggregates results across all clients at the server. This approach allows us to effectively utilize limited local samples while preserving data privacy in the federated setting.

4.1 Federated Causal Skeleton Optimization Using Bootstrapping

The first phase of FedECD focuses on learning an optimized causal skeleton through a federated process that incorporates Bootstrapping. We use $\mathcal{S}$ to denote the current global skeleton, and $\mathcal{S}(i_1, i_2) = \mathcal{S}(i_2, i_1) = 1$ $(i_1, i_2 \in \{1, 2, \ldots, d\})$ to represent that there is an undirected edge between X_{i_1} and X_{i_2} in $\mathcal{S}$. We start with a fully connected undirected graph (skeleton) and iteratively remove false edges based on CI tests [30] performed on the local dataset of each client and the resampled sub-datasets generated by using Bootstrapping. The skeleton optimization process proceeds as follows.

1. Initialize the conditioning set size $|\boldsymbol{S}| = 0$ for any CI tests between X_{i_1} and X_{i_2} conditioning on a subset $\boldsymbol{S} \subseteq \mathcal{X} \setminus \{X_{i_1}, X_{i_2}\}$ $(i_1, i_2 \in \{1, 2, \ldots, d\})$.
2. For each client $c_k \in \mathcal{C}$, perform CI tests on its local dataset $\mathcal{D}^{c_k}$:

$$\mathcal{S}^{c_k}(i_1, i_2) = \mathcal{S}^{c_k}(i_2, i_1) = \begin{cases} 0, & \text{if } X_{i_1} \perp\!\!\!\perp X_{i_2} | \boldsymbol{S} \\ 1, & \text{otherwise.} \end{cases} \tag{3}$$

The server aggregates skeletons from all clients:

$$\mathcal{S}(i_1, i_2) = \frac{1}{m} \sum_{k=1}^{m} \mathcal{S}^{c_k}(i_1, i_2),$$

$$\mathcal{S}(i_1, i_2) = \begin{cases} 1, & \text{if } \mathcal{S}(i_1, i_2) \geq 0.5 \\ 0, & \text{otherwise.} \end{cases} \tag{4}$$

Determine the set of edges that may be removed: $\mathcal{E}_{\text{del}} = \{(i_1, i_2) | \mathcal{S}(i_1, i_2) = 0\}$.

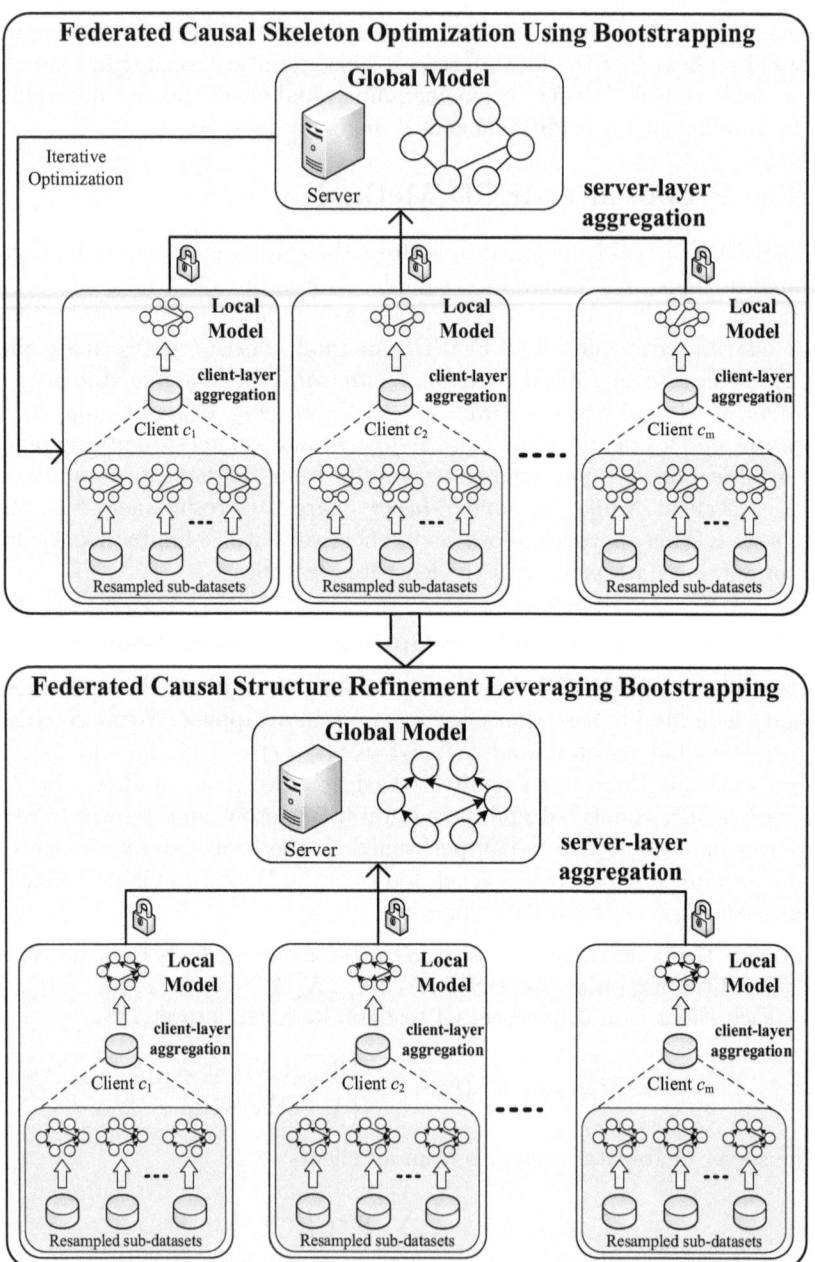

Fig. 2. The framework of FedECD, which consists of two phases.

3. For each client $c_k \in \mathcal{C}$: a) Generate B sub-datasets $\{\mathcal{D}_1^{c_k}, \mathcal{D}_2^{c_k}, ..., \mathcal{D}_B^{c_k}\}$ using Bootstrapping. b) For each sub-dataset $\mathcal{D}_j^{c_k}$, compute the weighted skeleton $\hat{\mathcal{S}}_j^{c_k}$:

$$\hat{\mathcal{S}}_j^{c_k}(i_1, i_2) = \begin{cases} w(\rho), & \text{if } (i_1, i_2) \in \mathcal{E}_{\text{del}} \wedge X_{i_1} \perp\!\!\!\perp X_{i_2} | \boldsymbol{S} \\ 0, & \text{otherwise}, \end{cases} \quad (5)$$

where $w(\rho)$ is a function mapping p-values ρ returned by CI tests to the $[0, 1]$ interval. c) Aggregate weighted skeletons within the client (***client-layer aggregation***):

$$\hat{\mathcal{S}}^{c_k}(i_1, i_2) = \frac{1}{B} \sum_{j=1}^{B} \hat{\mathcal{S}}_j^{c_k}(i_1, i_2). \quad (6)$$

4. The server aggregates weighted skeletons from all clients (***server-layer aggregation***) and updates the global skeleton:

$$\hat{\mathcal{S}}(i_1, i_2) = \frac{1}{m} \sum_{k=1}^{m} \hat{\mathcal{S}}^{c_k}(i_1, i_2),$$

$$\mathcal{S}(i_1, i_2) = \begin{cases} 0, & \text{if } (i_1, i_2) \in \mathcal{E}_{\text{del}} \wedge \mathcal{S}(i_1, i_2) > \tau \\ 1, & \text{if } (i_1, i_2) \in \mathcal{E}_{\text{del}} \wedge \mathcal{S}(i_1, i_2) \leq \tau, \end{cases} \quad (7)$$

where $\tau = 0.05$ is a predefined threshold.
5. If any edges are removed, the conditioning set size $|\boldsymbol{S}| = |\boldsymbol{S}| + 1$ and return to step 2. Otherwise, terminate the algorithm, yielding the optimal global causal skeleton $\mathcal{S}^*$.

This process optimizes the global causal skeleton by incrementally increasing the conditioning set size and leveraging Bootstrapping techniques, all while preserving data privacy in the FL setting. The use of weighted skeletons and aggregation at both ***client-layer*** and ***server-layer*** allows for a more robust estimation of the true causal skeleton, particularly in scenarios with limited local samples.

4.2 Federated Causal Structure Refinement Leveraging Bootstrapping

In the second phase, FedECD refines the causal structure by determining the direction of the edges using a Bootstrapping-based approach in the federated setting. This phase builds upon the optimized skeleton $\mathcal{S}^*$ from the first phase and aims to orient the edges to form a causal DAG [30]. The refinement process proceeds as follows.

1. For each $c_k \in \mathcal{C}$: a) Generate B Bootstrapped sub-datasets $\{\mathcal{D}_1^{c_k}, \mathcal{D}_2^{c_k}, ..., \mathcal{D}_B^{c_k}\}$ from $\mathcal{D}^{c_k}$. b) For each sub-dataset $\mathcal{D}_j^{c_k}$, learn a DAG $\mathcal{G}_j^{c_k}$ using a score-based method [32] constrained by $\mathcal{S}^*$:

$$\mathcal{G}_j^{c_k} = \arg\max_{\mathcal{G} \in \mathcal{G}(\mathcal{S}^*)} Score(\mathcal{G}, \mathcal{D}_j^{c_k}), \quad (8)$$

where $\mathcal{G}(\mathcal{S}^*)$ is the set of all DAGs consistent with $\mathcal{S}^*$, and $Score(\cdot)$ is a scoring function (e.g., BDeu [31]). c) Aggregate the B DAGs into a **client-layer** DAG $\mathcal{G}^{c_k}$ using majority voting:

$$\mathcal{G}^{c_k} = \sum_{j=1}^{B} \mathcal{G}^{c_k}_j,$$

$$\begin{cases} \mathcal{G}^{c_k}(i_1, i_2) = 1 \wedge \mathcal{G}^{c_k}(i_2, i_1) = 0 \; if \; \mathcal{G}^{c_k}(i_1, i_2) > \mathcal{G}^{c_k}(i_2, i_1) \\ \mathcal{G}^{c_k}(i_1, i_2) = \mathcal{G}^{c_k}(i_2, i_1) = 0 \quad if \; \mathcal{G}^{c_k}(i_1, i_2) = \mathcal{G}^{c_k}(i_2, i_1) = 0 \\ \mathcal{G}^{c_k}(i_1, i_2) = 0 \wedge \mathcal{G}^{c_k}(i_2, i_1) = 1 \; \text{otherwise}, \end{cases} \quad (9)$$

where $i_1 = 1, 2, \ldots, d$ and $i_2 = 1, 2, \ldots, (i_1 - 1)$.

2. The server aggregates the **client-layer** DAGs into a **server-layer** DAG $\mathcal{G}^*$:

$$\mathcal{G}^* = \sum_{k=1}^{m} \mathcal{G}^{c_k},$$

$$\begin{cases} \mathcal{G}^*(i_1, i_2) = 1 \wedge \mathcal{G}^*(i_2, i_1) = 0 \; if \; \mathcal{G}^*(i_1, i_2) > \mathcal{G}^*(i_2, i_1) \\ \mathcal{G}^*(i_1, i_2) = \mathcal{G}^*(i_2, i_1) = 0 \quad if \; \mathcal{G}^*(i_1, i_2) = \mathcal{G}^*(i_2, i_1) = 0 \\ \mathcal{G}^*(i_1, i_2) = 0 \wedge \mathcal{G}^*(i_2, i_1) = 1 \; \text{otherwise}, \end{cases} \quad (10)$$

where $i_1 = 1, 2, \ldots, d$ and $i_2 = 1, 2, \ldots, (i_1 - 1)$.

The resulting global DAG $\mathcal{G}^*$ represents the final causal structure learned by FedECD. This refined process leverages Bootstrapping to enhance the robustness of edge orientation in the federated setting, particularly when dealing with limited local samples. The use of majority voting at both **client-layer** and **server-layer** helps mitigate the impact of potential instabilities in individual DAG estimates.

5   Experimental Evaluation

5.1   Experiment Settings

Datasets. We use eight benchmark BN datasets [32], including *Child*, *Child3*, *Child5*, *Insurance*, *Insurance3*, *Insurance5*, *Alarm* and *Alarm3*[2], and each dataset contains 10,000 samples, allocated evenly across $\{5, 10, 15, 20, 25, 30\}$ clients.

Baselines. FedECD is compared with seven state-of-the-art FCD methods, including F2SL-Best, F2SL-Voting, F2SL-Avg, PC-stable-Best, PC-stable-Voting, PC-stable-Avg and FedPC [14][3]. Among them, F2SL [39] and PC-stable [5] are traditional CD algorithms[4]. We have adapted them with specific

---

[2] These benchmark Bayesian networks are publicly available at http://www.bnlearn.com/bnrepository/.

[3] The code is available at https://github.com/Xianjie-Guo/FedPC.

[4] The source codes of PC-stable and F2SL are available at https://github.com/kuiy/CausalLearner.

strategies to function in an FL setting. The suffix "-Best" indicates that the algorithm is first run independently on each client to generate m DAGs, after which the DAG with the highest Ar_F1 score is selected as the final output. The "-Voting" variant applies a voting method [26] to the algorithm, while "-Avg" means that the algorithm is first run independently on each client to obtain m DAGs, and then the average Ar_F1 score across the m DAGs is calculated.

Metrics. We adopt the Ar_F1 (the higher the better) and TPR (the higher the better) metrics [12] to evaluate the learned causal DAGs in FL settings.

$$Ar\_F1 = \frac{2 * Ar\_Precision * Ar\_Recall}{Ar\_Precision + Ar\_Recall}, \tag{11}$$

where the *Ar_Precision* denotes the number of correctly predicted arrowheads in the output divided by the number of edges in the output of an algorithm, while the *Ar_Recall* denotes the number of correctly predicted arrowheads in the output divided by the number of true arrowheads in a test causal DAG.

Implementation Details. All experiments were conducted on a computer with an Intel Core i9-10900 3.70-GHz CPU, NVIDIA GeForce RTX 3060 GPU, and 32 GB memory. The significance level for conditional independence (CI) tests is set to 0.01. All algorithms are implemented in MATLAB.

5.2   Results and Discussion

Figures 3, 4 demonstrate FedECD's superior performance across various scenarios, particularly when local sample sizes are limited:

- As the number of clients increases and local samples decrease, FedECD maintains robust performance while other algorithms decline sharply.
- For datasets like *Child, Child3,* and *Child5,* FedECD's performance remains stable even with 20–30 clients, where each client has very limited samples.
- This consistent performance in challenging scenarios highlights FedECD's effectiveness in addressing causal discovery with limited local samples in federated settings.

These observations highlight the efficacy of FedECD's resampling technique and two-layer aggregation strategy in real-world FL scenarios where client-level data scarcity is common.

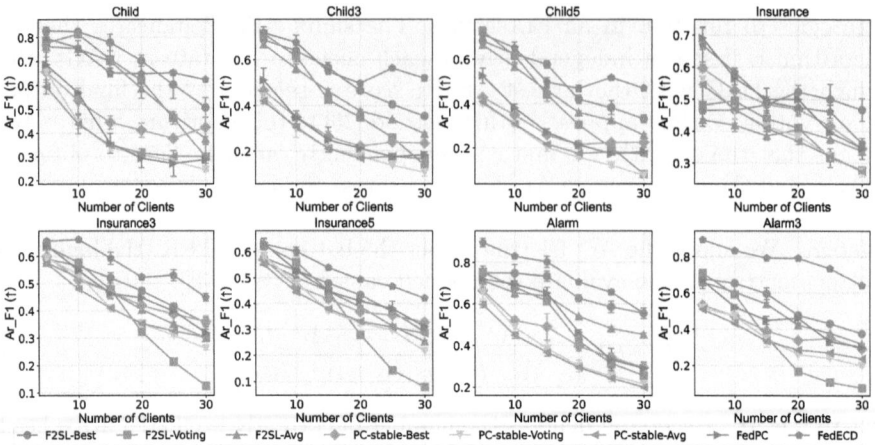

Fig. 3. Experimental results on benchmark BN datasets. (Ar_F1 metric).

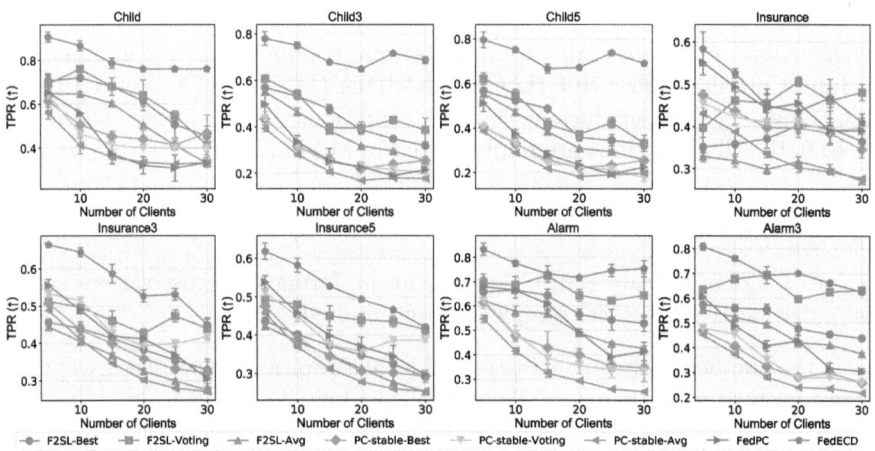

Fig. 4. Experimental results on benchmark BN datasets. (TPR metric).

6   Conclusions and Future Work

In this paper, we proposed FedECD, a novel FCD approach that effectively addresses the challenge of limited local samples in FL scenarios. The core innovation of FedECD lies in its two-phase structure, each employing a two-layer (*client-layer* and *server-layer*) aggregation strategy: (1) *Federated Causal Skeleton Optimization* and (2) *Federated Causal Structure Refinement*. In both phases, FedECD leverages resampling techniques at the *client-layer* to mitigate the impact of limited samples, while the *server-layer* aggregates results across all clients. FedECD significantly enhances the robustness and accuracy of causal discovery in federated settings with limited local samples, while preserving privacy. Experiments on benchmark Bayesian network datasets demonstrate FedECD's superior performance over existing FCD methods.

Future work will explore the application of FedECD to scenarios with hidden variables and mixed observational-interventional data.

Acknowledgments. This work was supported in part by the National Science and Technology Major Project (under grant 2020AAA0106100); the National Natural Science Foundation of China (under grant 62376087); and the China Scholarship Council (under grant 202306690023).

References

1. Abyaneh, A., Scherrer, N., Schwab, P., Bauer, S., Schölkopf, B., Mehrjou, A.: FED-CD: federated causal discovery from interventional and observational data. arXiv preprint arXiv:2211.03846 (2022)
2. Amalnerkar, E., Lee, T.H., Lim, W.: Reliability analysis using bootstrap information criterion for small sample size response functions. Struct. Multidiscip. Optim. **62**, 2901–2913 (2020)
3. Boyd, S., Parikh, N., Chu, E., Peleato, B., Eckstein, J., et al.: Distributed optimization and statistical learning via the alternating direction method of multipliers. Found. Trends® Mach. Learn. **3**(1), 1–122 (2011)
4. Cai, R., Huang, Z., Chen, W., Hao, Z., Zhang, K.: Causal discovery with latent confounders based on higher-order cumulants. In: International Conference on Machine Learning, pp. 3380–3407. PMLR (2023)
5. Colombo, D., Maathuis, M.H., et al.: Order-independent constraint-based causal structure learning. J. Mach. Learn. Res. **15**(1), 3741–3782 (2014)
6. Dwivedi, A.K., Mallawaarachchi, I., Alvarado, L.A.: Analysis of small sample size studies using nonparametric bootstrap test with pooled resampling method. Stat. Med. **36**(14), 2187–2205 (2017)
7. Gao, E., Chen, J., Shen, L., Liu, T., Gong, M., Bondell, H.: FedDAG: federated DAG structure learning. Trans. Mach. Learn. Res. (2023)
8. Guo, X., Wang, Y., Huang, X., Yang, S., Yu, K.: Bootstrap-based causal structure learning. In: Proceedings of the 31st ACM International Conference on Information & Knowledge Management, pp. 656–665 (2022)
9. Guo, X., Yu, K., Liu, L., Cao, F., Li, J.: Causal feature selection with dual correction. IEEE Trans. Neural Netw. Learn. Syst. **35**(1), 938–951 (2022)
10. Guo, X., Yu, K., Liu, L., Li, J.: FedCSL: a scalable and accurate approach to federated causal structure learning. In: Proceedings of the AAAI Conference on Artificial Intelligence, pp. 12235–12243 (2024)
11. Guo, X., et al.: Progressive skeleton learning for effective local-to-global causal structure learning. IEEE Trans. Knowl. Data Eng. (2024)
12. Guo, X., Yu, K., Liu, L., Li, P., Li, J.: Adaptive skeleton construction for accurate DAG learning. IEEE Trans. Knowl. Data Eng. **35**(10), 10526–10539 (2023)
13. Hesterberg, T.: Bootstrap. Wiley Interdisc. Rev. Comput. Stat. **3**(6), 497–526 (2011)
14. Huang, J., Guo, X., Yu, K., Cao, F., Liang, J.: Towards privacy-aware causal structure learning in federated setting. IEEE Trans. Big Data **9**(6), 1525–1535 (2023)

15. Jiang-She, Z.: A survey of selective ensemble learning algorithms. Chin. J. Comput. **34**(8), 1399–1410 (2011)
16. Kairouz, P., et al.: Advances and open problems in federated learning. Found. Trends® Mach. Learn. **14**(1–2), 1–210 (2021)
17. Kemp, K.: Concealed data practices and competition law: why privacy matters. Eur. Competition J. **16**(2–3), 628–672 (2020)
18. Lecca, P.: Machine learning for causal inference in biological networks: perspectives of this challenge. Front. Bioinform. **1**, 746712 (2021)
19. Li, L., et al.: Federated causal discovery from heterogeneous data. In: International Conference on Learning Representations (2024)
20. Li, Q., et al.: A survey on federated learning systems: vision, hype and reality for data privacy and protection. IEEE Trans. Knowl. Data Eng. **35**(4), 3347–3366 (2021)
21. Li, X., et al.: Interpretable deep learning: interpretation, interpretability, trustworthiness, and beyond. Knowl. Inf. Syst. **64**(12), 3197–3234 (2022)
22. Linardatos, P., Papastefanopoulos, V., Kotsiantis, S.: Explainable AI: a review of machine learning interpretability methods. Entropy **23**(1), 18 (2020)
23. Liu, C., Kuang, K.: Causal structure learning for latent intervened non-stationary data. In: International Conference on Machine Learning, pp. 21756–21777. PMLR (2023)
24. Mian, O., Kaltenpoth, D., Kamp, M., Vreeken, J.: Nothing but regrets-privacy-preserving federated causal discovery. In: International Conference on Artificial Intelligence and Statistics, pp. 8263–8278. PMLR (2023)
25. Moraffah, R., Karami, M., Guo, R., Raglin, A., Liu, H.: Causal interpretability for machine learning-problems, methods and evaluation. ACM SIGKDD Explor. Newsl. **22**(1), 18–33 (2020)
26. Na, Y., Yang, J.: Distributed Bayesian network structure learning. In: 2010 IEEE International Symposium on Industrial Electronics, pp. 1607–1611. IEEE (2010)
27. Ng, I., Zhang, K.: Towards federated Bayesian network structure learning with continuous optimization. In: International Conference on Artificial Intelligence and Statistics, pp. 8095–8111. PMLR (2022)
28. Pearl, J.: Probabilistic reasoning in intelligent systems: networks of plausible inference. Elsevier (2014)
29. Richens, J.G., Lee, C.M., Johri, S.: Improving the accuracy of medical diagnosis with causal machine learning. Nat. Commun. **11**(1), 3923 (2020)
30. Spirtes, P., Glymour, C.N., Scheines, R., Heckerman, D.: Causation, Prediction, and Search. MIT Press (2000)
31. Suzuki, J.: A theoretical analysis of the BDeu scores in Bayesian network structure learning. Behaviormetrika **44**, 97–116 (2017)
32. Tsamardinos, I., Brown, L.E., Aliferis, C.F.: The max-min hill-climbing Bayesian network structure learning algorithm. Mach. Learn. **65**, 31–78 (2006)
33. Vuković, M., Thalmann, S.: Causal discovery in manufacturing: a structured literature review. J. Manuf. Mater. Process. **6**(1), 10 (2022)
34. Wang, Z., Ma, P., Wang, S.: Towards practical federated causal structure learning. In: Joint European Conference on Machine Learning and Knowledge Discovery in Databases, vol. 14170, pp. 351–367. Springer (2023)
35. Yang, D., He, X., Wang, J., Yu, G., Domeniconi, C., Zhang, J.: Federated causality learning with explainable adaptive optimization. In: Proceedings of the AAAI Conference on Artificial Intelligence, pp. 16308–16315 (2024)
36. Yang, Q., Liu, Y., Chen, T., Tong, Y.: Federated machine learning: concept and applications. ACM Trans. Intell. Syst. Technol. **10**(2), 1–19 (2019)

37. Ye, Q., Amini, A.A., Zhou, Q.: Federated learning of generalized linear causal networks. IEEE Trans. Pattern Anal. Mach. Intell. (2024)
38. Yu, H., et al.: Mitigating herding in hierarchical crowdsourcing networks. Sci. Rep. **6**(1), 4 (2016)
39. Yu, K., Ling, Z., Liu, L., Li, P., Wang, H., Li, J.: Feature selection for efficient local-to-global Bayesian network structure learning. ACM Trans. Knowl. Discov. Data **18**(2), 1–27 (2023)
40. Zheng, X., Aragam, B., Ravikumar, P.K., Xing, E.P.: DAGs with no tears: continuous optimization for structure learning. In: Advances in Neural Information Processing Systems, vol. 31 (2018)

Author Index

© The Editor(s) (if applicable) and The Author(s), under exclusive license
to Springer Nature Switzerland AG 2025
H. Yu et al. (Eds.): FL 2024 Workshops, LNAI 15501, pp. 181–182, 2025.
https://doi.org/10.1007/978-3-031-82240-7